UNLOCKING THE POTENTIAL OF DIGITAL SERVICES TRADE IN ASIA AND THE PACIFIC

Edited by Jong Woo Kang, Matthias Helble, Rolando Avendano, Pramila Crivelli, and Mara Claire Tayag

NOVEMBER 2022

ASIAN DEVELOPMENT BANK

CONTENTS

TABLES, FIGURES, AND BOXES

TABLES

FIGURES

BOXES

FOREWORD

Digital services are on a fast track to deeper relevance in daily life. Mobility restrictions during the coronavirus disease (COVID-19) pandemic accelerated their development, and the explosive expansion of internet connectivity and smartphones in recent years has transformed how services and goods are delivered, creating opportunities to find new markets across borders.

Growth in digital services trade in Asia and the Pacific has outpaced other regions for more than a decade. With the rise in global demand for digital services, it is important for economies in the region to evaluate their competitiveness and formulate strategies to develop opportunities in the digital economy.

The expert research featured in this volume reviews critical issues for expanding digital services trade within and outside of the region. It offers valuable insights into the long-term implications of easier, faster, and cheaper delivery of a range of services including financial, professional, and logistics functions that are increasingly integral for driving economic growth and welfare. Online-based services are helping to raise incomes by not only lowering trade costs by cutting out intermediary agents between buyers and sellers, but also spreading benefits to manufacturing industries and stimulating participation of businesses in global value chains.

To maximize gains, economies should equip workers with digital skills and knowledge, invest in information and communication technology infrastructure, and cultivate enabling environments through policy and regulatory reforms. The research in this volume emphasizes that freer access to the internet is the bedrock for nurturing an enabling environment for digital services trade. Indeed, deregulation of cross-border digital services is shown to boost real incomes more than trade liberalization. Allowing data to flow freely across borders and easing burdensome data localization requirements is important for realizing the development potential of digital services trade.

In the meantime, appropriate data protection and privacy measures could improve the security and usability of cross-border digital transactions. Making digital trade laws more business friendly across the plethora of trade agreements in Asia and the Pacific is another crucial step toward freeing up the income-generating potential of the digital economy.

The power of deregulation combined with regional cooperation on regulatory standards is a common theme. Yet the research in this volume also highlights legitimate concerns about balancing freer data flows with privacy and data security concerns in the delivery of digital services. Many developing economies will need support to successfully prevent fraudulent acts, money laundering, and the financing of terrorism. International taxation of digital services to ensure fairer taxation rights across borders also is an important issue. There has been some encouraging progress in capturing cross-border digital transactions as a source of national revenue, but there is still a long way to go. Given the great complexity of taxation regimes, regional cooperation is essential.

Our hope is that this collection of studies will encourage more discussion about what Asia and the Pacific can do to maximize efficiencies and enhance the competitiveness of its digital services trade. Policy makers in the region must seize growing opportunities from embracing this evolutionary transformation or risk missing out on these opportunities and falling behind.

Albert Park
Chief Economist and Director General
Economic Research and Regional Cooperation Department
Asian Development Bank

ACKNOWLEDGMENTS

The editorial team would like to thank all contributors to this book volume: Rolando Avendano, Lennon Yao-Chung Chang, Won Hee Cho, Pramila Crivelli, Bruno da Silva, Henry Gao, Matthias Helble, Jong Woo Kang, Minjung Kim, Antonella Liberatore, Han-Wei Liu, Ben Shepherd, Dominique Hannah Sy, Mara Claire Tayag, and Erik van der Marel. Comments were provided by Jane Drake-Brockman, Renata Fontana, and Go Nagata on the early version of papers by authors, which have been developed into respective chapters of this book. Matthias Helble pioneered the idea of conducting new, comprehensive research on digital services trade in Asia and the Pacific. The editors are also thankful for the comments and suggestions provided by the participants of the following workshops and events: "ADB Virtual Inception Workshop on Digital Services Trade" held on 1–3 March 2021; "ADB-ADBI Virtual Conference: Digital Services Trade—Opportunities and Risks for Developing Asia" held on 30 June–2 July 2021; "ERCD Workshop: AEIR 2022 Theme Chapter on Digital Services Trade—Opportunities and Risks for Asia and the Pacific" held on 28 September 2021; and "Virtual Workshop: Asian Economic Integration Report 2022" held on 28 October 2021.

This publication was prepared with support from the Regional Cooperation and Integration Division of the Economic Research and Regional Cooperation Department of the Asian Development Bank (ADB) under the overall supervision of Cyn-Young Park. It was funded by ADB's Technical Assistance 6753: Asian Economic Integration: Building Knowledge for Policy Dialogue, 2021–2022 (Subproject 2).

James Unwin edited the manuscript. Joseph Manglicmot typeset and produced the layout. Erickson Mercado created the cover design. Tuesday Soriano proofread the report, with assistance from Carol Ongchangco. Pia Asuncion Tenchavez, Amiel Bryan Esperanza, and Nanette Lozano provided administrative and secretarial support and helped organize the workshops. The editorial team, likewise, acknowledges the printing and publishing support by the Printing Services Unit of ADB's Corporate Services Department and the publishing team of the Department of Communications.

EDITORS

Jong Woo Kang is a principal economist at the Economic Research and Cooperation Department of the Asian Development Bank (ADB). He is a seasoned economist with extensive knowledge and experience on policy and strategic issues. He was senior advisor to the managing director general of ADB and senior economist at ADB's Strategy and Policy Department. He leads the annual publication of the *Asian Economic Integration Report*. Jong Woo's research interests include regional integration, inclusive growth, macroeconomic and international trade policies, and aid effectiveness. He has published research articles in academic journals such as *Journal of Development Economics, Journal of Applied Economics,* and *Journal of World Trade,* and written numerous blogs and opinion articles on global macroeconomy and international trade and finance. Before joining ADB, Jong Woo was a director at the Ministry of Finance and Economy of the Republic of Korea. He received his BA in economics and MA in public administration from Seoul National University (Republic of Korea), and PhD in economics from the University of Washington in the United States (US).

Matthias Helble is a senior economist at the Economic Research and Cooperation Department of ADB (currently on special leave to the Science Division of the World Health Organization [WHO]). Previously, he was a senior research fellow and cochair of the Research Department of the ADB Institute in Tokyo. His research interests include international trade, health, and development. His research has been published in many scientific journals and in the flagship reports of international organizations. His publication record also includes 11 edited books, including with Oxford University Press. Matthias began his professional career at the World Bank in Washington, DC, before joining the WHO in Geneva, Switzerland. He then worked as an economist for the World Trade Organization (WTO) and for the United Nations. Matthias holds graduate degrees in economics from the University of Tübingen (Germany), the University of Wisconsin-Madison (the US), and the Graduate Institute of International and Development Studies (PhD) in Geneva. During his doctoral studies he was a research fellow at Yale University.

Rolando Avendano is an economist at the Economic Research and Cooperation Department of ADB. His research focuses on financial and international economics, with an emphasis on regional integration, cross-border investment, and competitiveness in emerging economies. Before joining ADB, he worked for the Organisation for Economic Co-operation and Development (OECD) in Paris. Rolando was partnership coordinator of PARIS21 (OECD Statistics and Data Directorate), an economist with the Director's Office and the Americas Desk (OECD Development Centre), and a research associate with the OECD Trade Directorate and Economics Department. Previously, he was a lecturer at the Engineering Faculty of University of Los Andes (Colombia), and a research associate at University College London. Rolando is a French and Colombian national and holds a BSc in industrial engineering from University of Los Andes (Colombia) and a master's and PhD in economics from the Paris School of Economics.

Pramila Crivelli is an economist at ADB's Economic Research and Cooperation Department. Her main fields of specialization are applied econometrics in international trade policy, regional trade agreements, trade negotiations, rules or origin, nontariff measures, and geographic indications. At ADB, her work focuses on trade agreements, aid for trade, the digital economy, and on supporting the Asia-Pacific Economic Cooperation regional forum. Prior to joining ADB in November 2020, she was an assistant professor at the Goethe University Frankfurt leading the Chair of International Trade. Pramila's work has been published in academic peer-reviewed journals including the *Journal of International Economics* and *The World Economy*. She accumulated extensive experience in applied economic policy and technical cooperation, serving as an economic affairs officer at the United Nations Conference on Trade and Development, researching at the European University Institute and the WTO, and consulting for clients in Asia and Africa. Pramila has expertise in delivering capacity building and advisory services to governments, public and private institutions, and trade negotiators in multilateral and regional forums. She received her PhD in economics from the University of Geneva.

Mara Claire Tayag is a senior economics officer at the Regional Cooperation and Integration Division of ADB's Economic Research and Cooperation Department. At ADB, she is part of the teams that produce the *Asian Economic Integration Report* and *Asia-Pacific Regional Cooperation and Integration Index*. She conducts research on regional cooperation and integration, provides technical and project management support, and handles the overall coordination for the preparation and dissemination of ADB publications. Mara manages a team of consultants for the maintenance and improvement of the Asia Regional Integration Center, a portal on regional cooperation and integration-related databases and information. Before joining ADB, she was an economist at one of the Philippines' largest conglomerates, a research manager at private consulting firms, and assistant professor in economics at the University of the Philippines in Los Baños, Laguna. Mara has a master's degree in economics from the University of the Philippines School of Economics.

AUTHORS

Rolando Avendano is an economist at the Regional Cooperation and Integration Division, Economic Research and Cooperation Department of the Asian Development Bank (ADB).

Lennon Yao-Chung Chang is a senior lecturer in cyber criminology and cybersecurity in the School of Social Science at Monash University, Australia.

Won Hee Cho is a graduate student at the Paris School of Economics and former senior economics research associate (consultant) in the Regional Cooperation and Integration Division, Economic Research and Cooperation Department of ADB.

Pramila Crivelli is an economist at the Regional Cooperation and Integration Division, Economic Research and Cooperation Department of ADB.

Bruno da Silva is an international tax consultant (base erosion and profit shifting or BEPS) and specialist at ADB, an adjunct professor at Texas A&M University School of Law, and a visiting professor at Portuguese Catholic University.

Henry Gao is a professor of law at the Singapore Management University and a senior fellow at the Centre for International Governance Innovation.

Matthias Helble is a senior economist at the Economic Research and Cooperation Department of ADB (currently on special leave to the Science Division of the World Health Organization).

Jong Woo Kang is a principal economist at the Regional Cooperation and Integration Division, Economic Research and Cooperation Department of ADB.

Minjung Kim is a senior researcher and professor in the Center for International Commerce and Strategy, Institute for International Affairs and Graduate School of International Studies at Seoul National University, Republic of Korea.

Antonella Liberatore is the Head of Trade and Business Statistics in the Statistics and Data Directorate at the Organisation for Economic Co-operation and Development.

Han-Wei Liu is a senior lecturer at Monash Business School and a member of the Monash Data Futures Institute at Monash University, Australia.

Ben Shepherd, the principal of Developing Trade Consultants, is a trade economist and international development consultant.

Dominique Hannah Sy is a cofounder of a social enterprise based in the Philippines and a former economic analyst (consultant) on financial integration in the Regional Cooperation and Integration Division, Economic Research and Cooperation Department of ADB.

Mara Claire Tayag is a senior economics officer at the Regional Cooperation and Integration Division of ADB's Economic Research and Cooperation Department.

Erik van der Marel is the chief economist at the European Centre for International Political Economy, an associate professor at the Université Libre de Bruxelles, and a consultant economist at the World Bank.

ABBREVIATIONS

ADB	Asian Development Bank
APEC	Asia-Pacific Economic Cooperation
ASEAN	Association of Southeast Asian Nations
ATM	automatic teller machine
BaTIS	Balanced Trade in Services
CPTPP	Comprehensive and Progressive Trans-Pacific Partnership
DDoS	distributed denial of service
DEA	Digital Economy Agreement
DID	difference-in-difference
DoS	denial of service
DPA	Digital Partnership Agreement
DST	digital services taxes
DSTRI	Digital Services Trade Restrictiveness Index
DVA	domestic value added
EPA	Economic Partnership Agreement
ETR	effective tax rate
FTA	free trade agreement
FVA	foreign value added
GATS	General Agreement on Trade in Services
GATT	General Agreement on Tariffs and Trade
GDPR	General Data Protection Regulation
GST	goods and services tax
GVC	global value chain
ICT	information and communication technology
IIR	income inclusion rule
MFN	most favored nation
MNE	multinational enterprise
MOU	memorandum of understanding
OECD	Organisation for Economic Co-operation and Development
PDC	pure double counting

PE	permanent establishment
PIPL	Personal Information Protection Law
PPML	Poisson pseudo-maximum likelihood
PRC	People's Republic of China
PTA	preferential trade agreement
QDMTT	qualified domestic minimum top-up tax
R&D	research and development
RCA	revealed comparative advantage
RCEP	Regional Comprehensive Economic Partnership
ROK	Republic of Korea
RTA	regional trade agreement
SPS	sanitary and phytosanitary
STRI	Services Trade Restrictiveness Index
STTR	subject to tax rule
TISMOS	Trade in Services by Mode of Supply
UN	United Nations
UNCTAD	United Nations Conference on Trade and Development
UNDP	United Nations Development Programme
UNICEF	United Nations Children's Fund
USMCA	United States–Mexico–Canada Agreement
UTPR	undertaxed payments rule
VAT	value-added tax
WPEC	Work Programme on Electronic Commerce
WTO	World Trade Organization

1 | INTRODUCTION AND OVERVIEW

Rolando Avendano and Matthias Helble

1.1 Background

Measures to contain the coronavirus disease (COVID-19) pandemic forced economic actors across the globe to find digital solutions to restrictions such as social distancing almost overnight. Digital delivery increased for a wide range of services such as audiovisual, banking, education, and health care. The sudden shift toward a more digital-based and enabled economy also propelled international trade to move rapidly into the digital space, while pandemic-induced travel restrictions accelerated the trend. For example, the World Trade Organization (WTO) recorded a sharp drop in the trade of health services received by the movement of patients (mode 2 trade) or delivered by health service providers (mode 4 trade) in 2020 (World Bank and WTO 2022). At the same time, health services trade delivered remotely (mode 1 trade) increased considerably. The objective of this book is to look beyond this sudden switch in gears, to gain better understanding of the implications of the long-term shift toward increased trade in digitally delivered international services.

The trend toward a more digital economy started well before COVID-19. Many industries recognized the potential of digital solutions to increase their productivity, including in their cross-border transactions. As one of the drivers of Industry 4.0, the digital sector was already growing at a significant pace before the pandemic. According to WTO (2019), information and communication technology registered the fastest export growth among the services sectors in 2018, increasing by 15%. Indeed, from 2005 to 2019, the average annual growth rates of both exports and imports in digitally deliverable services were higher than exports in non-digitally deliverable service sectors and total services.

The Asia and Pacific region is at the forefront of this trend. Figure 1.1 shows the region experienced faster growth than the rest of the world in digitally deliverable services from 2005 to 2020. Exports and imports in digitally deliverable services in Asia and the Pacific grew at an average annual rate of 10.1% and 8.0%, against a 6.9% global average for exports and 6.7% for imports over that period.

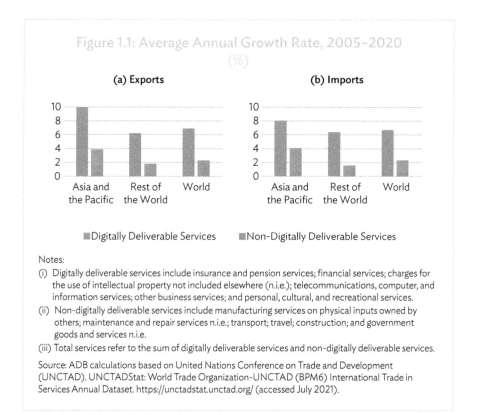

Figure 1.1: Average Annual Growth Rate, 2005–2020 (%)

Notes:
(i) Digitally deliverable services include insurance and pension services; financial services; charges for the use of intellectual property not included elsewhere (n.i.e.); telecommunications, computer, and information services; other business services; and personal, cultural, and recreational services.
(ii) Non-digitally deliverable services include manufacturing services on physical inputs owned by others; maintenance and repair services n.i.e.; transport; travel; construction; and government goods and services n.i.e.
(iii) Total services refer to the sum of digitally deliverable services and non-digitally deliverable services.

Source: ADB calculations based on United Nations Conference on Trade and Development (UNCTAD). UNCTADStat: World Trade Organization-UNCTAD (BPM6) International Trade in Services Annual Dataset. https://unctadstat.unctad.org/ (accessed July 2021).

Of the digitally deliverable services, telecommunications, computer, and information services (SI in Figure 1.2) grew fastest. This was attributable to telecommunications and computer services having become more easily available and affordable and, as a result, more services being increasingly tradable and possible to deliver remotely (UNCTAD 2019). Furthermore, exports of all service items in the Asia and Pacific region grew at faster rates than in the rest of the world, suggesting that the region has been thriving in digital services across all services industries.

South Asia and Southeast Asia led the overall growth in digital services exports to the world (Figure 1.3). Singapore dominates in Southeast Asia, producing two-thirds (67%) of the subregion's digital services exports. In parallel, the Philippines emerged as a top digital services exporter, producing almost one-eighth (13%) of the subregion's digital services exports. The Philippines' top service item is other business sectors, which contributed almost 70% of its digital services exports from 2005 to 2019. While smaller in comparison, digitally deliverable services trade in other Asian economies has grown substantially.

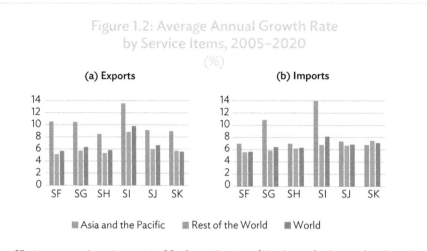

Figure 1.2: Average Annual Growth Rate
by Service Items, 2005–2020
(%)

(a) Exports   (b) Imports

■ Asia and the Pacific   ■ Rest of the World   ■ World

SF = insurance and pension services; SG = financial services; SH = charges for the use of intellectual property; SI = telecommunications, computer, and information services; SJ = other business services; SK = personal, cultural, and recreational services.

Notes:
(i) Economy groupings follow the Asian Economic Integration Report classification of the Asian Development Bank (ADB).
(ii) Asia and the Pacific includes all developing and developed ADB-member economies.
(iii) Rest of the World includes all economies except Asia and the Pacific.

Source: ADB calculations based on United Nations Conference on Trade and Development (UNCTAD). UNCTADStat: World Trade Organization-UNCTAD (BPM6) International Trade in Services Annual Dataset. https://unctadstat.unctad.org/ (accessed July 2021).

Digital services are playing an increasingly significant role globally. Digitally deliverable services exports are beginning to overtake non-digitally deliverable services exports across the world, which suggests economies are expanding their capacity to produce digitally enabled services. Growth in shares for the digitally deliverable services exports within the period has been particularly prolific for Asia and the Pacific (Figure 1.4). From a 35% share in total services exports in 2005, it increased to 60% in 2020. In contrast, the rest of the world exhibited growth in shares from 46% in 2005 to 54% in 2019.

An increased share of digitally delivered services was also evident for imports (Figure 1.5). From 34% of total services imports in 2005, it increased to 41% in 2019. Meanwhile, the rest of the world exhibited growth in shares, from 46% in 2005 to 55% in 2019.

Trends show that global demand for digital services is rising and accelerating. Both public and private sectors have been looking for ways to expand digital capacities in order to increase efficiency. Consequently, it is now essential for economies to evaluate their competitiveness in the sector and formulate strategies accordingly.

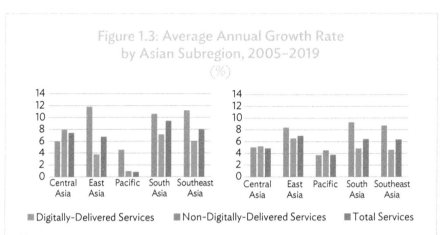

Figure 1.3: Average Annual Growth Rate
by Asian Subregion, 2005–2019
(%)

■ Digitally-Delivered Services   ■ Non-Digitally-Delivered Services   ■ Total Services

Notes:
(i) Digitally deliverable services include insurance and pension services; financial services; charges for the use of intellectual property not included elsewhere (n.i.e.); telecommunications, computer, and information services; other business services; and personal, cultural, and recreational services.
(ii) Non-digitally deliverable services include manufacturing services on physical inputs owned by others; maintenance and repair services n.i.e.; transport; travel; construction; and government goods and services n.i.e.
(iii) Total services refer to the sum of digitally deliverable services and non-digitally deliverable services.

Source: ADB calculations based on the World Trade Organization–Organisation for Economic Co-operation and Development Balanced Trade in Services Dataset (BaTIS). https://www.wto.org/english/res_e/statis_e/trade_datasets_e.htm (accessed July 2021).

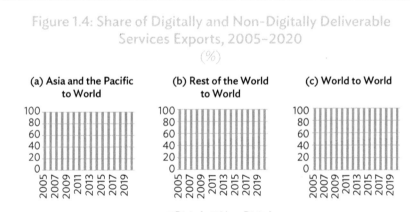

Figure 1.4: Share of Digitally and Non-Digitally Deliverable
Services Exports, 2005–2020
(%)

(a) Asia and the Pacific to World   **(b) Rest of the World to World**   **(c) World to World**

■ Digital   ■ Non-Digital

Notes:
(i) Digital includes insurance and pension services; financial services; charges for the use of intellectual property not included elsewhere (n.i.e.); telecommunications, computer, and information services; other business services; and personal, cultural, and recreational services.
(ii) Non-digital includes manufacturing services on physical inputs owned by others; maintenance and repair services n.i.e.; transport; travel; construction; and government goods and services n.i.e.

Source: ADB calculations using the World Trade Organization–Organisation for Economic Co-operation and Development Balanced Trade in Services Dataset (BaTIS). https://www.wto.org/english/res_e/statis_e/trade_datasets_e.htm (accessed July 2021).

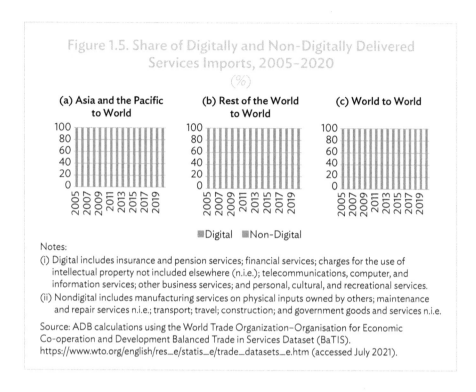

Figure 1.5. Share of Digitally and Non-Digitally Delivered
Services Imports, 2005–2020
(%)

Notes:
(i) Digital includes insurance and pension services; financial services; charges for the use of
   intellectual property not included elsewhere (n.i.e.); telecommunications, computer, and
   information services; other business services; and personal, cultural, and recreational services.
(ii) Nondigital includes manufacturing services on physical inputs owned by others; maintenance
   and repair services n.i.e.; transport; travel; construction; and government goods and services n.i.e.

Source: ADB calculations using the World Trade Organization–Organisation for Economic
Co-operation and Development Balanced Trade in Services Dataset (BaTIS).
https://www.wto.org/english/res_e/statis_e/trade_datasets_e.htm (accessed July 2021).

This book attempts to provide analysis of the most critical issues on digitally
delivered services trade with a focus on Asia and the Pacific. As such, the following
research questions are particularly interesting:

(i)   How can digitally delivered services be defined?
(ii)   What trends can be observed in digitally delivered services, and
        which subsectors exhibit the largest growth rates?
(iii)   Which subregions and economies have shown the strongest growth
        in digitally delivered services?
(iv)   What factors are driving trade in digitally delivered services?
(v)   How is trade in digitally delivered services addressed in trade
        agreements?
(vi)   How can cybersecurity be achieved for digitally delivered services?
(vii)   How can digitally delivered services be taxed in the most effective
        and fair way?

These questions are timely as the world has just entered a new phase of
rapid growth of digitally delivered services. As digitally delivered services reach
substantial volumes, it is now possible to better gauge their possible impact.

This book is targeted at the general audience seeking to better understand
the challenges and risks associated with trade in digital services. So far, the empirical
literature on this topic is relatively thin. This book aims to help close the gap.

The authors also hope that the book can provide useful guidance for trade policy makers. By shedding light on the main drivers and policies related to digital services, the book aims to equip government officials with the basic knowledge on digital services trade and could help orient policy makers in undertaking the necessary domestic reforms to reduce the digital divide.

Digital services trade has become an essential element of trade policy, in particular in ongoing and forthcoming trade negotiations. The book aims to equip government officials with up-to-date knowledge and valuable tools in supporting the development of digital services trade. Traditional thinking about trade barriers, such as tariffs, no longer inform negotiations about trade in services being delivered remotely. Policies that hinder the free flow of data across borders, such as data localization requirements, although having legitimate policy objectives in many cases, can negatively impact trade in such services. As these services are typically intangible, taxation is another challenge. Accordingly, the book aims to provide a comprehensive overview of issues at the core of digitally enabled services trade and to help negotiate trade deals that are commensurate to opportunities of the digital economy. Several of the issues, such as cybersecurity and taxation, are not only key for trade negotiations but are at the core of digital ecosystems. By highlighting the major challenges in the area of policy and regulations, the book also contributes to raise awareness and understanding on the difficulties that developing countries may face in embracing new digital services trade opportunities and in overcoming the growing digital divide. It could therefore serve to orient the future aid for trade agenda toward additional support in the area of "soft infrastructure" that has captured only little attention so far.

1.2   Chapter Overviews

Chapter 2 by Antonella Liberatore, Rolando Avendano, and Won Hee Cho introduces a conceptual framework for the measurement of digital services trade, building on the *Handbook on Measuring Digital Trade* by the Organisation for Economic Co-operation and Development (OECD), the WTO, and the International Monetary Fund (IMF). Having a solid framework allows the magnitude of this type of trade to be measured and to better understand its evolution. Applying the framework to Asia and the Pacific, the authors show that digital services trade has increased significantly over the past 15 years, both within the region and with the rest of the world. East Asia and South Asia are identified as the subregions driving this trend. Business services and telecommunications, as well as computer and information services, are the biggest contributors to Asia's growth in digitally deliverable services trade. While there is marked heterogeneity by subregion about the main digitally deliverable services, the predominant mode of supply is mode 1.

In Chapter 3, Jong Woo Kang, Rolando Avendano, Pramila Crivelli, Dominique Hanna Sy, and Won Hee Cho aim to better understand factors affecting competitiveness in digital services across economies. They divide possible factors into four main categories: human capital, infrastructure, investment, and policies. Using a gravity model for 235 exporting and 236 importing economies from 2005 through 2019, the authors find that higher human capital, better digital infrastructure, higher investment in telecommunications, and a more open internet regime were associated with more digital services trade. Interestingly, non-digital services trade in Asia and the Pacific showed significantly less or none of these associations. Using a Frankel and Romer framework, the study also finds that increasing bilateral trade in digital services is associated with a rise in output and gross national income per capita. This suggests that Asian economies may consider the expansion of digital services as a possible development strategy. To do so, the authors conclude that more investment in human capital, digital infrastructure, an open internet, and regional cooperation is needed.

In Chapter 4, Ben Shepherd uses ADB's Multiregional Input-Output Tables (MRIOT) to produce measures to estimate the extent to which digitally delivered services are used in global value chains (GVCs). The author uncovers that digitally delivered services are an important part of the GVC landscape in Asia and the Pacific as they complement strong development in the region's manufacturing sector. The chapter then presents a quantitative general equilibrium model of world trade based on ADB MRIOT for 2019 to estimate the effects on trade liberalization and deregulation of digitally delivered services. The results show that deregulation has a larger impact on real incomes than trade liberalization, because it affects the prices on the internal market more strongly. Moreover, the estimations reveal that reducing trade costs in digitally delivered services can have spillover effects to other sectors and increase the participation in GVCs.

Chapter 5 by Erik van der Marel studies how regulatory measures that restrict the flow of electronic data between economies impact digitally delivered services in Asia and the Pacific. The chapter focuses on three data-related policies: (i) data localization policies, (ii) local storage requirements, and (iii) conditional flow regimes. Using a difference-in-difference (DID) approach, the results indicate that data localization and local storage requirements reduced trade at the global level. In Asia and the Pacific, data localization and strict rules on data flows seem to be particularly burdensome for digital services trade. The results suggest that to benefit fully from the development opportunities offered by digital services trade, an open regime for cross-border data flows is important.

Henry Gao provides a comprehensive analysis on the regulation of digital services trade in trade agreements in Chapter 6. Starting with multilateral regulation, the author views the General Agreement on Trade in Services (GATS) as being in need of improvement for dealing effectively with e-commerce activities, especially with respect to classification, obligations, and exceptions. The chapter then presents the three main approaches for digital trade regulations by the United States (US), the European Union (EU), and the People's Republic of China (PRC). While the US is promoting the free flow of data across borders and trying to ensure that overly restrictive privacy regimes do not hamper the commercial interests of firms, the key concern for the PRC is data security; while for the EU, it is to safeguard the privacy of the individual. Finally, the chapter studies how digital trade is dealt with in 53 free trade agreements (FTAs) in Asia and the Pacific and finds that improvements in the FTA chapters dealing with digital trade are needed to better harness the opportunities of digital trade.

In Chapter 7, Minjung Kim explores recent developments in digital trade negotiations between the Republic of Korea and its trading partners, focusing on e-commerce rules. The author first examines e-commerce provisions contained in major FTAs of the Republic of Korea and compares them with the rules included in the latest and most advanced digital economy partnership agreements. That comparison reveals that digital trade rules in FTAs of the Republic of Korea have gradually developed, from removing customs duties and ensuring free flow of data, to obligations of nondiscriminatory treatment and restrictions on regulating the location of computing facilities, to rules for certain technical standards. The author concludes that, as digital trade law is increasingly influencing cross-border business transaction, the respective rules need to be made more conducive for business.

Chapter 8 by Yao-chung Lennon Chang and Han-Wei Liu highlights the importance of ensuring cybersecurity and preventing cybercrime in promoting digital trade in services. Chang and Liu define cybersecurity and cybercrime by describing their main features. The authors then provide an overview of international and national responses to tackle cybercrime and cybersecurity concerns. They evaluate the role of the WTO and conclude that it is not well equipped to explicitly address the issues. Finally, the chapter looks at recent preferential trade agreements and finds they have developed new ways to tackle trade concerns related to cybersecurity. In concluding, the authors issue a reminder that many developing countries lack adequate regulatory frameworks and the financial resources to tackle cyberthreats effectively.

In Chapter 9, Bruno da Silva and Rolando Avendano explore challenges in levying taxes on digital services trade. The nature of digital services and the reduced need for a physical presence to deliver them render taxation complicated. Most measures Asian economies have taken for taxing digital services are either indirect taxes on imported digital services, withholding taxes, anti-avoidance taxes, digital permanent establishment, or digital services taxes. The chapter introduces the two taxation pillars of the OECD/G20 base erosion and profit shifting project and examines possible implications for cross-border digital services. Under Pillar One, taxes can be levied on digital services providers independent from their physical presence. Under Pillar Two, a global minimum corporate tax for multinational enterprises is introduced. Finally, the authors discuss the attempt to tax income from digital transactions under the UN Model Tax Convention.

Chapter 10 by Jong Woo Kang, Pramila Crivelli, and Mara Claire Tayag concludes with policy recommendations.

Bibliography

United Nations Conference on Trade and Development (UNCTAD). 2019. *Digital Economy Report 2019: Value Creation and Capture. Implications for Developing Countries*. Geneva.

World Bank and World Trade Organization (WTO). 2022. *Trade Therapy: Deepening Cooperation to Strengthen Pandemic Defenses*. Washington, DC and Geneva.

WTO. 2019. *World Trade Report 2019: The Future of Services Trade*. Geneva.

———. 2021. *World Trade Report 2021: Economic Resilience and Trade*. Geneva.

2 | TRENDS IN DIGITAL SERVICES TRADE IN ASIA AND THE PACIFIC

Antonella Liberatore, Rolando Avendano, and Won Hee Cho

2.1 Defining Digital Trade

International trade statistics are traditionally compiled around "what" is being traded: which goods and services. However, digitalization is changing that, transforming the way goods and services are produced, traded, and delivered. The focus has shifted from "what" to "how."

Several approaches have emerged for improving the measurement of international trade in goods and services while acknowledging the effects from digitalization. The United Nations Conference on Trade and Development (UNCTAD) (2019) examines trade in digitally delivered services and the scope of value creation in the information and communication technology (ICT) sector, including telecommunications and computer services. The Asian Development Bank (ADB) (2021a) proposes an input-output framework to measure the digital economy and contribution to national and global production processes. The 2019 *Handbook on Measuring Digital Trade* by the Organisation for Economic Co-operation and Development (OECD), the World Trade Organization (WTO), and the International Monetary Fund (IMF) provides a statistical definition and conceptual framework for the measurement of digital trade (Figure 2.1).

In this framework, digital trade is all (international) trade which is digitally ordered and/or digitally delivered. Digitally ordered trade comprises "the international sale or purchase of a good or service, conducted over computer networks by methods specifically designed for the purpose of receiving or placing orders."[1] Digitally delivered trade is defined as "international transactions that are delivered remotely in an electronic format, using computer networks specifically designed for the purpose."

In the current framework, it is considered that only services (not goods) can be digitally delivered. Hence, digital trade in services should encompass all internationally traded services that are either digitally ordered, or digitally

---

[1] The definition of digitally ordered trade is equivalent to the OECD's definition of e-commerce (OECD 2011).

delivered, or both. From the measurement perspective, the concepts of "ordering" and "delivering" are not mutually exclusive, and many digitally delivered services are also digitally ordered.[2]

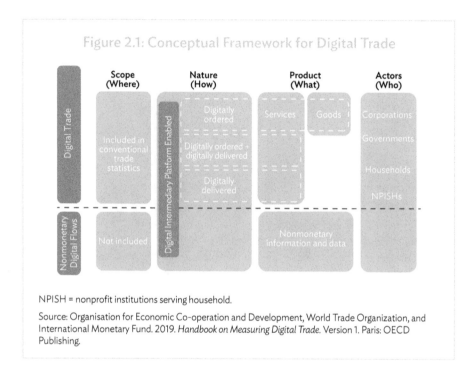

Figure 2.1: Conceptual Framework for Digital Trade

NPISH = nonprofit institutions serving household.

Source: Organisation for Economic Co-operation and Development, World Trade Organization, and International Monetary Fund. 2019. *Handbook on Measuring Digital Trade*. Version 1. Paris: OECD Publishing.

However, it is important to remember that for services, certainly more than for goods, the "how" became an important aspect long before the advent of digitalization. The General Agreement on Trade in Services (GATS) identifies four ways of delivering services internationally, or four modes of supply, defined based on the location of the supplier and the consumer when services are rendered, the nationality of the supplier, and the way in which the service is provided (United Nations et al. 2002, paragraph 2.15). Mode 1, or cross-border supply, takes place when a service is supplied from the territory of one WTO member into the territory of any other, implying that both the supplier and the consumer remain in their respective territories when the service is rendered and consumed.

---

[2] However, it is also likely that many digitally delivered services transactions are not digitally ordered. For instance, roaming mobile communications charges incurred while abroad are digitally delivered but not digitally ordered; also, most large-scale transactions in services between firms, and especially intra-firm services, may also be digitally delivered but not digitally ordered (OECD, WTO, and IMF 2019).

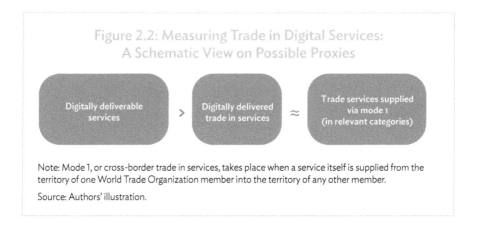

Figure 2.2: Measuring Trade in Digital Services: A Schematic View on Possible Proxies

Note: Mode 1, or cross-border trade in services, takes place when a service itself is supplied from the territory of one World Trade Organization member into the territory of any other member.

Source: Authors' illustration.

It is thus clear that the GATS definition of mode 1 greatly overlaps with the coverage of digitally delivered services, although it is worth noting that some services are deemed to be supplied via mode 1 but are not digitally deliverable (such as transport) and that some services can be digitally delivered and consumed abroad (i.e. via mode 2). Additionally, the notion of digital delivery is also very close to the pre-existing concept of "ICT-enabled services," defined as "services products delivered remotely over ICT networks" in UNCTAD (2015).

With the objective of achieving better alignment with mode 1 delivery and ICT-enabled services, while at the same time making measurement efforts easier, a second version of the Handbook on Measuring Digital Trade provides a simplified definition of digitally delivered trade which includes "all international transactions that are delivered remotely over computer networks" (OECD-WTO-IMF-UNCTAD, forthcoming).

Figure 2.2 illustrates the relationships between the different statistical concepts. Importantly, these relationships apply to both the original (2019) and the updated (forthcoming) definition of digitally delivered trade.

While digital transformation entails that more services become tradable across borders through digital tools, new services business models are also created, which are inherently *digital* (e.g., based on data analytics or cloud computing). Within this group, services provided by digital intermediation platforms are particularly relevant. The services provided by digital intermediation platforms are defined as "online, fee-based, intermediation services enabling transactions between multiple buyers and multiple sellers, without the intermediation platform taking economic ownership of the goods or rendering services that are being sold (intermediated)" (OECD, WTO, and IMF 2019). Digital intermediation platforms not charging a fee, involving nonmonetary transactions, are out of the scope to measure digital trade in this framework.[3]

The *Handbook on Measuring Digital Trade* template (OECD, WTO, and IMF 2019), by providing a way to report digital trade transactions in a harmonized way, can support efforts for improving statistics in digital trade for goods and services. In the case of services, it would allow identification of digitally delivered services and services that are digitally ordered, including through a breakdown by service category. The second (forthcoming) edition of the Handbook will provide some conceptual clarifications as well as enhanced compilation guidance to assist compilers in producing better digital trade statistics.

2.2   Digital Trade In Services: What Can We Currently Measure?

Existing statistics do not (yet) allow the separate identification of digitally ordered or digitally delivered trade in services. While some countries have produced estimates of digitally delivered trade, reliable global estimates are not yet available.

In particular, accurate estimates of "digitally ordered" trade are difficult to achieve based on current data sources and compilation methodologies. However, it seems reasonable that many digitally delivered services are also digitally ordered.

The "digitally delivered" part is somewhat easier to measure. Many national statistical offices use surveys to compile trade in services statistics, and the most direct way to produce estimates of digitally delivered trade would be to ask respondents to indicate, for each service exported or imported, the amount (or percentage) that was remotely delivered. The United States, the United Kingdom, Canada, and other countries have recently started to phase in similar approaches to produce first estimates of digitally delivered trade. Most often, these efforts aim at also gathering information on services trade through mode 1, since by definition all digitally delivered cross-border services transactions are mode 1. Hence, the share of cross-border exports or imports that were digitally delivered also provide a (lower bound) view of mode 1 service delivery (for those same products). Likewise, surveys aimed at measuring mode 1 delivery provide an upper-bound estimate of cross-border digitally delivered trade in those service categories where digital delivery is relevant.[4]

---

[3] Some platforms provide "free" (advertising-driven) services to users. These are excluded from the measurement framework.

[4] For instance, while transport services are mostly supplied through mode 1, they cannot be considered digitally delivered. On the contrary, computer or business services supplied via mode 1 are most likely digitally delivered.

Although gradually more countries have been compiling this information, those efforts remain sporadic and reliable global estimates of digitally delivered (or mode 1) trade are not yet available.

Recent initiatives do, however, shed light on the potential of available official statistics to capture these trends. Notably, the UNCTAD-led Partnership on Measuring ICT for Development introduced the concepts of *ICT-enabled services* and *potentially ICT-enabled services* in an effort to identify the "digital" component in existing statistics (UNCTAD 2015). While *ICT-enabled services* are defined as "services delivered remotely over ICT networks," *potentially ICT-enabled services* refer to those services that in principle can be delivered remotely over ICT networks, as opposed to those that require physical proximity or movement of physical objects or people.

Building on the above definitions, this chapter considers the scope of services that can in principle be digitally delivered as largely overlapping with the UNCTAD-developed list of potentially ICT-enabled services.[5] The concept of *potentially ICT-enabled services* is therefore broadly equivalent to that of *digitally deliverable services* and can be used as a reasonable proxy for *digitally delivered services* trade.

Table 2.1 identifies in bold an initial list of services categories that are considered digitally deliverable (or potentially ICT-enabled). The list includes not only inherently digital services like telecommunications and computer services, but also services whose ability to be traded internationally is greatly enhanced by digital tools, such as insurance and financial services, services related to intellectual property, and many types of business services.

Results of UNCTAD-led pilot surveys conducted in Costa Rica and Thailand confirm, as expected, that digitally deliverable services (or potentially ICT-enabled services) are, most of the time, digitally delivered.[6] Although some service categories likely include a component of non-digital transactions, this component is likely to account for a minor share.

Existing statistics on international trade in services (on a balance of payments basis) for the service categories can provide reasonable upper-bound estimates of trade in digitally delivered services. When possible, this chapter presents trends and insights on trade in digitally deliverable services for ADB members, following the definition provided in Table 2.1. When detailed categories are not available, figures follow a less detailed breakdown, as specified in the "parent category" column of Table 2.1.

---

[5] Minor differences in coverage exist—OECD, WTO, and IMF (2019). Chapter 4 provides more details. Those differences have marginal weight in total services trade.

[6] A survey in Costa Rica, for instance, showed that 97% of exports in digitally deliverable services were digitally delivered. UNCTAD. Meeting: UNCTAD Training to Help Launch New Pilot Survey on International Trade in ICT-Enabled Services. https://unctad.org/meeting/unctad-training-help-launch-new-pilot-survey-international-trade-ict-enabled-services.

Table 2.1: Digitally Deliverable Services

Code	Service Description	Digitally Deliverable	Parent Category
SA	Manufacturing services on input owned by others		Manufacturing services on input owned by others
SB	Maintenance and repair services n.i.e.		Maintenance and repair services n.i.e.
SC	Transport services		Transport services
SD	Travel		Travel
SE	Construction		Construction
SF	**Insurance and pension services**	✓	**Insurance and pension services**
SG	**Financial services**	✓	**Financial services**
SH	**Charges for the use of intellectual property n.i.e.**	✓	**Charges for the use of intellectual property n.i.e.**
SI1	**Telecommunication services**	✓	**Telecommunication, computer, and information services**
SI2	**Computer services**	✓	**Telecommunication, computer, and information services**
SI3	**Information services**	✓	**Telecommunication, computer, and information services**
SJ1	**Research and development services**	✓	**Other business services**
SJ2	**Professional and management consulting services**	✓	**Other business services**
SJ3	**Technical, trade-related, and other business services**	✓[a]	**Other business services**
SK1	**Audiovisual and related services**	✓	**Personal, cultural, and recreational services**
SK2	**Other personal, cultural, and recreational services**	✓[a]	**Personal, cultural, and recreational services**
SL	Government goods and services n.i.e.		Government goods and services n.i.e.

n.i.e. = not included elsewhere.

Note: Items in bold are services categories that are considered digitally deliverable, or potentially information and communication technology (ICT)-enabled.

[a] For technical, trade-related, and other business services, subcomponents such as operational leasing services, waste treatment and depollution and trade-related services are not considered to be digitally deliverable; in other personal cultural and recreational services, other personal services (covering social services, membership dues of business associations, domestic services) are not generally considered to be yet digitally deliverable. In both cases, however, the traded values in those categories are negligible and therefore including them in the aggregate of digitally deliverable services does not affect the observed trends.

Source: Based on Organisation for Economic Co-operation and Development, World Trade Organization, and International Monetary Fund. 2019. *Handbook on Measuring Digital Trade*. Version 1. Paris: OECD Publishing.

2.3   Trends in Asia and the Pacific

2.3.1   Global Landscape

Asia's participation in digital services trade and their economic development suggests there is room for improvement. Overall, a mild positive relationship exists between gross national income (GNI) per capita and the digitally deliverable services exports share (Figure 2.3). High-income economies seem to have a competitive advantage on exporting digitally deliverable services, possibly because generally they are endowed with more advanced technologies and better access to technological goods and services than lower-income economies.

The relationship between economic size and share of digital services exports in total exports is less clear, with European and North American countries better positioned than most developing regions.

Even relatively advanced economies in Asia and the Pacific such as Australia and the Republic of Korea hover low on the scale in comparison. On balance, it seems that economic size does not necessarily determine competitiveness in digitally deliverable services.

2.3.2   Regional Trends

Three main data sources illustrate trends in digitally deliverable services trade: (i) WTO–UNCTAD trade in services database, which provides the most recent overview of services trade trends from 2005 to 2020, allowing to observe the effects of COVID-19; (ii) WTO–OECD Balanced Trade in Services Dataset (BaTIS), which provides a comprehensive picture on bilateral trade in services flows from 2005 to 2019; and (iii) WTO's Trade in Services by Mode of Supply (TISMOS). These data sources have been reconciled to ensure consistency.[7]

---

[7] The WTO–UNCTAD trade in services dataset is the most comprehensive set of official statistics on services trade and is publicly available via UNCTADStat. It presents exports and imports of commercial services in conformity with the Extended Balance of Payments Services Classification (EBOPS 2010), based on the sixth edition of the IMF's *Balance of Payments and International Investment Position Manual* (BPM6). It is also the starting point for the WTO–OECD BaTIS (released in January 2021), an analytical dataset providing a complete bilateral matrix of services trade for 2005 to 2019, covering 202 economies and the 12 main EBOPS 2010 service categories. Both WTO–UNCTAD and BaTIS cover data from balance of payments, which include modes of supply 1, 2, and 4 in the GATS definition. Supplementary data and information—such as on data availability and differences, as well as charts and tables on trends—for the three datasets on trade in services are presented in online Annex 1b of ADB's *Asian Economic Integration Report 2022* available at http://aric. adb.org/pdf/aeir2022_onlineannex1.pdf.

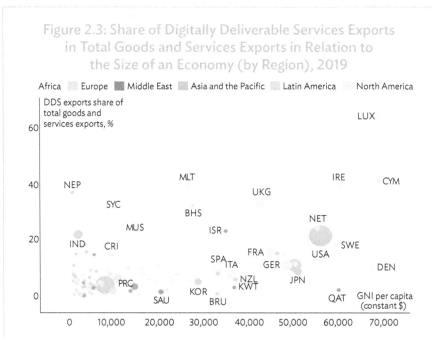

Figure 2.3: Share of Digitally Deliverable Services Exports in Total Goods and Services Exports in Relation to the Size of an Economy (by Region), 2019

BHS = The Bahamas, BRU = Brunei Darussalam, CRI = Costa Rica, CYM = Cayman Islands, DEN = Denmark, DDS = digitally deliverable services, FRA = France, GER = Germany, GDP = gross domestic product, GNI = gross national income, IND = India, IRE = Ireland, ISR = Israel, ITA = Italy, JPN = Japan, KOR = Republic of Korea, KWT = Kuwait, LUX = Luxembourg, MLT = Malta, MUS = Mauritius, NEP = Nepal, NET = Netherlands, NZL = New Zealand, PRC = People's Republic of China, QAT = Qatar, SAU = Saudi Arabia, SPA = Spain, SWE = Sweden, SYC = Seychelles, UKG = United Kingdom, USA = United States.

Notes: The x-axis is GNI per capita (constant 2010 $), while along the y-axis is the share of digitally deliverable services exports as percentage of total goods and services exports (log-transformed). The size of the circle is determined by the GDP (constant 2010 $). The figure plots 144 economies. Only those with complete data were included. Economy groupings follow the Asian Economic Integration Report classification.

Sources: Authors' calculations using World Trade Organization–Organisation for Economic Co-operation and Development Balanced Trade in Services Dataset (BaTIS)—BPM6. https://www.wto.org/english/res_e/statis_e/trade_datasets_e.htm; and World Bank. World Development Indicators. https://databank.worldbank.org/source/world-development-indicators (both accessed August 2021).

Trends between 2005 and 2019 confirm total services and digitally deliverable services trade in Asia and the Pacific is growing. Globally, the region is the world's second-largest trader of total services and digital services, after the European Union (Figure 2.4a). From $403.4 billion in 2005, the region's digitally deliverable services trade increased to $1.4 trillion in 2019 (Figure 2.4b). As a result, Asia's global share in digitally deliverable services trade grew from 17% to 24% over the same period. In 2020, digital services trade represented 55% of total services trade in the region. Other emerging regions, including the Middle East and Latin America, experienced considerably less growth over this period.

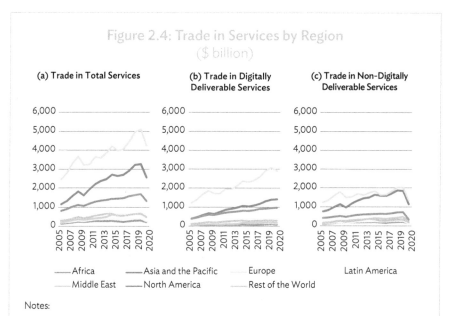

Figure 2.4: Trade in Services by Region ($ billion)

Notes:

(i) Digitally deliverable services include insurance and pension services; financial services; charges for the use of intellectual property not included elsewhere (n.i.e.); telecommunications, computer, and information services; other business services; and personal, cultural, and recreational services.

(ii) Non-digitally deliverable services include manufacturing services on physical inputs owned by others; maintenance and repair services n.i.e.; transport; travel; construction; and government goods and services n.i.e.

(iii) Total services is the sum of digitally deliverable services and non-digitally deliverable services.

(iv) Economy groupings follow the Asian Economic Integration Report classification. All economies not included in the integration indicators groupings are classified as Rest of the World.

(v) Figures in conformity with the sixth edition of the International Monetary Fund *Balance of Payments and International Investment Position Manual* (BPM6) as well as the 2010 edition of the *Manual on Statistics of International Trade in Services* (United Nations et al. 2012).

Source: United Nations Conference on Trade and Development (UNCTAD). UNCTADStat: World Trade Organization–UNCTAD (BPM6) International Trade in Services Annual Dataset. https://unctadstat.unctad.org/ (accessed July 2021).

Growth in global and regional services trade was upended with the onset of COVID-19 in early 2020. Global trade in total services contracted by 21% from 2019 to 2020. Digital services trade was relatively resilient globally, with a 3% year-on-year contraction (Figure 2.4b), while non-digital services plunged by 39% (Figure 2.4c). Asia and the Pacific experienced a moderate increase of 1% in digital services trade in 2020, while other regions experienced slowdown. Consistent with the global decline, trade in non-digital services in Asia and the Pacific contracted by 38% in 2020.

Asia's participation in digital services trade has increased within and outside the region (Table 2.2). From $120.8 billion in intraregional trade in digital services in 2005, it tripled its volume to $483.5 billion by 2019. The region has also strengthened linkages with other regions, notably in Europe (where Asia's share in digital services trade grew to 11.9% in 2019) and in North America (26.3%).

Table 2.2: Shares of Digitally Deliverable Services Trade, 2019 (%)

Reporter	Africa	Asia and the Pacific	Europe	Latin America	Middle East	North America	Rest of the World
				Partner			
Africa	3.3	20.7	45.0	1.8	4.1	19.6	5.6
Asia and the Pacific	1.5	38.8	27.5	2.0	3.3	22.2	4.7
Europe	1.4	11.9	58.2	2.2	2.8	14.2	9.2
Latin America	0.9	13.1	33.5	5.3	1.7	41.0	4.5
Middle East	2.1	22.6	44.9	1.7	5.6	17.2	5.9
North America	1.7	26.3	39.1	7.3	3.0	12.3	10.2
Rest of the World	1.0	11.6	56.4	1.7	2.1	22.6	4.4

Notes: Orange cells indicate increased shares from 2005 and red indicates decreased shares from 2005. The table indicates the share of bilateral trade from one region to another (extraregional) and one region to its own region (intraregional) in 2019. The bilateral trade levels are presented in ADB's *Asian Economic Integration Report 2022* online Annex 1 (Tables 1b.3 and 1b.4) available at http://aric.adb.org/pdf/aeir2022_onlineannex1.pdf.

Source: Authors' calculations using World Trade Organization–Organisation for Economic Co-operation and Development Balanced Trade in Services Dataset (BaTIS)—BPM6. https://www.wto.org/english/res_e/statis_e/trade_datasets_e.htm (accessed May 2021).

The data confirm a fast-growing share of Asia's digital services trade in total services trade, from 43% in 2005 to 55% in 2020 (Figure 2.5). Indeed, the surge in 2020 as a result of COVID-19 was larger than the accrued improvements observed during the previous decade. Digital services thrived in grueling circumstances during the pandemic. If these trends are generally positive, they also highlight Asia's lower share of digital services trade in total services trade in comparison to the rest of the world.

Services trade has grown faster in Asia and the Pacific than in most other regions (Figure 2.6). Between 2005 and 2020, total services trade in the region grew by 6.0%, well above the 4.5% global average and only comparable to the expansion in the Middle East. Digitally deliverable services, in particular, expanded at an average 9.0% annually, compared with a 6.8% global average. Growth in digital services exports (10%) has outpaced imports (8%) in Asia and the Pacific. That rapidity could be explained in part by noting that many Asian economies started from a lower baseline than developed economies.

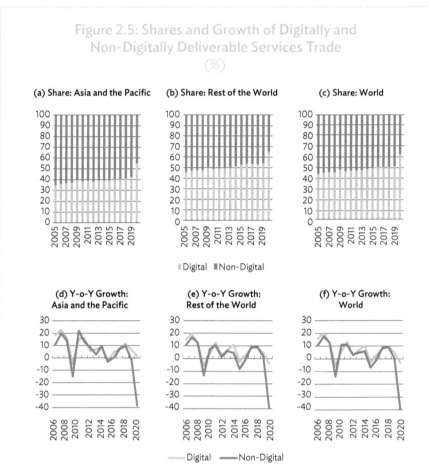

Figure 2.5: Shares and Growth of Digitally and Non-Digitally Deliverable Services Trade (%)

y-o-y = year-on-year.

Notes:
(i)   The values refer to the digitally and non-digitally deliverable services trade (exports plus imports) with the world.
(ii)   The following groupings were used: (a) 43 economies from Asia and the Pacific, (b) 160 economies (all economies in the dataset minus Asia and the Pacific), and (c) world aggregate.
(iii)   Digital includes insurance and pension services; financial services; charges for the use of intellectual property not included elsewhere (n.i.e.); telecommunications, computer, and information services; other business services; and personal, cultural, and recreational services.
(iv)   Non-digital includes manufacturing services on physical inputs owned by others; maintenance and repair services n.i.e.; transport; travel; construction; and government goods and services n.i.e.
(v)   The data conform with the sixth edition of the International Monetary Fund's *Balance of Payments and International Investment Position Manual* (BPM6) as well as the 2010 edition of the *Manual on Statistics of International Trade in Services* (United Nations et al. 2012).

Source: Authors' calculations using United Nations Conference on Trade and Development (UNCTAD). UNCTADStat: World Trade Organization-UNCTAD (BPM6) International Trade in Services Annual Dataset. https://unctadstat.unctad.org/ (accessed July 2021).

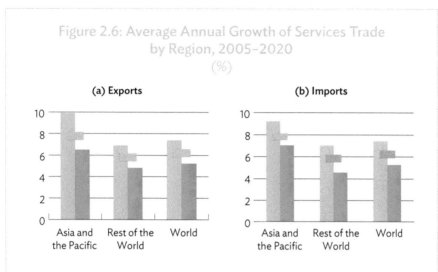

Figure 2.6: Average Annual Growth of Services Trade by Region, 2005–2020 (%)

Notes:
(i) The values refer to the digitally and non-digitally deliverable services exports and imports with the world.
(ii) The following groupings were used: (a) 43 economies from Asia and the Pacific, (b) 160 economies (all economies in the dataset minus Asia and the Pacific), and (c) world aggregate.
(iii) Digital includes insurance and pension services; financial services; charges for the use of intellectual property not included elsewhere (n.i.e.); telecommunications, computer, and information services; other business services; and personal, cultural, and recreational services. Non-digital includes manufacturing services on physical inputs owned by others; maintenance and repair services n.i.e.; transport; travel; construction; and government goods and services n.i.e.
(iv) The data conform with the sixth edition of the International Monetary Fund's *Balance of Payments and International Investment Position Manual* (BPM6) as well as the 2010 edition of the *Manual on Statistics of International Trade in Services* (United Nations et al. 2012).

Source: Authors' calculations using United Nations Conference on Trade and Development (UNCTAD). UNCTADStat: World Trade Organization–UNCTAD (BPM6) International Trade in Services Annual Dataset. https://unctadstat.unctad.org/ (accessed July 2021).

2.3.3 Subregional Trends

With the People's Republic of China (PRC) playing a major role, East Asia (excluding Japan) is the most dynamic region trading digital services in developing Asia (Figure 2.7). In general, exports grew faster than imports in most subregions between 2005 and 2020, led by Southeast Asia (average annual export growth of 11.2%) and South Asia (10.6%), followed by East Asia (9.8%), Central and West Asia (6.0%), and the Pacific (4.7%). Digital services are now important sectors in a number of economies in Southeast Asia and South Asia.

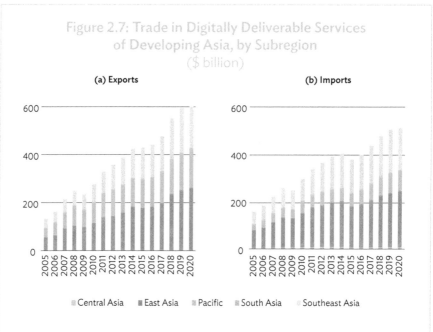

Figure 2.7: Trade in Digitally Deliverable Services
of Developing Asia, by Subregion
($ billion)

(a) Exports   (b) Imports

Central Asia   East Asia   Pacific   South Asia   Southeast Asia

Notes:
(i) Economy groupings follow the Asian Economic Integration Report classification of the Asian Development Bank (ADB).
(ii) Digitally deliverable services include insurance and pension services; financial services; charges for the use of intellectual property not included elsewhere; telecommunications, computer, and information services; other business services; and personal, cultural, and recreational services.
(iii) The data conform with the sixth edition of the International Monetary Fund's *Balance of Payments and International Investment Position Manual* (BPM6) as well as the 2010 edition of the *Manual on Statistics of International Trade in Services* (United Nations et al. 2012).

Source: Authors' calculations using United Nations Conference on Trade and Development (UNCTAD). UNCTADStat: World Trade Organization-UNCTAD (BPM6) International Trade in Services Annual Dataset. https://unctadstat.unctad.org/ (accessed July 2021).

Among subregions, East Asia accounts for the highest volume of digital services trade with the rest of the world (Figure 2.8). It received a volume worth more than $110.5 billion in 2005, which increased to $351.0 billion in 2019. Aside from intraregional trade (30.7%), North America (31.6%) and Europe (29.8%) were top contributors to East Asia. A similar picture emerges for Southeast Asia, with Europe (33.7%) and North America (21.9%) as important providers of digital services for the subregion.

Asia's top exporters and importers of digitally deliverable services point to the central role of some economies in the region's emergence as a digital services hub. Figure 2.9 lists the most dynamic economies that are exporting and purchasing digital services.

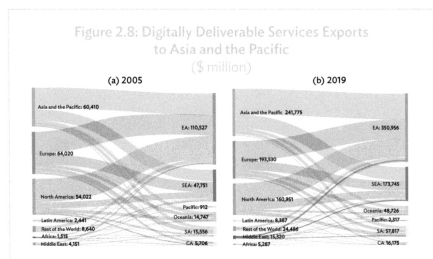

Figure 2.8: Digitally Deliverable Services Exports to Asia and the Pacific ($ million)

CA = Central Asia, EA = East Asia, SA = South Asia, SEA = Southeast Asia.

Notes: Bilateral trade flows from the different regions of the world to various Asian subregions in 2005 and 2019. Economy groupings follow the Asian Economic Integration Report classification. All economies not included in the integration indicators groupings are classified as Rest of the World. Digitally deliverable services include insurance and pension services; financial services; charges for the use of intellectual property not included elsewhere; telecommunications, computer, and information services; other business services; and personal, cultural, and recreational services.

Source: World Trade Organization–Organisation for Economic Co-operation and Development Balanced Trade in Services Dataset (BaTIS)—BPM6. https://www.wto.org/english/res_e/statis_e/trade_datasets_e.htm (accessed May 2021).

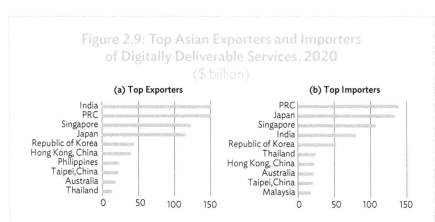

Figure 2.9: Top Asian Exporters and Importers of Digitally Deliverable Services, 2020 ($ billion)

PRC = People's Republic of China.

Notes: Digitally deliverable services include insurance and pension services; financial services; charges for the use of intellectual property not included elsewhere; telecommunications, computer, and information services; other business services; and personal, cultural, and recreational services. The data conform with the sixth edition of the International Monetary Fund's *Balance of Payments and International Investment Position Manual* (BPM6) and the 2010 edition of the *Manual on Statistics of International Trade in Services* (United Nations et al. 2012).

Source: Authors' calculations using United Nations Conference on Trade and Development (UNCTAD). UNCTADStat: World Trade Organization–UNCTAD (BPM6) International Trade in Services Annual Dataset. https://unctadstat.unctad.org/ (accessed July 2021).

2.3.4   Sector Trends

Overall, services trade displayed steady growth until the arrival of the pandemic. Figure 2.10 underlines the predominance of three main services sectors in the region: travel services (SD), transport (SC), and other business services (SJ). Travel and transport (which includes passenger transport) suffered greatly, given the need for physical presence, and were severely affected by tightened restrictions to international travel. Other business services contracted much less as most services in this category can be digitally delivered and do not require physical proximity.

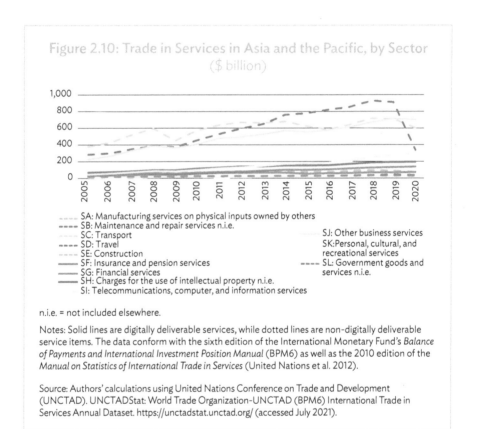

Figure 2.10: Trade in Services in Asia and the Pacific, by Sector ($ billion)

SA: Manufacturing services on physical inputs owned by others
SB: Maintenance and repair services n.i.e.
SC: Transport
SD: Travel
SE: Construction
SF: Insurance and pension services
SG: Financial services
SH: Charges for the use of intellectual property n.i.e.
SI: Telecommunications, computer, and information services
SJ: Other business services
SK: Personal, cultural, and recreational services
SL: Government goods and services n.i.e.

n.i.e. = not included elsewhere.

Notes: Solid lines are digitally deliverable services, while dotted lines are non-digitally deliverable service items. The data conform with the sixth edition of the International Monetary Fund's *Balance of Payments and International Investment Position Manual* (BPM6) as well as the 2010 edition of the *Manual on Statistics of International Trade in Services* (United Nations et al. 2012).

Source: Authors' calculations using United Nations Conference on Trade and Development (UNCTAD). UNCTADStat: World Trade Organization-UNCTAD (BPM6) International Trade in Services Annual Dataset. https://unctadstat.unctad.org/ (accessed July 2021).

Figure 2.11 further dissects trends in digitally deliverable services, in particular for telecommunications, computer, and information services (SI); other business services (SJ); and personal, cultural, and recreational services (SK). Trade in computer services, which includes, for example, computer software, cloud computing, and data storage services, displayed the steepest and most continuous growth, increasing eightfold from $31 billion in 2005 to $256 billion in 2020 (Figure 2.11a). For trade in other business services, growth since 2005 has been steady for professional and management consulting services, including legal services, accounting, auditing, advertising, and market research services. Finally, the region's trade in personal, cultural, and recreational services, which includes health and education, expanded—though it remains relatively modest in size.

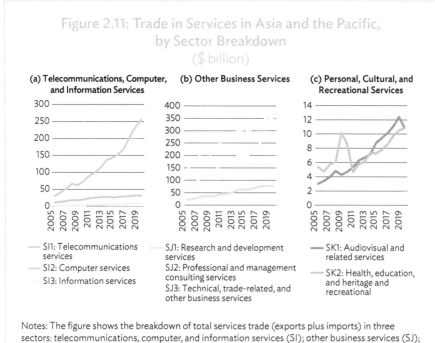

Figure 2.11: Trade in Services in Asia and the Pacific, by Sector Breakdown ($ billion)

(a) Telecommunications, Computer, and Information Services

SI1: Telecommunications services
SI2: Computer services
SI3: Information services

(b) Other Business Services

SJ1: Research and development services
SJ2: Professional and management consulting services
SJ3: Technical, trade-related, and other business services

(c) Personal, Cultural, and Recreational Services

SK1: Audiovisual and related services
SK2: Health, education, and heritage and recreational

Notes: The figure shows the breakdown of total services trade (exports plus imports) in three sectors: telecommunications, computer, and information services (SI); other business services (SJ); and personal, cultural, and recreational services (SK). The data conform with the sixth edition of the International Monetary Fund's *Balance of Payments and International Investment Position Manual* (BPM6) as well as the 2010 edition of the *Manual on Statistics of International Trade in Services* (United Nations et al. 2012).

Source: Authors' calculations using United Nations Conference on Trade and Development (UNCTAD). UNCTADStat: World Trade Organization-UNCTAD (BPM6) International Trade in Services Annual Dataset. https://unctadstat.unctad.org/ (accessed July 2021).

These trends attest to the changing composition of the region's services trade toward digital services (Figure 2.12). Between 2005 and 2020, digital services trade expanded, in particular, telecommunications, computer, and information services (13.8%); followed by financial services (10.6%); other business services (8.2%); insurance and pension services (7.7%); charges for the use of intellectual property not included elsewhere (7.5%); and personal, cultural, and recreational services (7.4%). The COVID-19 shock exacerbated this trend. Between 2019 and 2020, the region's trade in telecommunications, computer, and information services grew by 8.1%; followed by financial services (4.3%), and insurance and pension services (3.9%). In contrast, other business services recorded a mild (-1.4%) contraction.

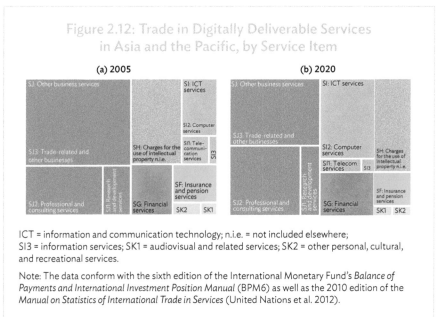

Figure 2.12: Trade in Digitally Deliverable Services in Asia and the Pacific, by Service Item

(a) 2005   (b) 2020

ICT = information and communication technology; n.i.e. = not included elsewhere; SI3 = information services; SK1 = audiovisual and related services; SK2 = other personal, cultural, and recreational services.

Note: The data conform with the sixth edition of the International Monetary Fund's *Balance of Payments and International Investment Position Manual* (BPM6) as well as the 2010 edition of the *Manual on Statistics of International Trade in Services* (United Nations et al. 2012).

Source: Authors' illustration using United Nations Conference on Trade and Development (UNCTAD). UNCTADStat: World Trade Organization-UNCTAD (BPM6) International Trade in Services Annual Dataset. https://unctadstat.unctad.org/ (accessed July 2021).

Asian subregions show some differences in digital services trade participation (Figure 2.13). Other business services and telecommunications, computer, and information services are dominant in most Asian subregions. Other business services account for almost 50% of digital services in most subregions, and for 80% in the Pacific. Telecommunications, computer, and information services exports are notably larger in South Asia. In general, the COVID-19 pandemic disrupted the volume, if not the composition, of digital services trade in most subregions, except for the Pacific. Box 2.1 presents some examples of digitally deliverable services.

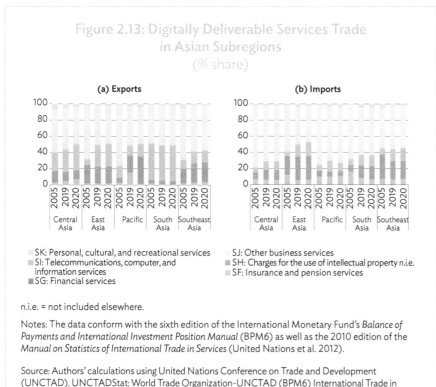

Figure 2.13: Digitally Deliverable Services Trade
in Asian Subregions
(% share)

(a) Exports **(b) Imports**

SK: Personal, cultural, and recreational services
SI: Telecommunications, computer, and
information services
SG: Financial services

SJ: Other business services
SH: Charges for the use of intellectual property n.i.e.
SF: Insurance and pension services

n.i.e. = not included elsewhere.

Notes: The data conform with the sixth edition of the International Monetary Fund's *Balance of Payments and International Investment Position Manual* (BPM6) as well as the 2010 edition of the *Manual on Statistics of International Trade in Services* (United Nations et al. 2012).

Source: Authors' calculations using United Nations Conference on Trade and Development (UNCTAD). UNCTADStat: World Trade Organization-UNCTAD (BPM6) International Trade in Services Annual Dataset. https://unctadstat.unctad.org/ (accessed July 2021).

2.3.5   Modes of Supply

To complement the information provided in WTO-UNCTAD and BaTIS on digitally deliverable services, the WTO's Trade in Services by Mode of Supply (TISMOS) provides estimates of trade in services broken down by the four modes of supply, as defined in the General Agreement on Trade in Services (GATS).

By including services provided through having commercial presence (besides modes 1, 2, and 4), TISMOS depicts a more comprehensive picture of global trade in services. Indeed, mode 3 (commercial presence) is Asia's predominant mode of services supply, both for exports and for imports, mirroring the global trend. Globally, the mode 3 share remained stable, around 60%, between 2005 and 2017. Over the same period, Asia's services imports as a share of mode 1 increased from 13% to 14%, while exports as a share of mode 1 declined from 14% to 11%.

Leaving aside commercial presence, TISMOS data confirm the relative importance of mode 1 within the identified cluster of digital services and for refining the upper-bound estimates of digital services presented so far.[8] In some cases, the international supply of digital services may require physical presence of the service supplier in the territory of the consumer and so involve a non-negligible mode 4 component. Figure 2.14 replicates Figure 2.8 but highlights, for digital services, the actual mode of supply.[9] As expected, mode 1 is the predominant mode of supply in Asia's services exports.

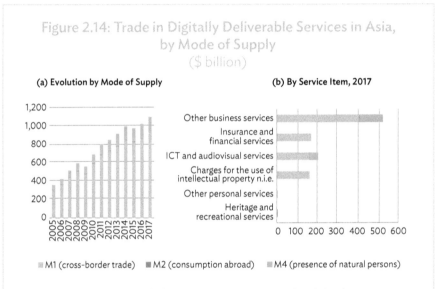

Figure 2.14: Trade in Digitally Deliverable Services in Asia, by Mode of Supply ($ billion)

ICT = information, computer, and telecommunication; n.i.e. = not included elsewhere; TISMOS = Trade in Services Data by Mode of Supply.

Notes: Other business services exclude trade-related services. The World Trade Organization (WTO) defines the modes of supply as: M1 (cross-border trade)—from the territory of one WTO member into the territory of any other member; M2 (consumption abroad)—in the territory of one member to the service consumer of any other member; and M4 (presence of natural persons)—by a service supplier of one member, through the presence of natural persons of a member in the territory of any other member. Data for 2017, which is the latest available year in TISMOS.

Source: WTO and Directorate-General for Trade of the European Commission. TISMOS. https://www.wto.org/english/res_e/statis_e/trade_datasets_e.htm (accessed July 2021).

---

[8] Notwithstanding the (minor) differences between digital delivery and mode 1. See the section on the measurement framework and definitions on pages 10-13.

[9] It has to be noted, however, that TISMOS includes estimations by the WTO.

Figure 2.15 provides a further decomposition of services grouped under other business services and telecommunications, computer, and information services, with each service category broken down by mode of supply. Although the assumption that digitally deliverable services are remotely delivered still holds in most cases, the figures suggest that for services such as computer, legal, accounting, management consulting, and research and development, the physical presence of the supplier is still important for service delivery. Box 2.2 presents brief case studies on the role of digitalization for the shift in the delivery mode of services and implications for the region.

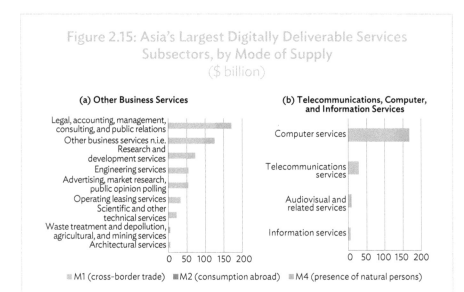

Figure 2.15: Asia's Largest Digitally Deliverable Services Subsectors, by Mode of Supply
($ billion)

(a) Other Business Services

(b) Telecommunications, Computer, and Information Services

M1 (cross-border trade)   M2 (consumption abroad)   M4 (presence of natural persons)

n.i.e. = not included elsewhere.

Notes: Other business services exclude trade-related services. The World Trade Organization (WTO) defines the modes of supply as: M1 (cross-border trade)—from the territory of one WTO member into the territory of any other member; M2 (consumption abroad)—in the territory of one member to the service consumer of any other member; and M4 (presence of natural persons)—by a service supplier of one member, through the presence of natural persons of a member in the territory of any other member.

Source: WTO and Directorate-General for Trade of the European Commission. Trade in Services Data by Mode of Supply (TISMOS). https://www.wto.org/english/res_e/statis_e/trade_datasets_e.htm (accessed July 2021).

Box 2.1: Recent Developments in Digitally Deliverable Services in Developing Asia

Asia's expansion in digitally deliverable services exports encompasses a wide range of industries, geographic hubs, and ecosystems. Some examples from the region in the six categories defined in the conceptual framework are presented here.

Insurance and Pension Services (SF). Digital technologies are redefining how insurance services are being accessed and distributed, with big data, data analytics, and artificial intelligence (AI) increasingly used for underwriting and the pricing of risk. Other digitally enabled services in the industry include claims management, data management, new insurance service offerings, marketing and distribution, platforms, and partnerships. For example, the People's Republic of China (PRC) online insurer ZhongAn has automatized more than 95% of claim underwriting and settlement rates, with more than 70% of customer service claims managed through AI.

Financial Services (SG). Financial services driven by digital technologies—or fintech—have evolved quickly, with big data, cloud computing, and distributed ledger technology becoming ubiquitous in the sector. Fintech adoption in Asia and the Pacific has grown substantially over the past 2 years, with digital payments accounting for 86% of Asia's fintech transaction value.[a] The increasing use of digital payments by governments-to-individuals (G2P) or governments-to-companies (G2B) has contributed to this trend.[b]

Card and e-money are dominant and rising cashless payment instruments in Asia and the Pacific. Singapore's Coda Payments helps digital content providers monetize their products and operates as a platform for processing transactions for purchases online and charge them to prepaid accounts. Another payments platform, Nium, focuses on business-to-business (B2B) transactions and supports businesses to accept and make online payments. Also, Japan's Crowd Credit provides debt capital to peer-to-peer lending platforms, nonbank financial institutions, microfinance institutions, and renewable energy businesses.

Charges for the use of intellectual property not included elsewhere (SH). Services in this category include payments and receipts between residents and nonresidents for the authorized use of proprietary rights (such as patents, trademarks, copyrights, industrial processes and designs including trade secrets and franchises) and for the use, through licensing agreements, of produced originals or prototypes and related rights.

Telecommunications, Computer, and Information Services (SI). Information and communication technology services are the fastest growing component of the global trade in services. Services including the internet, mobile telephony, and data transmission provide the basic infrastructure for other services to be provided digitally. The provision of high-speed connectivity, 5G, and the development industry-specific software has accelerated this expansion.

Other Business Services (SJ). Increasing multinational activity and outsourcing has led to a considerable rise in exports of other business services, including research and development services, professional and management consulting services (such as legal, accounting, advertising, and management consulting services), architectural, engineering, scientific, and other technical services.

continued on next page

Box 2.1 *continued*

The Philippines is one of the major hubs for the services exports through business process outsourcing (BPOs) such as call centers and high-end outsourcing or knowledge process outsourcing and business process management. About 788 companies provide IT-BPO services to domestic and international firms including Accenture, Citi, Convergys, HSBC, and JP Morgan. In legal services, the PRC law firms are pursuing international strategies. FenXun Partners provides legal counseling to investors doing business in the PRC and now advises the PRC firms expanding overseas.

Personal, Cultural, and Recreational Services (SK). Services included in this group include audiovisual and creative industries (audiovisual production, movies, and television programming rights to use audiovisual products), health services, education services, heritage, and recreational services. While trade in some of these sectors is still relatively small, it is growing rapidly.

Digital health services thrived during the coronavirus disease (COVID-19) pandemic to reduce patients' exposure and avoid overburdening the national health systems. Cross-border health services include shipment of laboratory samples, screening, diagnosis, and teleconsultations. In several economies such as the PRC and Indonesia, digital health services grew during the pandemic. Education services were already on the rise before the pandemic, with school and university closures exacerbating this trend. While many of the virtual education initiatives during the pandemic targeted domestic demand, some economies expanded their foreign operations. The expansion of massive open online courses has opened opportunities in this regard. Malaysia, Singapore, and several other regional economies have also pursued an internationalization strategy to become important global education hubs.

[a] Asian Development Bank. 2021. *Asian Economic Integration Report 2021: Making Digital Platforms Work for Asia and the Pacific.* Manila.

[b] In the context of services trade, the Extended Balance of Payments Services Classification (EBOPS 2010) definition of financial services include, among others, brokerage and market-seeking services, underwriting and private placement services, credit card and other related services, financial management services, and electronic funds transfers.

Sources: Authors based on Baur, Yew, and Xin (2021); and Osborne Clarke (2020).

Box 2.2: Key Features of Digital Services Trade
in Developing Asia

Digital services have been the fastest growing area of trade in recent years. Their contribution within manufacturing and services exports (excluding information and communication technology) has grown globally and in Asia and the Pacific, underscoring their indirect (embedded) contribution to exports. Using mode 1 data as a proxy for digital services trade, trade (exports and imports) for these economies is dominated by business, professional, and computer and information services, followed by financial and insurance services. There is a significant shift from mode 4 toward mode 1, indicating the growing role of digital services trade as opposed to that based on the mobility of people.

Three profiles among the selected economies can be identified. The first group consists of large and established exporters, which are competitive in digital services exports with consistently strong performance in this area, depend on such exports, and are engaged in direct exports to varied export markets. The second group includes other middle- and upper middle-income economies. Although their exports of digital services are large, growth is strong, and their significance in overall services exports is high and growing, their competitiveness essentially still lies in manufacturing and not in digital services, and performance in digital services exports seems to be linked to growth in other parts of the economy (like manufacturing and e-commerce). The third group includes jurisdictions that are showing varied performance. They tend to have high growth in digital services exports but at a nascent stage, with a limited basket and export markets. They have potential, but growth remains weak.

The economies also show characteristics distinctive of their stage as digital services exporters. They differ greatly in the scale and diversity of export segments, from conventional call center and business process outsourcing (BPOs) services, to domain and skill-specific outsourcing, to higher value-added segments such as artificial intelligence (AI)-based solutions and predictive analytics.[a] There is also a distinct difference between economies with global presence (e.g., the Philippines) with offshore delivery centers worldwide, and regional exporters (e.g., Fiji, Indonesia, Mongolia). These economies differ in the extent and nature of integration of digital services exports with other economies.[b]

An examination of the digital readiness and regulatory environment for the selected economies reveals differences and helps identify scope for improvement. What emerges is a gap in technological infrastructure and the startup environment, followed by inadequacies in human capital and the ease of doing business. There are restrictions to trade arising from infrastructure and connectivity issues, as well as conditions on electronic transactions, data protection, and other regulatory requirements.

The Philippine Case

The Philippines has a large and globally competitive information technology (IT)-BPO industry. The country currently accounts for over 12% of the global IT-BPM market and is expected to cover 15% of the global outsourcing market by 2022.[c] Exports are diversified spanning subsectors: contact centers, knowledge process outsourcing and back offices, software development, animation, game development, medical transcription, and engineering design.

continued on next page

Box 2.2 *continued*

Contact center services are the most important segment. The industry generated $24.7 billion in revenue in 2018, with call centers accounting for about half of the total. Contact center services are provided to companies such as Accenture, Transcom, and Concentrix. The country is the second-largest offshore location for global shared services, driven by high growth areas such as data analytics, automation, and security. The Philippines is also an important player in business segments such as transcription, engineering services outsourcing, high-value services for specific industry verticals, and animation and game development. According to industry experts, potential also exists in indirect digitally enabled services, AI-based knowledge process outsourcing, construction design, and platform-enabled trade. Key industry verticals and applications include financial, accounting, travel and hospitality, health care, content moderation, network services, cybersecurity, and digital customer experience management (CXM).

The Philippines shows a broad diversity in services provided and its client base. The online advertising segment, which has grown due to online video platforms, is expected to grow to $79 million by 2030.[d] In the animation and games development segment, the Philippines provides services to international game developers and producers such as France's Ubisoft. Other clients include Disney, Cartoon Network, DreamWorks, Nintendo, and Warner Brothers. The Philippines is a prominent offshore-nearshore location for health services delivery in care management, medical coding, transcriptions, claims processing, telemedicine, and health analytics, given the presence of many United States (US)-registered nurses and its mix of medical know-how and customer servicing skills.

Key Features in Developing Asia

Several salient features emerge for developing Asia's digital services trade:

- Economies are distinctive of their stage as digital services exporters. They differ greatly in export scale and diversity, from conventional call center and BPO-type services, to domain and skill-specific outsourcing, to higher value-added segments such as AI-based solutions and predictive analytics.
- Market size emerges as both an opportunity and a constraint. While large markets can support digital services solutions that are exportable or can provide the human resources needed to export a wide range of digital services, small markets (e.g., Mongolia) can provide a laboratory to experiment with niche solutions and applications.
- Digital literacy and adoption are important. Digital transformation in key sectors such as education, banking and finance, business-to-business (B2B) trade, and commerce has been important, and the growth of online financial transactions, in particular, appears an important facilitator of digital services trade.
- The role of investment (foreign direct investment and venture capital funding in unicorns) emerges as important for growth prospects in digital services exports for most economies. Thus, modalities of digital services exports may be bundled to include different modes of delivery.
- Several factors that can be leveraged to boost exports of digital services include well-recognized cost-based arbitrage, availability of skills, location, language, digital infrastructure, and less recognized factors such as "servicification" (increasing use, production, and supply of services by manufacturers), e-commerce, digital innovation, and domestic market-led scale economies. Several economies have potential for indirect exports of digital services in certain products (automotive, health devices).

continued on next page

Box 2.2 *continued*

- All economies reflect the importance and complementarities of digital services imports alongside exports, indicating the importance of supporting two-way trade and cross-border data flows. Trade openness has a bearing on ability to export.

[a] Some economies are present in all parts of the digital services export value chain, whereas others are present in specific segments. More mature economies want to move toward higher value digital services, based on innovation and in specific domains or verticals.
[b] In the case of the People's Republic of China, digital services exports are linked to strengths in manufacturing, e-commerce, and the wider digital economy. For the Philippines, digital services exports are related to overseas demand with potential export-related spinoff effects. In Indonesia, it is largely the domestic market which creates opportunities for expanding digital services exports. For Mongolia, the emergence of technology-based startups with innovative solutions is a potential source for digital services exports.
[c] Everest Group. 2020. *Recalibration of Industry Growth Forecasts 2020–22.* Manila: IT and Business Process Association of the Philippines.
[d] Hinrich Foundation. 2020. *The Data Revolution: How the Philippines Can Capture the Digital Trade Opportunity at Home and Abroad.* Scottsdale, AZ: Digital Trade Research Project.

Source: Chanda (2021).

Bibliography

Abbas, R. 2021. Top-25 InsurTechs in Asia Revealed. *Asia Insurance Review.* June. https://www.asiainsurancereview.com/Magazine/ReadMagazineArticle?aid=44573.

ASEAN Secretariat. RCEP Agreement Legal Text. https://rcepsec.org/legal-text/ (accessed July 2021).

Asia-Pacific Centre for Security Studies. Countries of the Asia-Pacific. https://apcss.org/about/ap-countries/ (accessed July 2021).

Asian Development Bank (ADB). 2021a. *Capturing the Digital Economy: A Proposed Measurement Framework and Its Applications.* Manila.

———. 2021b. *Asian Economic Integration Report 2021: Making Digital Platforms Work for Asia and the Pacific.* Manila.

Baldwin, R. 2011. Trade and Industrialization after Globalization's Second Unbundling: How Building and Joining a Supply Chain Are Different and Why It Matters. *NBER Working Paper.* 17716. Cambridge, MA: National Bureau of Economic Research.

———. 2019. *The Globotics Upheaval: Globalisation, Robotics and the Future of Work.* Oxford University Press.

Baur, A., H. Yew, and M. Xin. 2021. The Future of Healthcare in Asia: Digital Health Ecosystems. *McKinsey.com.* 21 July. https://www.mckinsey.com/industries/healthcare-systems-and-services/ourinsights/the-future-of-healthcare-in-asia-digitalhealth-ecosystems.

Bukht, R. and R. Heeks. 2017. Defining, Conceptualising and Measuring the Digital Economy. *Development Informatics Working Papers Series.* No. 68. Manchester, UK: University of Manchester.

Chanda, R. 2021. Trade in Digital Services in Developing Asia. Background Paper for the *Asian Economic Integration Report 2022* on "Advancing Digital Services Trade in Asia and the Pacific." Manuscript.

Everest Group. 2020. *Recalibration of Industry Growth Forecasts 2020–22.* Manila: IT and Business Process Association of the Philippines.

Hinrich Foundation. 2020. *The Data Revolution: How the Philippines Can Capture the Digital Trade Opportunity at Home and Abroad.* Scottsdale, AZ: Digital Trade Research Project.

Organisation for Economic Co-operation and Development (OECD). 2011. *OECD Guide to Measuring the Information Society.* Paris: OECD Publishing.

OECD and World Trade Organization (WTO). 2021. *The OECD-WTO Balanced Trade in Services Database (BPM6 edition).* Paris: OECD Publishing.

OECD, WTO, and International Monetary Fund (IMF). 2019. *Handbook on Measuring Digital Trade, Version 1.* Paris: OECD Publishing.

OECD, WTO, IMF, and United Nations Conference on Trade and Development (UNCTAD). Forthcoming. Handbook on Measuring Digital Trade, Version 2. Paris: OECD Publishing.

Osborne Clarke. 2020. *The Future of Insurance in Asia-Pacific: Navigating InsurTech Issues in the Digital Era.* London. https://www.osborneclarke.com/wp-content/uploads/2020/03/InsurTech-in-Asia-Osborne-Clarke-March-2020.pdf.

United Nations, European Commission, IMF, OECD, UNCTAD, and World Trade Organization (WTO). 2002. *Manual on Statistics of International Trade in Services.* Geneva; Luxembourg; New York; Paris; and Washington, D.C.

United Nations, Statistical Office of the European Union, IMF, OECD, UNCTAD, World Tourism Organization, and WTO. 2012. *Manual on Statistics of International Trade in Services 2010.* Geneva; Luxembourg; Madrid; New York; Paris; and Washington, D.C.

UNCTAD. 2015. International Trade in ICT Services and ICT-Enabled Services: Proposed Indicators from the Partnership on Measuring ICT for Development. *Technical Notes on ICT for Development.* No. 3. Geneva: United Nations.

————. 2019. *Digital Economy Report 2019: Value Creation and Capture— Implications for Developing Countries.* Geneva: United Nations.

————. UNCTADStat: WTO-UNCTAD (BPM6) International Trade in Services Annual Dataset. https://unctadstat.unctad.org/ (accessed July 2021).

World Bank. World Development Indicators. https://databank.worldbank.org/source/world-development-indicators (accessed July 2021).

World Trade Organization (WTO). *WTO-OECD Balanced Trade in Services Dataset (BaTIS)—BPM6.* https://www.wto.org/english/res_e/statis_e/trade_datasets_e.htm (accessed July 2021).

3

FACTORS AFFECTING THE COMPETITIVENESS OF DIGITAL SERVICES TRADE

Jong Woo Kang, Rolando Avendano, Pramila Crivelli, Dominique Hannah Sy, and Won Hee Cho

3.1 Introduction

Growth of trade in digital services has exceeded that of non-digitally deliverable services and total services over the past 15 years. Digital services growth in that time has been faster in Asia and the Pacific than in any other region of the world (Figure 3.1). As an example, exports and imports in digitally deliverable services in the region grew at an average annual rate of 9.9% and 9.2%, compared with a 7.4% global average.

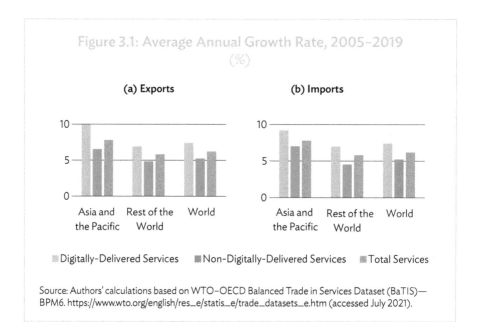

Figure 3.1: Average Annual Growth Rate, 2005–2019
(%)

(a) Exports   (b) Imports

Digitally-Delivered Services   Non-Digitally-Delivered Services   Total Services

Source: Authors' calculations based on WTO–OECD Balanced Trade in Services Dataset (BaTIS)—BPM6. https://www.wto.org/english/res_e/statis_e/trade_datasets_e.htm (accessed July 2021).

The Asia and Pacific region's lead in digital services trade growth may not necessarily indicate increasing competitiveness. One metric to assess the competitiveness at the economy or regional level is revealed comparative advantage (RCA). RCA, although having drawbacks in accurately assessing an economy's status of competitiveness, can provide a snapshot of an economy's and region's trade performance relative to the world. RCA is based on the share of an economy's digitally deliverable services exports out of its total goods and services exports with respect to the share of digitally deliverable services exports out of total exports for the world. Formally, it is defined by

$$RCA_{it}^{DST} = \frac{X_{iwt}^{DST}}{X_{iwt}} \bigg/ \frac{X_{wwt}^{DST}}{X_{wwt}}$$

(3.1)

where X_{iwt}^{DST} is economy i's digitally deliverable services exports to the world at time t,
X_{iwt} is economy i's total good and services exports to the world at time t,
X_{ww}^{DST} is the world's digitally deliverable services exports at time t, and
X_{wwt} is the world's total goods and services exports at time t.

An economy's share of digitally deliverable services exports is greater than the global share if its RCA index exceeds 1.

Figure 3.2a shows that Asia and the Pacific—along with Latin America, Africa, and the Middle East—does not have RCA in digital services trade. Europe and North America display RCA in digitally deliverable services, with RCA indexes greater than 1 for 2005 to 2019. The Middle East had the lowest RCA across all regions from 2005 to 2014 but, in subsequent years, overtook Asia and the Pacific, Latin America, and Africa to approach the world average. Given that the development of digital technologies and complexity of production are also correlated with economic development, a higher RCA for richer economies seems natural.

Within Asia and the Pacific, developed economies have a somewhat higher RCA than developing economies, at 0.65 compared with 0.59 (Figure 3.2b). South Asia emerges as the sole subregion with an RCA greater than 1 at 1.06 over the 15-year period, 2005–2019 (Figure 3.2c). As shown in Figure 3.2d, some South Asian economies, along with Southeast Asian economy the Philippines, lead the entire region. Of these, Nepal consistently held the highest RCA of digitally deliverable services exports. Nepal specializes in services exports, which contributed 60% of GDP in 2019 (ADB 2021), and it is very competitive in telecommunications exports (Sáez et al. 2015).

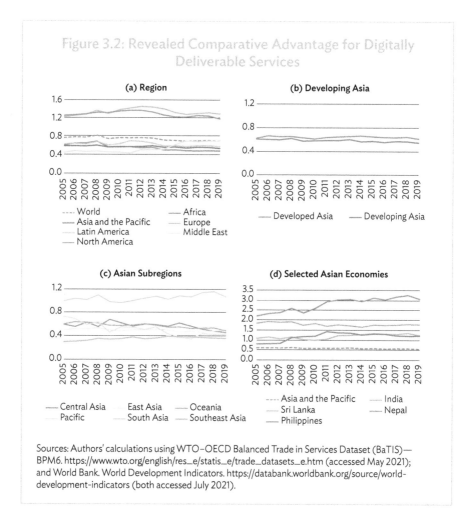

Figure 3.2: Revealed Comparative Advantage for Digitally Deliverable Services

3.2 Factors Affecting Digital Services Sector Competitiveness

One benchmark to assess a country's competitiveness in digital services is their export performance, given that competitiveness reflected into high productivity could translate into larger outputs, and further into better export performance. In explaining trade flows based on comparative advantage, the literature has identified factor endowments such as human and physical capital, and country institutions and policies (Chor 2010). Among the inputs affecting competitiveness, traditional factors of production, digital infrastructure, and the policy environment are the most important. In other words, assessment of competitiveness in digital services, as in this chapter, must examine the factors of (i) human capital, (ii) digital connectivity, (iii) investment in information and communication technology (ICT), and (iv) the policy and regulatory environment.

Human Capital

Keeping up with the fast-changing technological landscape entails making transformative shifts in human capital development strategies. Digital services production requires human capital equipped with technical skills, including for human–machine interaction (Grigorescu et al. 2021). Improved productivity in digital services requires improvements in education to equip people with new and relevant competencies.

In the 21st century, digital literacy programs embedded in grades K-12 are essential, so that children can engage in responsible technology usage and learn the tools needed to thrive in an ever-changing digital world (Loveless n.d.). However, in a study by Learning.com, 75% of fifth and eighth grade students lacked proficiency in technological skills (Robacker 2017). It is now more important than ever to integrate digital literacy in the educational curriculum.

Digital competency underpins the bedrock of digital economy and characterizes how inclusive a society can be in helping people gain the benefits of digital services and digital services trade. Investing in improving digital skills is often recommended for raising economic growth and competitiveness (Froy, Giguère, and Meghnagi 2012; Spante et al. 2018). The Asia and Pacific region saw a substantial growth in hiring workers with digital skills recently, according to a report from the Asia-Pacific Economic Cooperation (APEC 2021). The report highlights the gap between workforce supply and demand and stresses the urgent need for economies in the region to invest in digital upskilling and reskilling of their workforce.

Data from the United Nations Children's Fund (UNICEF) point to Europe leading the way in internet accessibility for students by a large margin (Figure 3.3). Eighty-eight percent of children in school attendance age (of about ages 3–17, depending on the country) have an internet connection at home. This trend is followed by Asia and the Pacific (49%), the Middle East (41%), and Latin America and the Caribbean (40%). Meanwhile, Africa falls behind in making the internet a viable resource to its students, with a penetration rate of only 14%.

The overall level of education is still the key metric of human capital development, and a vast body of literature links digital adoption to education. Caselli and Coleman (2001) include educational attainment as a significant determinant of personal computer adoption. Chinn and Fairlie (2007) find that after controlling for the effects of income, differences in years of education explain more than a tenth of the gap in computer literacy among countries.

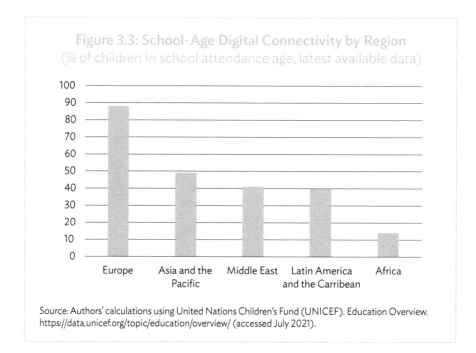

Figure 3.3: School-Age Digital Connectivity by Region (% of children in school attendance age, latest available data)

Source: Authors' calculations using United Nations Children's Fund (UNICEF). Education Overview. https://data.unicef.org/topic/education/overview/ (accessed July 2021).

The International Labour Organization (ILO) surveys of crowd workers in 2015 and 2017 also find that more educated people are more likely to participate in digital contract work (Berg et al. 2018).

Expected years of schooling have increased steadily across all regions of the world, with an annual global average growth rate of 0.7% (Figure 3.4a). Growth in Africa stands out, where expected schooling increased from 9.1 years in 2005 to 10.7 years in 2019. That annual average growth rate of 1.2% compares with 0.9% in Asia and the Pacific, where expected schooling rose from 11.8 years in 2005 to 13.3 years in 2019.

Within Asia and the Pacific, there are varying degrees of progress (Figure 3.4b). Oceania (Australia and New Zealand) is an obvious outlier with 20.4 expected years of schooling. Both countries are among those with the highest number of years of education in the world. Next to Oceania, East Asia has the highest expected schooling years, at 15.4 years in 2019. On the other hand, South Asia has the shortest expected schooling but biggest improvement in the past 15 years. The subregion recorded an average annual growth of 1.6%, well above the average for the Asia and Pacific region of 0.9%. Expected schooling improved from 9.5 years in 2005 to 11.8 in 2019. Pakistan's case is notable, as it increased its schooling from 5.7 to 8.3 expected years over 2005–2019. Its annual average growth in expected years of schooling was 2.8%, well above the subregion's 1.6%.

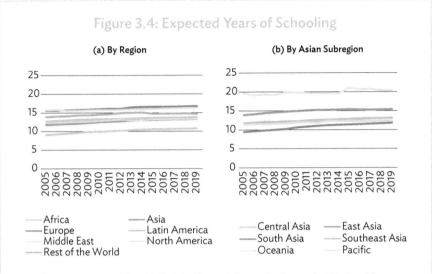

Figure 3.4: Expected Years of Schooling

(a) By Region

(b) By Asian Subregion

Africa · Asia · Europe · Latin America · Middle East · North America · Rest of the World

Central Asia · East Asia · South Asia · Southeast Asia · Oceania · Pacific

Note: Economy groupings follow ADB's Asian Economic Integration Report classification. All economies not included in the integration indicators groupings are classified as "Rest of the World."

Source: ADB calculations using United Nations Development Programme. Human Development Data Center. http://hdr.undp.org/en/data (accessed July 2021).

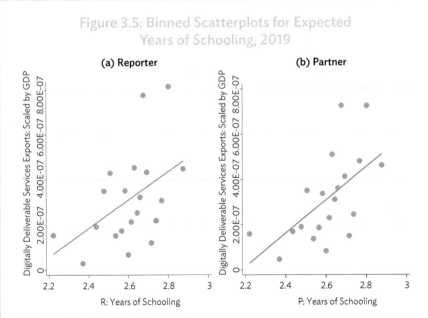

Figure 3.5: Binned Scatterplots for Expected Years of Schooling, 2019

(a) Reporter

(b) Partner

GDP = gross domestic product, P = partner, R = reporter.

Sources: Authors' calculations using WTO–OECD Balanced Trade in Services Dataset (BaTIS)—BPM6. https://www.wto.org/english/res_e/statis_e/trade_datasets_e.htm; and United Nations Development Programme. Human Development Index. http://hdr.undp.org/en/content/human-development-index-hdi (both accessed July 2021).

Figure 3.5 plots binned scatterplots for the expected years of schooling for reporters and partners. For both entities, longer-schooling years are associated with an increase of digital services exports.

Digital Connectivity

Enabling firms to bring services to large numbers of connected customers across the globe is a prerequisite for increasing the scale, scope, and speed of digital services trade. According to the Organisation for Economic Co-operation and Development (OECD), rapid technological developments facilitate the rise of services in international cross-border trade. This is associated with being able to deliver more rapidly and "on demand," so that consumers can access services instantly. The availability, quality, and cost of telecommunications infrastructure, internet and mobile penetration and accessibility, along with the adoption of digital and mobile technologies, play major roles in determining patterns of digital services trade. In some developing countries, lack of availability, high cost, and uneven quality of broadband and internet services remain significant challenges.

Internet Penetration. Literature links broadband and internet adoption to increased productivity, where the internet is seen as a tool that can support businesses to flourish and hire employees (OECD 2012, 2016). According to Haltenhof (2019), internet connectivity and exports of services are positively correlated. Consequently, improving bilateral internet connections promotes bilateral services trade in data-intensive sectors. The study claims that the greatest effects are observed for services sectors in finance, computers and information, and other business services. Moreover, higher internet penetration in developing countries is correlated with higher level of exports to developed countries, suggesting that access to the internet affects the export performance of firms in developing countries (Clarke and Wallsten 2004). A study of 151 countries from 1990 and 2006 showed that a doubling of internet usage led to a 2% to 4% increase in services trade (Choi 2009).

For the past years, broadband subscriptions have been increasing steadily. This was more pronounced in mobile-broadband subscriptions. According to the International Telecommunication Union (ITU), fixed broadband subscription increased from 5.2% in 2007 to 14.8% in 2019, while mobile-broadband subscription grew from 4.0% in 2007 to 74.2% in 2019. While Figure 3.6 indicates that the number of subscriptions has been consistently growing, it also displays the digital divide across the three economy groups.

Higher levels of internet penetration are positively associated with digital services trade (Figure 3.7).

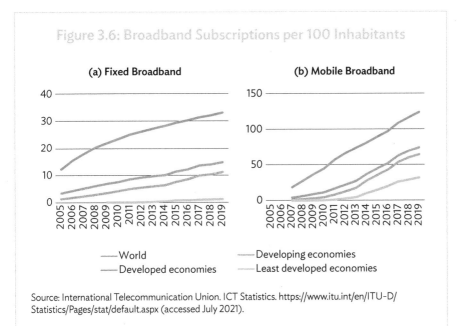

Figure 3.6: Broadband Subscriptions per 100 Inhabitants

Source: International Telecommunication Union. ICT Statistics. https://www.itu.int/en/ITU-D/Statistics/Pages/stat/default.aspx (accessed July 2021).

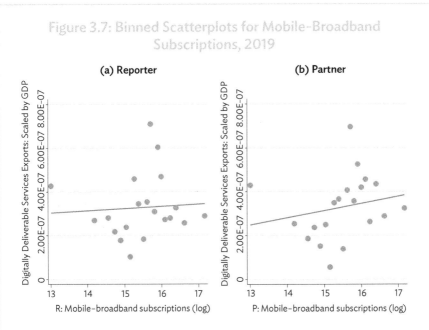

Figure 3.7: Binned Scatterplots for Mobile-Broadband Subscriptions, 2019

GDP = gross domestic product, P = partner, R = reporter.

Sources: Authors' calculations using WTO–OECD Balanced Trade in Services Dataset (BaTIS)—BPM6. https://www.wto.org/english/res_e/statis_e/trade_datasets_e.htm; and International Telecommunication Union. ICT Statistics. https://www.itu.int/en/ITU-D/Statistics/Pages/stat/default.aspx (both accessed July 2021).

Internet Speed. A reliable internet with high-speed connection increases productivity. Switching from normal speed to fast broadband substantially improves both firm and labor productivity (Dalgic and Fazlioglu 2020; Grimes, Ren, and Stevens 2012). For businesses using technologies such as videoconferencing, online payments, and other e-commerce functions, a high-speed connection is necessary (DataKom 2016). This is particularly true of firms that consume large volumes of data and for which greater bandwidth is essential.

Actual internet speed and usage are also important. Some may have internet access, but not at a usable speed. Figure 3.8 illustrates the positive relationship between digital services exports and the digital services trade and international internet bandwidth per user. It is also of note that international bandwidth capacity is more strongly related with digital services exports than with the mobile-broadband subscription level. This suggests that internet speed and quality should be more important as a factor in the expansion of digital services trade than simple internet availability.

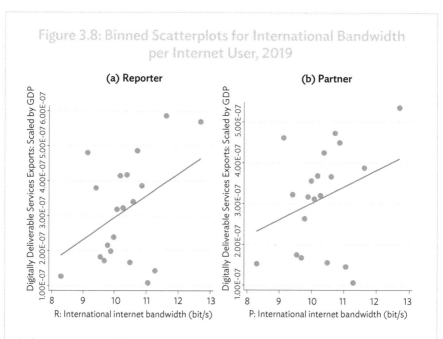

Figure 3.8: Binned Scatterplots for International Bandwidth per Internet User, 2019

bit/s = bits per second, GDP = gross domestic product, P = partner, R = reporter.

Sources: Authors' calculations using WTO–OECD Balanced Trade in Services Dataset (BaTIS)—BPM6. https://www.wto.org/english/res_e/statis_e/trade_datasets_e.htm; and International Telecommunication Union. ICT Statistics. https://www.itu.int/en/ITU-D/Statistics/Pages/stat/default.aspx (both accessed July 2021).

Investments

Digital solutions are defined as "other internet-based players and digital enablers, such as electronic and digital payment operators, cloud players and other service providers" (UNCTAD 2017). With increasing digitalization of industries, it is important to adopt digital solutions that cater to the needs of businesses. Firms that invest in and apply ICT are generally in a better position to become more productive, competitive, and profitable (UNCTAD 2011). As a result, new digital solutions are opening doors for companies of all sizes to engage in domestic and international trade (UNCTAD 2019).

Investments in telecommunications, ICT infrastructure, and digital payments enable digitally deliverable businesses to thrive. Figure 3.9 shows that investments in telecommunication infrastructure are positively associated with digital services trade.

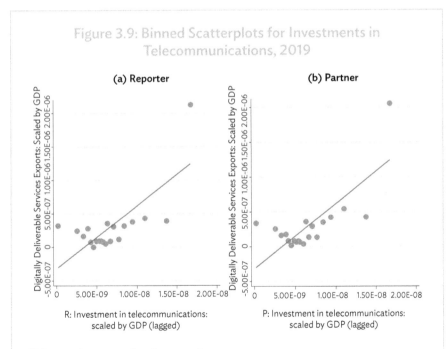

Figure 3.9: Binned Scatterplots for Investments in Telecommunications, 2019

GDP = gross domestic product, P = partner, R = reporter.

Sources: Authors' calculations using WTO–OECD Balanced Trade in Services Dataset (BaTIS)—BPM6. https://www.wto.org/english/res_e/statis_e/trade_datasets_e.htm; and International Telecommunication Union. ICT Statistics. https://www.itu.int/en/ITU-D/Statistics/Pages/stat/default.aspx (both accessed July 2021).

Policies and Regulatory Environment

The ecosystem for digital services trade requires a conducive overall business and regulatory environment. Stakeholders typically highlight the importance of transparency in regulations, the ease of data transfers, an open trade and investment regime, and supporting incentives for innovation. Many countries are also making efforts to build trust in supporting data flows. Creating trust should come with regulatory cooperation between countries and developing trade agreements or other arrangements that bolster privacy and consumer protection.

Internet freedom, or the ability of individuals to access the internet without state surveillance, censorship, or other barriers, could foster digital services trade. Hindley and Smith (1984) propose that services trade is constrained by government control over communications, media, and broadcasting. In the digital sphere, Topornin, Pyatkina, and Bokov (2021) characterize barriers to international data transfers, restrictions on digital payment systems, and many unique and opaque standards of filtering and blocking as potential tools of digital protectionism.

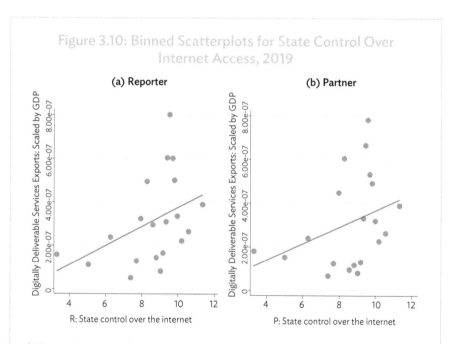

Figure 3.10: Binned Scatterplots for State Control Over Internet Access, 2019

GDP = gross domestic product, P = partner, R = reporter.

Sources: Authors' calculations based on WTO–OECD Balanced Trade in Services Dataset (BaTIS)—BPM6. https://www.wto.org/english/res_e/statis_e/trade_datasets_e.htm; and CATO Institute. Human Freedom Index. https://www.cato.org/human-freedom-index/2020 (both accessed July 2021).

Figure 3.10 shows how freedom of information positively influences digital services trade outcomes for both reporter and partner. It uses the CATO Institute's measure of "state control over internet access," which is a component from the Institutional Profiles Database question: "Freedom of information: Freedom of access, navigation, and publication on the internet (0 = no freedom of internet access; 10 = complete freedom of navigation and publication)."

3.3   Empirical Analysis

The impact of various factors affecting digital services trade can be tested empirically. Using the factors affecting digital services trade competitiveness that were identified in Section 3.2, we run a gravity model to determine the relationship between the dependent and various independent variables. Table 3.1 shows the selected variables and their sources.

Table 3.1: Data and Sources

Category	Variable	Notes	Source
Dependent variable	Digital services trade exports	Sum of all digitally deliverable items (SF, SG, SH, SI, SJ, SK).	BaTIS
Independent (human capital)	Expected years of schooling	Number of years of schooling that a child of school-entrance age can expect to receive if prevailing patterns of age-specific enrollment rates persist throughout the child's life. Log-transformed.	UNDP
Independent (infrastructure)	Mobile-broadband subscriptions	Active mobile-broadband subscriptions; scaled to population. Interpolated using nearest-neighbor algorithm. Log-transformed.	ITU
	International internet bandwidth per internet user	Expressed in bit/s. Log-transformed.	ITU
Independent (investment)	Annual investment in telecommunication services	Expressed in $, log-transformed; annual investments made by entities providing telecommunication networks and/or services in the country. Log-transformed. Lagged.	ITU

continued on next page

Table 3.1 *continued*

Category	Variable	Notes	Source
Independent (policies)	State control over the internet	Freedom of information: Freedom of access, navigation, and publication on the internet (10 = complete freedom of internet access; 0 = no freedom of navigation and publication). Interpolated using nearest-neighbor algorithm.	Cato Institute

BaTIS = WTO–OECD Balanced Trade in Services dataset; bit/s = bits per second; ITU = International Telecommunication Union; n.i.e. = not included elsewhere; OECD = Organisation for Economic Co-operation and Development; SF = insurance and pension services; SG = financial services; SH = charges for the use of intellectual property n.i.e.; SI = telecommunications, computer, and information services; SJ = other business services; SK = personal, cultural, and recreational services; UNDP = United Nations Development Programme; WTO = World Trade Organization.

Sources: Authors' compilation from WTO–OECD Balanced Trade in Services Dataset (BATIS)—BPM6. https://www.wto.org/english/res_e/statis_e/trade_datasets_e.htm; CATO Institute. Human Freedom Index. https://www.cato.org/human-freedom-index/2020; International Telecommunication Union. ICT Statistics. https://www.itu.int/en/ITU-D/Statistics/Pages/stat/default.aspx; and United Nations Development Programme. Human Development Index. http://hdr.undp.org/en/content/human-development-index-hdi (all accessed July 2021).

Table 3.1 lists the variables used in the regression. Each category was represented by at least one time-varying independent variable. Besides the variables of interest, we include economy-pair fixed effects that absorb classical gravity model controls, such as the log-transformed simple distance between the bilateral economies, contiguity, common official language, colony, time difference, common currency, common religion, and others. We do, however, include separate runs for the baseline regression without bilateral fixed effects, while including these traditional gravity variables in Appendix Table A3.1. We include reporter-time and partner-time fixed effects to account for factors such as economic size that vary by the economy and time dimensions. A regional trade agreement (RTA) indicator variable from the World Trade Organization's RTA database is also added.

Model Specification

The dataset covers a total of 235 reporter (exporter) economies and 236 partner (importer) economies. For the dependent variable, we use digitally deliverable services exports. Equation 3.2 below shows the model specification. Each variable of interest is interacted by an economy pair, transforming them into bilateral values to better account for pairwise synergy effects.

$$DDS_{ijt} = \alpha + I_{it} + I_{jt} + I_{ij} + \gamma_1 \ln(Educ_{it} * Educ_{jt}) + \delta_1 \ln(Infra_{it} * Infra_{jt}) + \zeta_1 \ln(Inv_{it} * Inv_{jt}) + \eta_1 (Pol_{it} * Pol_{it}) + \varepsilon_{ijt} \tag{3.2}$$

where $i = 1,..,235$, and i refers to reporter (exporter) economy i,
        $j = 1,..,236$, and j refers to partner (importer) economy j,

t = 2005,...,2019, and t refers to year t,
I_{it} are reporter-time fixed effects,
I_{jt} are partner-time fixed effects,
I_{ij} are time-invariant bilateral fixed effects,
$Educ$ refers to the vector of human capital variables,
$Infra$ refers to the vector of infrastructure variables,
Inv refers to the vector of investment variables, and
Pol refers to the vector of policy variables.

We employ the Poisson pseudo-maximum likelihood (PPML) as the primary estimation method for equation 3.2. Santos Silva and Tenreyro (2006) posit that PPML may be used in the presence of zero trade flows. As a Poisson estimator, it directly applies the multiplicative form of the equation, hence resolving Jensen's inequality. Additionally, this method remains robust against heteroscedasticity, which is endemic in trade research. These characteristics make PPML particularly suited to gravity model estimation, and its use has been documented extensively in the literature (Head and Mayer 2014).

We use the *ppmlhdfe* package by Correia, Guimarães, and Zylkin (2019). This package accelerates the estimation of parameter values in PPML models with high-dimensional fixed effects, as in gravity models. This is achieved with improvements to the iteration algorithm of the least-squares estimation and with deletions to separated observations, which do not add additional information to the estimation. The Ramsey regression equation specification error test (RESET) is used post-estimation to check the robustness of the PPML specification.

To obtain information on patterns across different regions and sectors, several iterations of the baseline model have been estimated. Aside from digital services trade, non-digital services trade was used as a dependent variable. Moreover, regressions were run across Asian and non-Asian regional groupings, with various interaction variables to gauge disparities. Besides regional analysis, several interaction effects were estimated to examine the nuances in digital services determinants for different Asia trade flows and developing Asia. As a diagnostic measure, regressions were run for observations in the BaTIS dataset, which were not derived from the gravity model.

Results

For all results, only variables of interest are reported. For iterations on the baseline regression, such as those including interactions effects, all standard variables are shown in the full tables in Appendix Table A3.2 for Asia and Table A3.3 for developing Asia. All pseudo R-squared values indicate that the model explains over 90% of the variation in digital services trade, which is within the typical range of gravity models. Moreover, all Ramsey test statistics are insignificant (do not reject the null hypothesis), indicating no evidence of specification error.

Results of the baseline regression for digital services exports are shown in the first column of Table 3.2. Consistent with expectations, nearly all variables of interest appear to positively drive digital services trade. Human capital, as measured in expected years of education for the adult population, seems to bolster digital services trade at a 1% significance level. The parameter values for this factor imply that a 1% increase in average education years in the bilateral level of education boosts digital services trade by about 0.122%, all else equal.[1]

Table 3.2: Baseline Regression Results

Dependent Variable:	(1) Digitally Deliverable Services Exports	(2) Non-Digitally Deliverable Services Exports
Mean years of schooling	0.1221***	0.0486
	(0.0265)	(0.0193)
Mobile-broadband subscriptions	0.0015***	0.0026
	(0.0003)	(0.0003)
International internet bandwidth (bit/s)	0.0027***	0.0021***
	(0.0004)	(0.0005)
Investment in telecommunications, lagged (log)	0.0018***	0.0028***
	(0.0004)	(0.0003)
State control over the internet	0.0027***	0.0018***
	(0.0003)	(0.0004)
RTA dummy variable	0.0101	0.0062**
	(0.0160)	(0.0153)
Constant	5.3189***	4.6169***
	(0.2350)	(0.2731)
Exporter-year fixed effects	Yes	Yes
Importer-year fixed effects	Yes	Yes
Bilateral fixed effects	Yes	Yes
Observations	112,540	112,540
Pseudo R-squared	0.993	0.989
Ramsey test: Prob > chi2	0.747	0.162

bit/s = bit per second, RTA = regional trade agreement.

Note: Numbers in parentheses are robust standard errors, clustered by economy pair: *** $p < 0.01$, ** $p < 0.05$, * $p < 0.10$.

Sources: Authors' calculations using data from WTO–OECD Balanced Trade in Services Dataset (BaTIS)—BPM6. https://www.wto.org/english/res_e/statis_e/trade_datasets_e.htm; CATO Institute. Human Freedom Index. https://www.cato.org/human-freedom-index/2020; International Telecommunication Union. ICT Statistics. https://www.itu.int/en/ITU-D/Statistics/Pages/stat/default.aspx; United Nations Development Programme. Human Development Index. http://hdr.undp.org/en/content/human-development-index-hdi (accessed July 2021).

---

[1] Coefficients of continuous variables, which are log-transformed, are interpreted as elasticities in the PPML model.

Results also indicate that mobile-broadband subscriptions have a highly significant positive association to digital services exports, on the exporter side. This is statistically significant at the 1% level. Furthermore, faster international internet bandwidth also appears correlated with greater digital services trade, highlighting the importance of digital infrastructure in fostering trade.

Similarly, investments relating to digital services, as measured by the annual investment in telecommunications, has a positive relationship with digital services trade. This covariate may reflect the government's priority on investing in digital infrastructure.

Moreover, it appears that more internet freedom is conducive to trade, showing a positive and highly significant association. This is consistent with the literature on services trade, where enhanced freedom of information supports a thriving trade environment.

Finally, we examine the regional trade agreement dummy, which appears to hold no statistical significance once accounting for the rich array of fixed effects employed in the model.

As a comparison, the results for non-digital services trade are also examined in the second column of Table 3.2. As seen, while non-digital services exports seem to benefit from internet bandwidth and telecommunications investment, it is notable that the covariates on schooling and mobile-broadband subscriptions uniquely enhance digital trade. Moreover, in direct contrast to digital services, the existence of an RTA between the two nations seems to drive non-digital services trade at a statistically significant level in line with expectations. Intuitively, digitally deliverable services are not as dependent on traditional economic arrangements and are subject to different rules and barriers. Nonetheless, an existing economic relationship does appear to foster services trade for certain sectors.

From the first two columns of Table 3.3, there is clear heterogeneity in the determinants of digital services trade across Asian and non-Asian economies. On human capital, the years of education of a nation's populace seem to bolster trade, although to a slightly greater magnitude and level of significance outside of Asia.

On the infrastructure aspect, Asian economies notably benefit at a 1% significance level from mobile-broadband subscriptions, which indicates that greater access to the internet is a driving factor of digital trade. In contrast, non-Asian economies show a positive but insignificant parameter value. Also, internet speed does not appear to universally drive exports, remaining statistically insignificant for Asia, while positive for digital services trade from non-Asian nations.

On investment, this again appears to significantly bolster trade of both Asian and non-Asian digital services. However, it appears to have a greater magnitude for non-Asian economies (0.0024 against 0.0012), which may highlight the relative maturity of Asian telecommunications infrastructure.

Table 3.3: Digitally Deliverable and Non-Digitally Deliverable Services Determinants by Region

	(1) Digitally Deliverable Services		(2) Non-Digitally Deliverable Services	
Dependent Variable:				
Region:	**Asia**	**Non-Asia**	**Asia**	**Non-Asia**
Mean years of schooling (log)	0.1536***	0.3389***	0.0185	0.0437
	(0.0479)	(0.0557)	(0.0830)	(0.0438)
Mobile-broadband subscriptions (log)	0.0019***	0.0003	0.0035***	0.0041***
	(0.0003)	(0.0004)	(0.0004)	(0.0005)
International internet bandwidth (bit/s)	0.0007	0.0028***	0.0036	0.0015***
	(0.0007)	(0.0005)	(0.0016)	(0.0005)
Investment in telecommunications, lagged (log)	0.0012***	0.0024***	0.0020	0.0005*
	(0.0003)	(0.0004)	(0.0006)	(0.0003)
State control over the internet	0.0027***	0.0025***	0.0004	0.0029
	(0.0004)	(0.0004)	(0.0009)	(0.0006)
RTA dummy variable	0.0130	0.0004	0.0231	0.0095
	(0.0306)	(0.0179)	(0.0428)	(0.0123)
Constant	5.2891***	4.3834***	5.0767***	5.8115***
	(0.2926)	(0.3810)	(0.4702)	(0.2106)
Exporter-year fixed effects	Yes	Yes	Yes	Yes
Importer-year fixed effects	Yes	Yes	Yes	Yes
Bilateral fixed effects	Yes	Yes	Yes	Yes
Observations	20,893	91,647	20,893	91,647
Pseudo R-squared	0.992	0.993	0.990	0.989
Ramsey test: Prob > chi2	0.786	0.934	0.772	0.784

bit/s = bit per second, RTA = regional trade agreement.

Notes:
(i) Non-Asia = all economies outside of the Asia and Pacific region.
(ii) Numbers in parentheses are robust standard errors, clustered by economy pair: *** $p < 0.01$, ** $p < 0.05$, * $p < 0.10$.

Sources: Authors' calculations using data from WTO–OECD Balanced Trade in Services Dataset (BaTIS)—BPM6. https://www.wto.org/english/res_e/statis_e/trade_datasets_e.htm; CATO Institute. Human Freedom Index. https://www.cato.org/human-freedom-index/2020; International Telecommunication Union. ICT Statistics https://www.itu.int/en/ITU-D/Statistics/Pages/stat/default.aspx; and United Nations Development Programme. Human Development Index. http://hdr.undp.org/en/content/human-development-index-hdi (accessed July 2021).

On the policy aspect, increased freedom to navigate the internet is a positive determinant of digital services everywhere, and it is significant at the 1% level. This highlights the continuing importance of the level of state control or censorship of the internet in digitally deliverable services trade.

The third and fourth columns of Table 3.3 regress the same functional equation on services trade that is other than digital services (non-digital services trade) for each region. Compared with the results in the first two columns, education, digital infrastructure, investment, and internet freedom appear to follow the same overall directions, though to a much-diminished scale and statistical significance. For instance, mean years of schooling does not appear to significantly drive non-digitally deliverable services for Asian economies. It is also weakly significant for non-Asian economies, although with a coefficient that is less than half of that for digitally deliverable services. On the other hand, mobile internet users, a factor that was significant for Asia and the Pacific, remains significant for non-digital services trade. Similarly, both internet bandwidth and investment remain positive and significant for non-Asian economies.

A further point of contrast is in the index of state control over the internet, which is statistically insignificant for Asia and Pacific trade in non-digitally deliverable services. These findings underscore the unique nature of digitally deliverable services trade over more traditionally delivered services, with digital services trade in the region being more strongly driven by education, internet access (as measured by mobile internet users), and internet freedom, as compared to non-digital services trade.

The nexus of financial access, technological progress, and development in digitally deliverable progress cannot be ignored. Table 3.4 analyzes the correlation of digital payments on trade in digital services within and outside Asia and the Pacific. To obviate the problem of multicollinearity, the infrastructure variables (mobile-broadband and internet speed) are dropped. Variables besides digital payments such as education, investment, and internet policy generally follow the directions and magnitudes reported in Table 3.3. The results indicate that the greater the usage of digital payments, the greater the volume of digitally deliverable services exports, more so for Asian economies.

Robustness Check

To further test the robustness of the data and specification, considering that most observations (over 70%) in the BaTIS database were derived using gravity modeling, we regressed the same equation with only the data points that were reported by the observing economies excluding those estimated. Full results can be found in Table 3.5. Overall, the directions of all variables are generally similar to the baseline model using all the balanced values of the BaTIS database; although, the level of significance is slightly lessened for the truncated dataset. Nonetheless, no wild swings are seen in relationships or scale, especially for digital services trade. This may point to the robustness of the full dataset for analysis.

Table 3.4: Digital Payments and Digitally Deliverable Services

Dependent Variable:	Digitally Deliverable Services	
Region:	Asia	Non-Asia
Mean years of schooling (log)	0.1152***	0.3157***
	(0.0745)	(0.0921)
Digital payments	0.3449***	0.1854***
	(0.1086)	(0.0521)
Investment in telecommunications (log) (lag)	0.0034***	0.0062***
	(0.0007)	(0.0010)
State control over the internet	0.0018*	0.0026*
	(0.0011)	(0.0014)
RTA dummy variable	0.0316	0.0249
	(0.0316)	(0.0215)
Constant	6.3511***	4.9348***
	(0.6129)	(0.7642)
Exporter-year fixed effects	Yes	Yes
Importer-year fixed effects	Yes	Yes
Bilateral fixed effects	Yes	Yes
Observations	14,470	61,406
Pseudo R-squared	0.993	0.995
Ramsey test: Prob > chi2	0.213	0.167

RTA = regional trade agreement.

Notes:
(i) Non-Asia = all economies outside of the Asia and Pacific region.
(ii) Numbers in parentheses are robust standard errors, clustered by economy pair: *** $p < 0.01$, ** $p < 0.05$, * $p < 0.10$.

Sources: Authors' calculations using data from WTO–OECD Balanced Trade in Services Dataset (BaTIS)—BPM6. https://www.wto.org/english/res_e/statis_e/trade_datasets_e.htm; CATO Institute. Human Freedom Index. https://www.cato.org/human-freedom-index/2020; International Telecommunication Union. ICT Statistics. https://www.itu.int/en/ITU-D/Statistics/Pages/stat/default.aspx; and United Nations Development Programme. Human Development Index. http://hdr.undp.org/en/content/human-development-index-hdi; World Bank (accessed July 2021 and September 2021).

Table 3.5: Diagnostics on BaTIS Dataset

Dependent Variable:	(1) Digitally Deliverable Services Exports	(2) Non-Digitally Deliverable Services Exports	(3) Digitally Deliverable Services Exports	(4) Non-Digitally Deliverable Services Exports
Mean years of schooling (log)	0.1720*** (0.0353)	0.1743*** (0.0305)	0.1386*** (0.0330)	0.0692** (0.0314)
Mobile-broadband subscriptions (log)	0.0017*** (0.0005)	0.0045*** (0.0009)	0.0015*** (0.0004)	0.0032*** (0.0006)
International internet bandwidth (bit/s)	0.0025*** (0.0005)	0.0030*** (0.0007)	0.0022*** (0.0005)	0.0022*** (0.0007)
Investment in telecommunications, lagged (log)	0.0023*** (0.0008)	0.0033*** (0.0006)	0.0016*** (0.0006)	0.0031*** (0.0006)
State control over the internet	0.0021*** (0.0005)	0.0045*** (0.0007)	0.0022*** (0.0004)	0.0027*** (0.0007)
RTA dummy variable	0.0140 (0.0247)	-0.0583** (0.0291)	0.0335 (0.0214)	-0.0098 (0.0217)
Constant	5.0819*** (0.4912)	2.9399*** (0.4877)	5.7491*** (0.3432)	4.5308*** (0.5112)
Exporter-year fixed effects	Yes	Yes	Yes	Yes
Importer-year fixed effects	Yes	Yes	Yes	Yes
Observations	17,892	20,589	28,697	31,464
Pseudo R-squared	0.991	0.988	0.993	0.990
Ramsey test: Prob > chi2	0.666	0.128	0.339	0.326
Mean years of schooling (log)	0.1720***	0.1743***	0.1386***	0.0692**

BaTIS = WTO–OECD Balanced Trade in Services dataset, bit/s = bits per second, RTA = regional trade agreement.

Note: Numbers in parentheses are robust standard errors, clustered by economy pair: *** $p < 0.01$, ** $p < 0.05$, * $p < 0.10$.

Sources: Authors' calculations using data from WTO–OECD Balanced Trade in Services Dataset (BaTIS)—BPM6. https://www.wto.org/english/res_e/statis_e/trade_datasets_e.htm; CATO Institute. Human Freedom Index. https://www.cato.org/human-freedom-index/2020; International Telecommunication Union. ICT Statistics. https://www.itu.int/en/ITU-D/Statistics/Pages/stat/default.aspx; and United Nations Development Programme. Human Development Index. http://hdr.undp.org/en/content/human-development-index-hdi (accessed July 2021).

3.4   Conclusions and Recommendations

Digital services trade is influenced by an economy's human capital, digital connectivity, investment, and policy and regulatory environment. Asia and the Pacific, while growing rapidly in digital services trade, still lag advanced economies in competitiveness. To shed light on where policy makers in the region can focus on to drive the development of digital services and digital services trade, this chapter illustrates the reasoning behind the key determinants of digital services trade. Further, we test empirically the impact of the potential determinants of digital services trade utilizing the BaTIS database and standard indicators for digital infrastructure and gravity controls.

Employing the best practice of PPML estimation, we find that all relevant pillars such as human capital, digital connectivity, investment, and policy environment are significant and positively associated factors for driving digital services trade development among all economies. This finding is robust against various specifications and for regional subsamples. These results are particularly relevant to digital services trade, with non-digital services trade in Asia not being significantly impacted by education or mobile-broadband subscriptions.

As digital services trade becomes increasingly important, several policy considerations are important to ensuring that all nations stand to benefit.

In the era of COVID-19 and after the pandemic, the value of upskilling and reskilling the workforce is paramount, especially considering existing skill-based barriers to the uptake of digital technology. As can be seen from the analysis in this chapter, the length of education is associated with greater trade in digitally deliverable services, suggesting that economies should strengthen national education systems. It is also becoming imperative to integrate digital literacy into the core curriculum to ensure that the youth are equipped with necessary digital tools to thrive amid rapid digital transformation.

As evident in the analysis, the value of digital services exports benefits to a larger extent from more broadband users and internet speed. Consequently, investing in digital connectivity and ICT infrastructure can help reap the great economic benefits offered by digital services trade. This highlights that governments and the private sector need to make further effort to narrow the gaps between frontier and other economies on this front.

The policy environment also affects the performance of digital services trade. Although this chapter has shown that internet freedom can be conducive to digital services trade, other policy measures, such as those on data flows, data protection, trade restrictiveness, and domestic regulations, can exert no less impact on digital services trade, calling for policy makers to ensure a fine balance between diverse policy objectives, including economic welfare, national security, and digital privacy.

Although this chapter's analysis shows that cross-border agreements are not yet significant in fostering digitally deliverable services trade, this might change as more and more international agreements enter into force, affecting the digital services trade landscape. The General Agreement on Trade in Services has general provisions that may support digital trade, such as market access, legal considerations, and most-favored treatment. However, many opportunities exist for nations to further improve cooperation in this sphere. Recently, the Digital Economy Partnership Agreements among Asian economies have risen to prominence, most notably in Singapore, Thailand, Australia, and the Republic of Korea (Government of Singapore, Ministry of Trade and Industry 2021). These agreements foster cooperation in digital payment systems, cross-border data flows, digital identity, and more—all of which promote multilateral digital economic trade. These nascent initiatives address the limitations of traditional regional trade agreements by establishing provisions that streamline processes, modernize payments systems, and harmonize data protection policies.

Bibliography

Asia-Pacific Economic Cooperation (APEC). 2021. *Investing in Digital Upskilling and Reskilling of APEC's Workforce Is Critical: Report.* 23 February. https://www.apec.org/Press/News-Releases/2021/0223_Digital.

Asian Development Bank (ADB). 2021. *Asian Development Outlook 2021: Financing a Green and Inclusive Recovery.* Manila.

Berg, J., M. Furrer, E. Harmon, U. Rani, and M. S. Silberman. 2018. *Digital Labour Platforms and the Future of Work: Towards Decent Work in the Online World.* Geneva: International Labour Organization.

Borchert, I., B. Gootiiz, J. Magdelieine, J. Marchetti, A. Mattoo, E. Rubio, and E. Shannon. 2019. Applied Services Trade Policy: A Guide to the Services Trade Policy Database and the Services Trade Restrictions Index. *Staff Working Paper.* ERSD-2019-14. Geneva: World Trade Organization. https://www.wto.org/english/res_e/reser_e/ersd201914_e.pdf.

Caselli, F., and W. J. Coleman. 2001. Cross-Country Technology Diffusion: The Case of Computers. *American Economic Review.* 91 (2). pp. 328–335.

CATO Institute. Human Freedom Index. https://www.cato.org/human-freedom-index/2020 (accessed July 2021).

Centre d'Etudes Prospectives et d'Informations Internationales (CEPII). Geography Database. http://www.cepii.fr/CEPII/en/bdd_modele/bdd_modele.asp (accessed July 2021).

Chinn, M. D., and R. W. Fairlie. 2007. The Determinants of the Global Digital Divide: A Cross-Country Analysis of Computer and Internet Penetration. *Oxford Economic Papers*. 59 (1). pp. 16–44.

Choi, C. 2009. The Effect of the Internet on Service Trade. *Economics Letters*. 109 (2010). pp. 102–104.

Chor, D. 2010. Unpacking Sources of Comparative Advantage: A Quantitative Approach. *Journal of International Economics*. 82 (2). pp. 152–167.

Clarke, G. and S. Wallsten. 2004. Has the Internet Increased Trade? Evidence from Industrial and Developing Countries. *World Bank Policy Research Working Paper*. No. 3215. Washington, DC: World Bank.

Correia, S., P. Guimarães, and T. Zylkin. 2019. PPMLHDFE: Fast Poisson Estimation with High-Dimensional Fixed Effects. *The Stata Journal: Promoting Communications on Statistics and Stata*. 20 (1). pp. 95–115.

Dalgic, B. and B. Fazlioglu. 2020. The Impact of Broadband Speed on Productivity: Findings from Turkish Firms. *Applied Economics Letters*. 27 (21). pp. 1764–1767.

DataKom. 2016. *How Slow Internet Speeds Can Impact Productivity*. 22 July. https://www.datakom.co.uk/2016/07/how-slow-internet-speeds-can-impact-productivity/.

Ferracane, M. and E. van der Marel. 2021. Regulating Personal Data: Linking Different Models to Digital Services Trade. *VoxEU*. 30 May. https://voxeu.org/article/regulating-personal-data-linking-different-models-digital-services-trade.

———. 2021. Regulating Personal Data: Background paper for the World Development Report 2021. *Policy Research Working Paper*. No. 9596. Washington, DC: World Bank.

Ferrarini, B. 2010. Trade and Income in Asia: Panel Data Evidence from Instrumental Variable Regression. *ADB Economics Working Paper Series*. No. 234. Manila: ADB.

Frankel, J. A. and D. H. Romer. 1999. Does Trade Cause Growth? *American Economic Review*. 89 (3). pp. 379–399.

Froy, F., S. Giguère, and M. Meghnagi. 2012. *Skills for Competitiveness: A Synthesis Report*. Paris: Organisation for Economic Co-operation and Development.

Government of Singapore, Ministry of Trade and Industry. 2021. *Digital Economy Partnership Agreement (DEPA)*. https://www.mti.gov.sg/Improving-Trade/Digital-Economy-Agreements/The-Digital-Economy-Partnership-Agreement.

Grigorescu, A., E. Pelinescu, A. E. Ion, and M. F. Dutcas. 2021. Human Capital in Digital Economy: An Empirical Analysis of Central and Eastern European Countries from the European Union. *Sustainability 2021*. 13 (2020). https://doi.org/10.3390/su13042020.

Grimes, A., C. Ren, and P. Stevens. 2012. The Need for Speed: Impacts of Internet Connectivity on Firm Productivity. *Journal of Productivity Analysis*. 37 (2). pp. 187–201.

Haltenhof, S. 2019. Services Trade and Internet Connectivity. *Research Seminar in International Economics Working Papers*. No. 668. Ann Arbor, MI: University of Michigan.

Head, K. and T. Mayer. 2014. Gravity Equations: Workhorse, Toolkit, and Cookbook. *Handbook of International Economics*. No. 4. pp. 131–195.

Hindley, B. and A. Smith. 1984. Comparative Advantage and Trade in Services. *World Economy*. 7 (4). pp. 369–390.

IMD. 2020. *IMD World Digital Competitiveness Ranking 2020*. https://imd.cld.bz/ IMD-World-Digital-Competitiveness-Ranking-2020/18/.

International Telecommunication Union (ITU). *World Telecommunication/ICT Indicators Database*. https://www.itu.int/en/ITU-D/Statistics/Pages/stat/ default.aspx (accessed July 2021).

Loveless, B. n.d. *The Importance of Digital Literacy in K-12*. https://www. educationcorner.com/importance-digital-literacy-k-12.html.

Martin, A. and J. Grudziecki. 2006. DigEuLit: Concepts and Tools for Digital Literacy Development. *Innovation in Teaching and Learning in Information and Computer Sciences*. 5 (4). pp. 249–267.

Organisation for Economic Co-operation and Development (OECD). n.d. Digital Trade. https://www.oecd.org/trade/topics/digital-trade/.

———. 2012. *OECD Internet Economy Outlook 2012*. Paris.

———. 2016. *Skills and Jobs in the Digital Economy: A Digital Economy Toolkit*. Paris.

———. 2018. *Implications of the Digital Transformation for the Business Sector*. Paris.

Robacker, T. 2017. More Than 75 Percent of Fifth and Eighth Graders Are Non-Proficient in 21st Century Skills, According to Learning.com Study. *Learning. com*. 22 August. https://www.learning.com/more-than-75-percent-of-fifth-and-eighth-graders-are-non-proficient-in-21st-century-skills-according-to-learning-com-study/.

Sáez, S., D. Taglioni, E. Van der Marel, C. H. Hollweg, and V. Zavacka. 2015. *Valuing Services in Trade: A Toolkit for Competitiveness Diagnostics*. Washington, DC: World Bank.

Santos Silva, J. M. C. and S. Tenreyro. 2006. The Log of Gravity. *The Review of Economics and Statistics*. 88 (4). pp. 641–658.

Spante, M., S. S. Hashemi, M. Lundin, A. Algers, and S. Wang. 2018. Digital Competence and Digital Literacy in Higher Education Research: Systematic Review of Concept Use. *Cogent Education*. 5 (1).

Topornin, N., D. Pyatkina, and Y. Bokov. 2021. Government Regulation of the Internet as Instrument of Digital Protectionism in Case of Developing Countries. *Journal of Information Science*. DOI:10.1177/01655515211014142.

United Nations Children's Fund (UNICEF). Education Overview. https://data. unicef.org/topic/education/overview/ (accessed July 2021).

United Nations Conference on Trade and Development (UNCTAD). 2011. *Information Economy Report 2011: ICTs as an Enabler for Private Sector Development*. Geneva.

———. 2017. *World Investment Report 2017*. Geneva.

———. 2019. *Digital Economy Report 2019*. Geneva.

United Nations Development Programme (UNDP). Human Development Data Center. http://hdr.undp.org/en/data (accessed July 2021).

World Bank. Goods Export (BoP, current US$). https://data.worldbank.org/ indicator/BX.GSR.MRCH.CD (accessed July 2021).

———. World Development Indicators. https://databank.worldbank.org/source/ world-development-indicators (accessed July 2021).

———. 2017. The Global Findex Database 2017. https://globalfindex.worldbank. org/#data_sec_focus (accessed September 2021).

World Trade Organization (WTO). 2019. *World Trade Statistical Review 2019*. https://www.wto.org/english/res_e/statis_e/wts2019_e/wts2019_e.pdf.

———. Regional Trade Agreements Database. https://rtais.wto.org/UI/ PublicMaintainRTAHome.aspx (accessed July 2021).

———. WTO–OECD Balanced Trade in Services Dataset (BATIS)—BPM 6. https:// www.wto.org/english/res_e/statis_e/trade_datasets_e.htm (accessed July 2021).

APPENDIXES

Table A3.1: Base Model with Gravity Variables

Dependent Variable:	(1) BaTIS DST Exports Balanced Value	(2) BaTIS Non-DST Exports Balanced Value
Mean years of schooling (log)	0.1757**	0.0924
	(0.0734)	(0.0588)
Mobile-broadband subscriptions (log)	0.0017***	0.0031***
	(0.0006)	(0.0006)
International internet bandwidth (bit/s) (log)	0.0006	0.0014
	(0.0012)	(0.0010)
Investment in telecommunications (log) (lag)	0.0028***	0.0028***
	(0.0008)	(0.0007)
State control over the internet	0.0010	-0.0009
	(0.0007)	(0.0007)
RTA dummy variable	0.1381***	0.2530***
	(0.0257)	(0.0193)
Distance	-0.3065***	-0.4255***
	(0.0164)	(0.0136)
Colonial relationship	0.0014	0.3938***
	(0.0324)	(0.0291)
Contiguity	0.0621*	0.4658***
	(0.0368)	(0.0260)
Common language	0.4597***	0.3160***
	(0.0348)	(0.0253)
Hours difference	-0.0462***	-0.0508***
	(0.0038)	(0.0030)
Common currency	0.3138***	0.1045***
	(0.0466)	(0.0295)
Common religion	0.3894***	0.2197***
	(0.0435)	(0.0296)
Constant	7.0649***	7.8384***
	(0.7195)	(0.6227)
Exporter-year fixed effects	Yes	Yes
Importer-year fixed effects	Yes	Yes
Bilateral fixed effects	No	No
Observations	119,368	119,368
Pseudo R-squared	0.958	0.935

BaTIS = WTO–OECD Balanced Trade in Services dataset, bit/s = bits per second, DST = digital services trade, RTA = regional trade agreement.

Note: Numbers in parentheses are robust standard errors, clustered by economy pair: *** $p < 0.01$, ** $p < 0.05$, * $p < 0.10$.

Sources: Authors' calculations using data from WTO–OECD Balanced Trade in Services Dataset (BaTIS)—BPM6. https://www.wto.org/english/res_e/statis_e/trade_datasets_e.htm; CATO Institute. Human Freedom Index. https://www.cato.org/human-freedom-index/2020; International Telecommunication Union. ICT Statistics. https://www.itu.int/en/ITU-D/Statistics/Pages/stat/default.aspx; and United Nations Development Programme. Human Development Index. http://hdr.undp.org/en/content/human-development-index-hdi (accessed July 2021).

Table A3.2: Asia Trade Interactions

Dependent Variable:	Digitally Deliverable Services			
Interaction Variable:	Mobile Broadband	Internet Bandwidth	Telecom Investment	Internet Regime
Mean years of schooling (log)	0.1159***	0.1261***	0.1219***	0.1221***
	(0.0264)	(0.0265)	(0.0263)	(0.0264)
Mobile-broadband subscriptions (log)	0.0006*	0.0014***	0.0015***	0.0015***
	(0.0003)	(0.0003)	(0.0003)	(0.0003)
International internet bandwidth per internet user (bit/s) (log)	0.0022***	0.0020***	0.0027***	0.0027***
	(0.0004)	(0.0005)	(0.0004)	(0.0004)
Investment in telecommunications, lagged (log)	0.0017***	0.0018***	0.0018***	0.0018***
	(0.0004)	(0.0004)	(0.0005)	(0.0004)
State control over the internet	0.0025***	0.0027***	0.0027***	0.0027***
	(0.0003)	(0.0003)	(0.0003)	(0.0004)
RTA dummy variable	-0.0010	-0.0003	0.0099	0.0100
	(0.0156)	(0.0159)	(0.0160)	(0.0165)
Asia Trade * Interaction Variable (Reference group: non-Asia trade)				
Asia intraregional	0.0008**	-0.0002	-0.0007	-0.0022***
	(0.0004)	(0.0008)	(0.0009)	(0.0008)
Asia outward	0.0015***	0.0021***	-0.0005	-0.0014**
	(0.0003)	(0.0006)	(0.0006)	(0.0007)
Asia inward	0.0018***	0.0028***	0.0012	-0.0019**
	(0.0003)	(0.0007)	(0.0008)	(0.0008)
Constant	5.6630***	5.3678***	5.2973***	5.4515***
	(0.2430)	(0.2339)	(0.2574)	(0.2268)
Exporter-year fixed effects	Yes	Yes	Yes	Yes
Importer-year fixed effects	Yes	Yes	Yes	Yes
Bilateral fixed effects	Yes	Yes	Yes	Yes
Observations	112,540	112,540	112,540	112,540
Pseudo R-squared	0.993	0.993	0.993	0.993
Ramsey test: Prob > chi2	0.527	0.527	0.809	0.774

bit/s = bits per second, RTA = regional trade agreement.

Notes:
(i) Non-Asia = all economies outside of the Asia and Pacific region.
(ii) Numbers in parentheses are robust standard errors, clustered by economy pair: *** $p < 0.01$, ** $p < 0.05$, * $p < 0.10$.

Sources: Authors' calculations using data from WTO–OECD Balanced Trade in Services Dataset (BaTIS)—BPM6. https://www.wto.org/english/res_e/statis_e/trade_datasets_e.htm; CATO Institute. Human Freedom Index. https://www.cato.org/human-freedom-index/2020; International Telecommunication Union. ICT Statistics. https://www.itu.int/en/ITU-D/Statistics/Pages/stat/default.aspx; and United Nations Development Programme. Human Development Index. http://hdr.undp.org/en/content/human-development-index-hdi (accessed July 2021).

Table A3.3: Developing Asia Interactions

Dependent Variable:	Digitally Deliverable Services			
Developing Asia Interaction:	Mobile Broadband	Internet Bandwidth	Telecom Investment	Internet Regime
Mean years of schooling (log)	0.1096***	0.1209***	0.1208***	0.1216***
	(0.0261)	(0.0263)	(0.0264)	(0.0264)
Mobile-broadband subscriptions (log)	0.0007**	0.0015***	0.0014***	0.0015***
	(0.0004)	(0.0003)	(0.0003)	(0.0003)
International internet bandwidth per internet user (bit/s) (log)	0.0023***	0.0026***	0.0027***	0.0027***
	(0.0004)	(0.0005)	(0.0004)	(0.0004)
Investment in telecommunications, lagged (log)	0.0016***	0.0018***	0.0016***	0.0018***
	(0.0004)	(0.0004)	(0.0005)	(0.0004)
State control over the internet	0.0025***	0.0027***	0.0026***	0.0026***
	(0.0003)	(0.0003)	(0.0003)	(0.0004)
RTA dummy variable	0.0063	0.0093	0.0092	0.0106
	(0.0159)	(0.0160)	(0.0160)	(0.0163)
R: Developing Asia * Interaction Variable	0.0009***	-0.0000	-0.0004	0.0005
	(0.0003)	(0.0006)	(0.0006)	(0.0006)
P: Developing Asia * Interaction Variable	0.0010***	0.0004	0.0017***	-0.0003
	(0.0003)	(0.0006)	(0.0006)	(0.0006)
Constant	5.7392***	5.3520***	5.3438***	5.3233***
	(0.2477)	(0.2373)	(0.2566)	(0.2320)
Exporter-year fixed effects	Yes	Yes	Yes	Yes
Importer-year fixed effects	Yes	Yes	Yes	Yes
Bilateral fixed effects	Yes	Yes	Yes	Yes
Observations	112,540	112,540	112,540	112,540
Pseudo R-squared	0.993	0.993	0.993	0.993
Ramsey test: Prob > chi2	0.527	0.405	0.809	0.774

bit/s = bits per second, P = partner, R = reporter, RTA = regional trade agreement.

Note: Numbers in parentheses are robust standard errors, clustered by economy pair: *** $p < 0.01$, ** $p < 0.05$, * $p < 0.10$.

Sources: Authors' calculations using data from WTO–OECD Balanced Trade in Services Dataset (BaTIS)—BPM6. https://www.wto.org/english/res_e/statis_e/trade_datasets_e.htm; CATO Institute. Human Freedom Index. https://www.cato.org/human-freedom-index/2020; International Telecommunication Union. ICT Statistics. https://www.itu.int/en/ITU-D/Statistics/Pages/stat/default.aspx; and United Nations Development Programme. Human Development Index. http://hdr.undp.org/en/content/human-development-index-hdi (accessed July 2021).

4
SERVICES, DIGITALLY DELIVERED TRADE, AND GLOBAL VALUE CHAINS IN ASIA

Ben Shepherd

4.1 Introduction and Motivation

Digital technology has become a major factor in global trade, and through it an engine of economic growth (Ferracane, Lee-Makiyama, and van der Marel 2018). The environment governing these transactions has seen substantial changes over recent years, involving policies, preferences, and technologies. Digitally delivered trade—that is to say, export and import transactions delivered using digital means— now provides benefits to producers and consumers alike, and is arguably helping drive productivity growth, which is the only reliable engine of long-run economic growth and increasing per capita incomes. As Ferracane, Lee-Makiyama, and van der Marel (2018) show, however, policies relating to digitally delivered sectors in Asia are mixed: some economies adopt relatively liberal stances, while others are among the most highly restrictive in the world.

The pandemic has accelerated the transformation toward digitally delivered trade. Not only have many activities—primarily services—that traditionally required in-person interaction moved online, but goods sectors have also increasingly shifted to online ordering and payment systems combined with advances in rapid delivery to keep crucial sectors afloat during a period where, in many economies, the protection of public health curtailed traditional retail interaction.

Conceptually, digital technology seems likely to play a major role in linking the large number of firms that participate in global value chains (GVCs). Lead firms depend on digital means to monitor production by suppliers and movement of goods within networked production structures. Similarly, digital payments make it possible for firms at different points in the chain to negotiate contracts and secure payments across borders, potentially at great distances. It is no coincidence that the "second unbundling" referred to by Baldwin (2011)—the geographic dispersion of production processes—coincides with the rise of information and communication technologies that began in the 1990s. Without such technologies, it would be difficult if not impossible to achieve the required degree of coordination in production.

An important policy issue is therefore the degree of linkage between the performance of goods market GVCs in sectors like electronics or apparel and in services, and the policy environment governing digitally delivered trade. If restrictive policies increase price and decrease availability of services provided digitally, then those services will be correspondingly less used as inputs in the production of manufactured goods and other services—potentially undermining trade performance and production efficiency. This analysis makes plain the importance of embodied services trade in the understanding of GVCs—i.e., the proportion of gross exports by sector that is made up of value added sourced in the services sector. It raises the question of the extent to which services provided digitally are used as inputs in the production of exports in other sectors. These backward and forward perspectives can be used in different contexts to better understand the role of input–output linkages, including those relating to services delivered digitally, in driving GVC performance and expansion.

Amid this trading environment, we seek to add to the literature in three ways. First, we identify digitally delivered services based on analysis by the Organisation for Economic Co-operation and Development (OECD) and use the ADB Multi-Regional Input–Output Tables (MRIOT) to produce consistent measures of their use within GVCs. We track this across economies and through time, focusing on Asia. Second, we analyze recently collected data on policy measures affecting digitally delivered trade. Finally, we build a quantitative general equilibrium model of world trade based on the ADB MRIOT for 2019. We use it to conduct counterfactual simulations based on plausible goals for policy liberalization and deregulation across economies affecting digitally delivered sectors. The model shows not only how policy changes affect trade flows and aggregate real income, but also how they influence GVC linkages. In other words, we are able to pinpoint the potential for the liberalization of digitally delivered trade to promote GVC integration across an economy, in other services sectors, and in goods. We also assess the ways in which this liberalization can promote structural change, by looking at the distribution of exports across primary, secondary, and tertiary aggregates.

After looking conceptually at digitally delivered trade and how it has trended through time, this chapter covers its effect on sectors, GVC linkages, and policies. We then develop a general equilibrium model of trade that incorporates GVC linkages and use this to conduct counterfactual simulations based on liberalization and deregulation of digitally delivered trade. The chapter ends by discussing the policy implications of the simulation findings.

4.2   Digitally Delivered Trade: Sectors, Linkages, and Policies

This section lays the groundwork for the rest of the chapter by developing a framework for understanding digitally delivered trade in terms of standard aggregates in the national accounts. Those insights help in measuring the degree of GVC integration exhibited by digitally delivered trade, focusing on Asian economies over 2000–2019. Finally, the section presents data on policies affecting digital trade for 2019, the most recent year for which data are available.[1]

4.2.1   Conceptualizing Digitally Delivered Trade

National accounts do not recognize "digital" as a sector or aggregate. Similarly, they do not identify ways in which other services are delivered, such as distinguishing between in-person versus digital provision. Services trade data do not distinguish provision by digital means from other means. In particular, they do not identify which of the four modes of supply recognized by the General Agreement on Trade in Services (GATS) is involved in particular cases. Standard services trade data are derived from the Balance of Payments, which mixes elements of GATS modes 1, 2, and 4. As such, it includes digitally delivered trade—which is relatively similar to the concept of GATS mode 1, or pure cross-border service provision—but also trade involving in-person interactions, either through movement of the consumer (mode 2) or the service provider (mode 4). Chapter 2 provides an overview of these issues, along with an identification of services that are digitally delivered, which is followed in this section.

Statisticians from the World Trade Organization (WTO) have made progress in moving beyond this by compiling data on Trade in Services by Mode of Supply (TISMOS). Since economies do not yet collect data by GATS mode of supply, the approach taken is to use information from surveys and external sources to construct first estimates of trade by mode. As such, TISMOS data are not directly observed, but instead are modeled estimates. They will be refined over time, but for the time being provide the best available information.

The TISMOS data make it possible to rank sectors according to the percentage of exports provided through GATS mode 1. This mode of supply is pure cross-border services trade, and essentially captures service provision by digital means. In other words, this mode is services trade that takes place by

---

[1]   No baseline year is free from external shocks to trade performance and GVC integration. For example, 2019 has the variable of the United States–People's Republic of China (PRC) trade conflict, but its effects were most keenly felt in goods markets rather than services. Nonetheless, this conflict primarily affects only two economies in the database, and is not a reason for preferring historical rather than current data.

phone, e-mail, data flows, and similar technologies, rather than in-person. A high proportion of mode 1 relative to other modes suggests that a significant proportion of a sector's trade is delivered digitally, and so the sector as a whole can be regarded as "digitally delivered."

Figure 4.1 shows results for this calculation using the major TISMOS aggregates. Results vary widely across sectors, with some services entries in TISMOS traded exclusively by mode 1, while others are not traded at all using that mode. Results differ somewhat among economies, but the pattern generally reflects the limited available information on the extent of pure cross-border trade in the total.

In interpreting the results, it is important to note that some pure cross-border services trade is not digital. Transport is a good example. Figure 4.1 shows it is heavily traded by mode 1, but clearly it is not digitally delivered; rather, the data capture the nature of transport movements in a physical sense. Putting royalties to one side, the key sectors are business services, telecommunications, financial services, and other personal services.

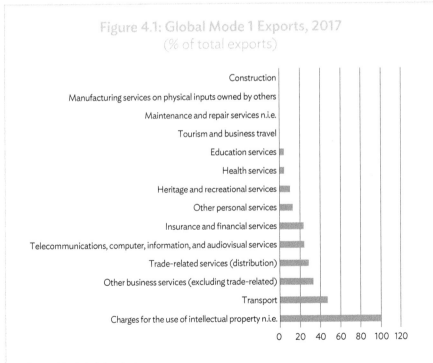

Figure 4.1: Global Mode 1 Exports, 2017
(% of total exports)

n.i.e. = not included elsewhere.

Source: World Trade Organization and Directorate-General for Trade of the European Commission. Trade in Services Data by Mode of Supply (TISMOS). https://www.wto.org/english/res_e/statis_e/ trade_datasets_e.htm (accessed June 2021).

Mapping these aggregates to sectors in national accounts is not straightforward, as the classifications involved are slightly different. However, in a general sense, the following ADB MRIOT sectors can be considered as digitally delivered,[2] on a broad reading:

- Post and telecommunications;
- Financial intermediation;
- Real estate activities;
- Renting of machinery and equipment, and other business activities; and
- Other community, social, and personal services.

While the analysis is necessarily approximate, given the extent of data available, this list presents a selection of sectors where digitally delivered trade is expected to account for an important share of total trade, and where, therefore, policy reforms could be expected to have the most significant impact on trade flows and input sourcing.

4.2.2   Measuring Global Value Chain Integration

Standard trade data are ill-suited to measuring GVC integration. The reason is that they include a large measure of double counting because they are recorded on the basis of gross shipments rather than value added. For example, if the Republic of Korea ships a cellphone component worth $100 to the People's Republic of China (PRC), which then adds a further $500 worth of components from other regional sources and $100 of assembly services, then ships the cellphone to the United States, the transaction is recorded as an export of $100 from the Republic of Korea to the PRC, and of $700 from the PRC to the United States. The value-added origins of the cellphone are lost in the standard accounting systems used for customs valuation.

Wang, Wei, and Zhu (2013) provide a consistent methodology for decomposing gross value trade data into value-added components by combining them with information from input–output tables. The methodology is set out in detail from the next paragraph. Intuitively the decomposition is split into three main aggregates: domestic value added (DVA), foreign value added (FVA), and pure double counting (PDC). DVA records the part of gross exports that can be sourced to industries located within the exporting economy, while FVA is that part attributable to imported intermediate goods and services. Finally, PDC records the part of gross exports that is double counted due to having moved across borders multiple times during production.

---

[2] ADB MRIOT sectors do not correspond exactly to TISMOS aggregates. Concordance is based on visual inspection, and matching to nearest categories, as well as information provided by the OECD Secretariat.

FVA as a proportion of gross exports gives a backward measure of GVC integration: the proportion of exports that is accounted for by imports of intermediate goods and services. To see the opposite perspective, it is necessary to zero in on a particular component of DVA that Wang, Wei, and Zhu (2013) term DVA_INTRex. This equates to production by domestic industries that is exported and used by other economies in the production of their own exports, and it is a typical measure of forward GVC participation from the perspective of industries in the exporting economy. We focus on it here, as we are interested in tracking forward linkages from the perspective of the sectors identified as digitally delivered—that is, we are interested in how other sectors use digitally delivered trade to produce their exports (forward linkages), not in how digitally delivered sectors use inputs from other sectors, by definition not digitally delivered, to produce their exports (backward linkages).

ADB provides a decomposition of gross exports from the MRIOT using the Wang, Wei, and Zhu (2013) methodology. Figure 4.2 shows results by sector, aggregating by summing all Asian economies in the database. For four of the five sectors, GVC forward linkages account for reasonably similar proportions of gross exports, at about 15%–20%. The exception is other community, social, and personal services, which is considerably lower at around 10%. In a static sense, there is clear evidence of significant GVC integration in digitally delivered sectors, focusing on forward linkages. However, the direction of change is also important: for three of the five sectors, forward integration between 2000 and 2019 increases only slightly; for the remaining two sectors, the proportion decreases, significantly so for post and telecommunications. The direction of change suggests that digitally delivered sectors are generally maintaining their importance in regional GVCs in a forward integration sense, but that importance is not really growing.

To provide a comparison, we can consider the sum of all forward integration across all sectors in the economy, goods and services combined. Again, considering Asian economies only, results indicate that forward linkages accounted for 16.9% of gross exports in 2000 and 18.4% in 2019. So aggregate GVC integration has been generally increasing over time, though more slowly than gross exports as a whole. For three of the five digitally delivered sectors—finance, real estate, and other business services—forward integration is generally higher than for all sectors taken together, while for the remaining sectors it is either slightly lower (telecom) or significantly lower (other community, social, and personal services). Moreover, in interpreting growth, it is important to note that forward GVC integration for the economy as a whole grew from 16.9% to 18.1% between 2000 and 2008, then decreased markedly because of the global financial crisis, returning to growth, though slow-paced, in the years after. So, the 2019 figure, although only a couple of percentage points higher than the 2000 figure, highlights the depth of the shock to production structures that occurred in 2009, as indicated by relatively slow growth in trade and GVC integration since then.

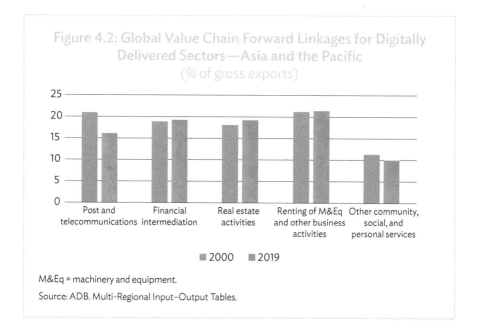

Figure 4.2: Global Value Chain Forward Linkages for Digitally Delivered Sectors—Asia and the Pacific (% of gross exports)

M&Eq = machinery and equipment.
Source: ADB. Multi-Regional Input–Output Tables.

Figure 4.3 looks at the data in a different way, retaining only the five digitally delivered sectors identified in Figure 4.2, and aggregating by exporting Asian economy. It shows that the digitally delivered sectors display substantial forward GVC integration in all economies for which data are available, although with considerable variation across economies. Interestingly, economies at a variety of income levels—not just high incomes—are well represented among those with the strongest forward GVC integration in digitally delivered sectors. Although results for some of the smaller economies have to be taken as indicative only (given the difficulties inherent in data collection and treatment), it is also generally true that both small and large economies can have relatively high forward GVC integration in digitally delivered sectors.

Figures 4.4 and 4.5 show the results of the analysis for backward linkages, again focusing on the five digitally delivered sectors. Backward linkages here capture the use of imported intermediates in these sectors. Figure 4.4 shows that much greater growth in backward linkages than forward linkages occurred over the sample period in post and telecommunications and in financial services. So, these sectors have developed overseas sourcing arrangements substantially over this period, while the other sectors have seen remote sourcing diminish or remain fairly steady. The contrast is clear when comparing with forward linkages, where changes were relatively small over time in all sectors. It is also evident in economy results for 2019 (Figure 4.5), where there is more dispersion in the proportion of backward linkages in gross exports than forward linkages. Levels of backward integration range from very low (Japan, for example) to very substantial (Singapore). Economy variation is also evident in forward linkages, but it is greater looking at use of imported intermediates in digitally delivered sectors. Otherwise, the patterns of integration differ substantially at this level of aggregation, depending on the direction of linkage. This result is typical in GVC analysis, as economies tend to specialize in different parts of the value chain, which implies different relationships to input sourcing and supply across borders.

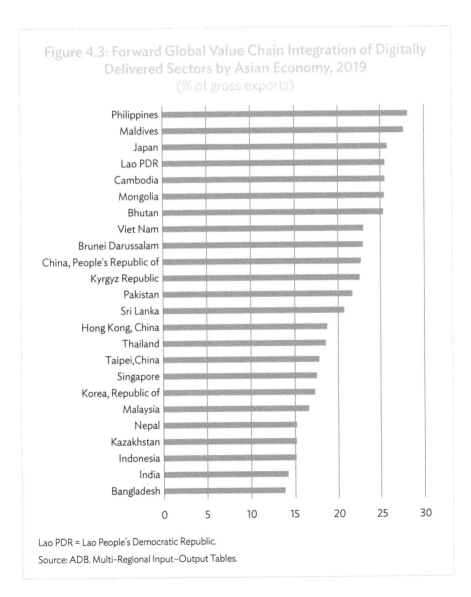

Figure 4.3: Forward Global Value Chain Integration of Digitally Delivered Sectors by Asian Economy, 2019
(% of gross exports)

Lao PDR = Lao People's Democratic Republic.

Source: ADB. Multi-Regional Input–Output Tables.

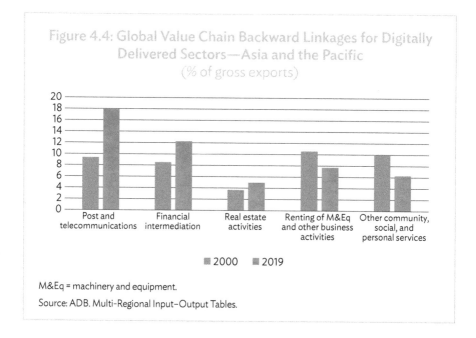

Figure 4.4: Global Value Chain Backward Linkages for Digitally Delivered Sectors—Asia and the Pacific (% of gross exports)

M&Eq = machinery and equipment.

Source: ADB. Multi-Regional Input–Output Tables.

Overall, the picture that emerges from this brief review is that digitally delivered sectors are an important part of the GVC landscape in Asia. This point is important from a policy perspective, because development policy in Asia often focuses on manufacturing as the engine of growth, even as evidence is compelling that economies that have grown rapidly in recent decades have not only developed their manufacturing but have also seen services production and trade increase significantly (Shepherd 2019).

4.2.3   Quantifying Policies Affecting Digitally Delivered Trade

Conceptually, it is clear that policy is one factor affecting the ability of firms to use digital technologies for international transactions. During the initial development of digital technologies, the sector itself was not particularly burdened by specific regulations. But as governments have come to recognize its economic importance and strategic potential, they have taken different approaches to facilitating or restricting both the activities of digital firms that provide the infrastructure for transactions, and the nature and extent of certain transactions.

To a large extent, work on quantifying policies affecting digitally delivered trade is more advanced than for digitally delivered trade itself. National accounts do not yet track digitally delivered trade flows, and therefore rely on estimates, inferences, and proxies; the same is not true of policies: they can be measured directly, using the general set of techniques developed for assessing trade restrictions in services more broadly (Dee 2005).

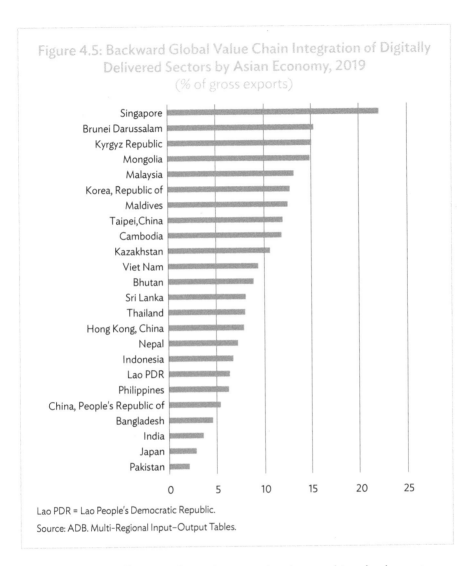

Figure 4.5: Backward Global Value Chain Integration of Digitally Delivered Sectors by Asian Economy, 2019 (% of gross exports)

Lao PDR = Lao People's Democratic Republic.

Source: ADB. Multi-Regional Input–Output Tables.

Whereas tariffs in goods markets are already stated in ad valorem terms, policy restrictions in services sectors—including those affecting digitally delivered trade—typically affect either the ability to contest markets or the cost of doing business once in a market. As such, they need to be quantified in a fundamentally different way from tariffs. The first step is to develop a regulatory questionnaire, typically based on consultations with sector experts and the private sector. The questionnaire, which can have a large number of individual questions, identifies policy measures that are believed to affect the ability of firms to trade, in this case digitally. The next step is to code restrictions quantitatively by assessing national regulations relevant to each question along a sliding scale from completely open (usually coded as the minimum value) to completely closed (usually coded as the maximum value). The third step is then to weigh and aggregate the individual data points for each question in the questionnaire to produce a single summary index of restrictiveness. An optional fourth step is to use an econometric model to relate restrictiveness to some measure of economic performance, such as trade values or trade costs, often with the objective of producing ad valorem equivalents of the bundle of policies captured by the index.

The European Centre for International Political Economy (Ferracane, Lee-Makiyama, and van der Marel 2018) and OECD apply variations on this approach to produce trade restrictiveness indexes for digitally delivered trade. We focus on the OECD version because it is publicly available in panel data format—i.e., over a number of years, which is important for the econometric estimations conducted in this chapter.

The OECD Digital Services Trade Restrictiveness Index (DSTRI) covers all OECD members and a selection of nonmembers, for the years 2014 through 2020 inclusive. Figure 4.6 shows 2020 results for Asian economies, to give an idea of how restrictiveness varies in a cross-sectional sense. Given that the DSTRI is an index number, the interpretation is ordinal only, not cardinal. That is, a score of 0.2 is more restrictive than a score of 0.1 (on a range of zero to one), but it is not "twice as restrictive"—that is an issue that can only be examined with further econometric modeling, as per the last analytical stage, which was referred to as an optional fourth step.

Figure 4.6 shows that patterns of restrictiveness in Asian economies vary substantially. Kazakhstan is the most restrictive economy in the dataset, followed by the PRC and Saudi Arabia (considered in the dataset as part of West Asia). Other economies are typically substantially less restrictive, with the lowest scores recorded in Japan, the Republic of Korea, and Malaysia.

Figure 4.7 looks at the data dynamically, focusing on the percentage change in the DSTRI between 2014 and 2020. The overwhelming takeaway is that policy regimes that have changed most have increased in restrictiveness, not liberalization. The change in the DSTRI is 50% or more in Japan, Kazakhstan, and Saudi Arabia. Only one economy in the sample, Indonesia, has witnessed major liberalization, with a fall in its DSTRI of 26% over 2014 to 2020. By and large, then, the Asian region has seen an emerging policy approach of greater restrictions to digitally delivered trade over the past half dozen years.

Another way of looking at the data is through the lens of heterogeneity. From this perspective, it is not only the restrictiveness of an economy's policies that matter for trade costs, but also how similar or different its policies are from those of trading partners. Data is perhaps an area, like services trade more broadly, where regulatory heterogeneity plays a significant part in determining the pattern of flows (Nordas 2016). For example, if one economy in a trading pair has strong

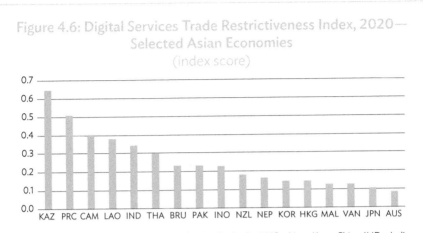

Figure 4.6: Digital Services Trade Restrictiveness Index, 2020—
Selected Asian Economies
(index score)

AUS = Australia; BRU = Brunei Darussalam; CAM = Cambodia; HKG = Hong Kong, China; IND = India;
INO = Indonesia; JPN = Japan; KAZ = Kazakhstan; KOR = Republic of Korea; LAO = Lao People's
Democratic Republic; MAL = Malaysia; NEP = Nepal; NZL = New Zealand; PAK = Pakistan;
PRC = People's Republic of China; THA = Thailand; VAN = Vanuatu.

Notes: Given that the Digital Services Trade Restrictiveness Index is an index number, the interpretation
is ordinal only, not cardinal. That is, a score of 0.2 is more restrictive than a score of 0.1 (on a range of
zero to one), but it is not "twice as restrictive."

Source: Organisation for Economic Co-operation and Development. OECD.Stat. https://stats.oecd.org/
Index.aspx?DataSetCode=STRI_DIGITAL (accessed October 2021).

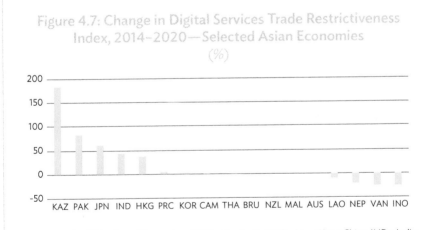

Figure 4.7: Change in Digital Services Trade Restrictiveness
Index, 2014–2020—Selected Asian Economies
(%)

AUS = Australia; BRU = Brunei Darussalam; CAM = Cambodia; HKG = Hong Kong, China; IND = India;
INO = Indonesia; JPN = Japan; KAZ = Kazakhstan; KOR = Republic of Korea; LAO = Lao People's
Democratic Republic; MAL = Malaysia; NEP = Nepal; NZL = New Zealand; PAK = Pakistan;
PRC = People's Republic of China; THA = Thailand; VAN = Vanuatu.

Note: No change in Australia, Brunei Darussalam, Malaysia, New Zealand, and Thailand.

Source: Author's calculations using data from Organisation for Economic Co-operation and
Development. OECD.Stat. https://stats.oecd.org/Index.aspx?DataSetCode=STRI_DIGITAL (accessed
October 2021).

rules about data privacy and the other does not, it may be difficult or impossible to move data in that direction as part of a broader economic transaction. Localization of data and servers may also impose additional costs in a case where those rules differ between economies, for instance, inside and outside a trade bloc. So, in addition to restrictiveness, there is good reason to believe that regulatory heterogeneity can play a role in driving trade costs.

Figure 4.8 shows results from a regulatory heterogeneity measure calculated by the OECD using the DSTRI. A higher score indicates a greater level of heterogeneity. The figure shows average levels (horizontal lines) and ranges for Asian economies, looking at intra-Asian trading relationships only. Economies differ substantially in the heterogeneity they exhibit with their partners. Kazakhstan, which had the most restrictive regime, also has the highest average heterogeneity with respect to other Asian economies, followed by the PRC. The lowest levels are in the Republic of Korea and Japan. To some extent, the more liberal economies also tend to display lower heterogeneity with trading partners but, as the chart shows, dispersion in scores is also substantial for most economies.

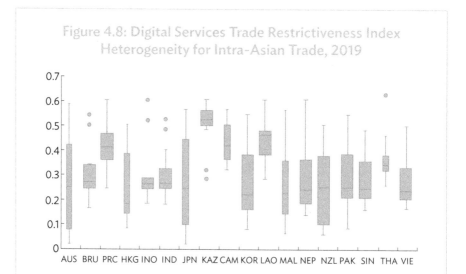

Figure 4.8: Digital Services Trade Restrictiveness Index Heterogeneity for Intra-Asian Trade, 2019

AUS = Australia; BRU = Brunei Darussalam; CAM = Cambodia; HKG = Hong Kong, China; IND = India; INO = Indonesia; JPN = Japan; KAZ = Kazakhstan; KOR = Republic of Korea; LAO = Lao People's Democratic Republic; MAL = Malaysia; NEP = Nepal; NZL = New Zealand; PAK = Pakistan; PRC = People's Republic of China; SIN = Singapore; THA = Thailand; VIE = Viet Nam.

Source: Author's calculations using data from Organisation for Economic Co-operation and Development. OECD.Stat. https://stats.oecd.org/Index.aspx?DataSetCode=STRI_DIGITAL (accessed October 2021).

Given the overall change in regional policy stance that emerges from the data, the time is ripe to look at the economic impacts of restrictions to digitally delivered trade. Broadly speaking, that is this chapter's objective. The next section introduces a general equilibrium trade model that provides a framework for analyzing empirically the effects of policies in the digital arena on trade flows by sector, as well as on GVC integration.

4.3   Results and Interpretation

The model set out in section 4.2 can serve as a framework for conducting counterfactual simulations.[3] We use it here to examine the trade and GVC impacts of trade liberalization and deregulation on digitally delivered sectors and define both terms. The exercise takes the form of a "thought experiment" because DSTRI data are available only for a small number of Asian economies; as a result, detailed policy simulations are not possible.

Defining trade liberalization is straightforward in terms of the framework set out in section 4.2: it is a reduction in trade costs that applies only to economy pairs that are not the same. For example, Australia reduces its trade costs in a particular way compared with other economies, but its internal trade costs remain constant. This definition allows us to contrast trade liberalization with deregulation, in which domestic trade costs also fall.

Taking this approach, we define two counterfactual simulations:

- Scenario 1 (Trade liberalization): All economies reduce international iceberg trade costs in digitally delivered sectors by 10% but leave intranational trade costs unchanged.
- Scenario 2 (Deregulation): All economies reduce international and intranational iceberg trade costs in digitally delivered sectors by 10%.

The data for the simulation model come from the ADB MRIOT, so we use the same sector classification as section 4.2.1. Digitally delivered sectors are therefore the following five: telecommunications, finance, real estate, other business services, and other community services.

Table 4.1 shows how intra-Asian trade flows change by sector under the two scenarios. Most goods sectors see a slight contraction under Scenario 1: the cost-decreasing effect of liberalization of digitally delivered sectors, which promotes trade by reducing the cost of an input bundle, is dominated by a substitution effect that draws resources into the digitally delivered sectors. This

---

[3] Details about the conceptional underpinnings of the model can be found in Appendix A4.1.

intuition is confirmed by figures for the digitally delivered sectors, which show very large rises. By contrast, in Scenario 2 trade shrinks more substantially in all goods sectors, and expands more modestly in the digitally delivered sectors. The intuition is that deregulation lowers both internal and external trade costs. Given the size of the internal market, a substantial amount of sourcing switches as a consequence: the substitution effect is stronger as the domestic market in digitally delivered sectors sees substantial increases. Table 4.1 does not show changes in real income. These are typically positive but modest in both scenarios; however, the real income changes are larger in Scenario 2 than in Scenario 1, which is a standard result in the trade literature: lowering intranational trade costs creates more "trade" because of the larger internal market, and therefore increases the possibilities of consumption since prices tend to fall when trade costs are reduced.

Table 4.1: Counterfactual Changes in Total
Intra-Asian Exports by Sector
(% of baseline)

Sector	Scenario 1	Scenario 2
Agriculture, hunting, forestry, and fishing	-1.131	-4.301
Mining and quarrying	-0.045	-3.644
Food, beverages, and tobacco	-0.480	-4.752
Textiles and textile products	-0.335	-5.454
Leather, leather products, and footwear	-0.523	-5.715
Wood and products of wood and cork	-0.305	-3.995
Pulp, paper, paper products, printing, and publishing	0.319	-1.394
Coke, refined petroleum, and nuclear fuel	-0.513	-2.824
Chemicals and chemical products	-0.243	-3.001
Rubber and plastics	0.657	-3.197
Other nonmetallic minerals	-0.507	-3.817
Basic metals and fabricated metals	0.009	-3.767
Machinery, n.e.c.	0.335	-4.187
Electrical and optical equipment	-0.130	-3.164
Transport equipment	0.266	-4.800
Manufacturing, n.e.c.; recycling	0.192	-4.205
Electricity, gas, and water supply	-0.084	-1.559
Construction	-1.877	-4.266
Sale, maintenance, and repair of motor vehicles and motorcycles; retail sale of fuel	0.627	-0.661

continued on next page

Table 4.1 *continued*

Sector	Scenario 1	Scenario 2
Wholesale trade and commission trade, except of motor vehicles and motorcycles	-0.656	-3.189
Retail trade, except of motor vehicles and motorcycles; repair of household goods	0.188	-2.163
Hotels and restaurants	-2.179	-4.226
Inland transport	-0.883	-2.012
Water transport	-0.523	-2.873
Air transport	-0.342	-4.085
Other supporting and auxiliary transport activities; activities of travel agencies	-1.585	-3.769
Post and telecommunications	**63.769**	**9.299**
Financial intermediation	**60.782**	**8.300**
Real estate activities	**54.791**	**9.948**
Renting of M&Eq and other business activities	**48.385**	**9.872**
Public administration and defense; compulsory social security	-2.114	-2.490
Education	3.734	-1.602
Health and social work	-0.271	-4.428
Other community, social, and personal services	**57.360**	**5.644**
Private households with employed persons	1.786	8.328

M&Eq = machinery and equipment, n.e.c. = not elsewhere classified.

Notes: Boldface indicates sectors subject to a change in trade costs. In Scenario 1 (Trade Liberalization), all economies reduce international iceberg trade costs in digitally delivered services by 10% but leave intranational trade costs unchanged. In Scenario 2 (Deregulation), all economies reduce international and intranational iceberg trade costs in digitally delivered services by 10%. Sector definitions are based on ADB Multi-Regional Input–Output Tables.

Source: Author's calculations.

Table 4.2 looks in more detail at GVC integration. As in Wang, Wei, and Zhu (2013), we first focus on forward linkages (DVA_INTRex). Both scenarios see increases in GVC forward integration as a percentage of gross exports, but the effect is typically more pronounced in Scenario 1 than Scenario 2. The reason is that forward linkages are measured on an international basis, so the emphasis is on effects in traded markets, not domestic ones. The five digitally delivered sectors see substantial increases in their GVC forward linkages, which means that other sectors are using them more intensively in the production of their own traded output. Even the deregulation scenario shows an increase in forward GVC integration for the sectors of interest relative to the baseline, due to the changed incentives to engage in international sourcing. From the perspective of value chains in the region, Table 4.2 suggests that liberalizing digitally delivered sectors can increase their breadth and depth, both in the affected sectors and elsewhere in the economy. The effect is to deepen value chain trade, not only in digitally delivered services but also in goods sectors and other services sectors.

Table 4.2: Forward Global Value Chain Participation by Sector—Intra-Asia (% of gross exports, baseline and counterfactuals)

Sector	Baseline	Scenario 1	Scenario 2
Agriculture, hunting, forestry, and fishing	14.645	14.805	14.618
Mining and quarrying	25.735	25.979	25.935
Food, beverages, and tobacco	6.779	6.873	6.876
Textiles and textile products	12.637	12.636	12.730
Leather, leather products, and footwear	5.583	5.605	5.690
Wood and products of wood and cork	15.585	15.828	15.818
Pulp, paper, paper products, printing, and publishing	20.383	20.905	20.757
Coke, refined petroleum, and nuclear fuel	21.409	21.237	21.260
Chemicals and chemical products	22.456	22.613	22.617
Rubber and plastics	24.210	24.581	24.497
Other nonmetallic minerals	13.805	13.932	14.004
Basic metals and fabricated metals	21.909	21.930	21.993
Machinery, n.e.c.	11.734	11.848	11.991
Electrical and optical equipment	20.880	21.057	21.231
Transport equipment	8.837	8.873	8.950
Manufacturing, n.e.c.; recycling	10.490	10.822	10.783
Electricity, gas, and water supply	17.740	18.080	18.052
Construction	6.942	7.146	7.227
Sale, maintenance, and repair of motor vehicles and motorcycles; retail sale of fuel	23.041	23.099	23.187
Wholesale trade and commission trade, except of motor vehicles and motorcycles	16.948	16.967	17.162
Retail trade, except of motor vehicles and motorcycles; repair of household goods	20.571	20.549	20.636
Hotels and restaurants	3.960	4.261	4.205
Inland transport	17.345	17.599	17.482
Water transport	20.346	20.080	19.996
Air transport	13.479	13.550	13.696

continued on next page

Table 4.2 *continued*

Sector	Baseline	Scenario 1	Scenario 2
Other supporting and auxiliary transport activities; activities of travel agencies	28.604	29.031	29.023
Post and telecommunications	**17.431**	**18.043**	**17.784**
Financial intermediation	**22.533**	**23.006**	**22.737**
Real estate activities	**21.284**	**21.980**	**22.014**
Renting of M&Eq and other business activities	**21.271**	**21.782**	**21.829**
Public administration and defense; compulsory social security	11.633	11.910	12.155
Education	4.219	4.232	4.534
Health and social work	2.150	2.102	2.225
Other community, social, and personal services	**5.529**	**6.044**	**5.833**
Private households with employed persons	20.469	21.280	22.337

M&Eq = machinery and equipment; n.e.c. = not elsewhere classified.

Notes: Boldface indicates sectors subject to a change in trade costs. In Scenario 1 (Trade Liberalization), all economies reduce international iceberg trade costs in digitally delivered services by 10% but leave intranational trade costs unchanged. In Scenario 2 (Deregulation), all economies reduce international and intranational iceberg trade costs in digitally delivered services by 10%. Sector definitions are based on ADB Multi-Regional Input–Output Tables.

Source: Author's calculations.

Moving to backward linkages, Table 4.3 shows that both scenarios result in modest increases in backward GVC integration across the board. These changes are largest in the five digitally delivered sectors, which is in line with the fact that the two scenarios include only shock trade costs in those sectors. Given that backward GVC integration, like forward integration, changes only slowly in proportional terms over time, the sector results are significant in the shocked sectors, as well as in some others. The general picture is similar to the one that emerged for forward linkages, in the sense that value chains generally deepen in the region, and this extends not only to the shocked sectors but to other parts of the economy (value chains for services and goods).

Table 4.4 takes a different approach, breaking out the results by economy. It reports changes in total intra-Asian exports and shows that all economies, except Cambodia and Viet Nam, see increases in total exports (summing over all sectors) under Scenario 1, but the changes are generally modest except in Hong Kong, China and Nepal. The first result is driven by the importance of the finance sector, while the second is driven by the "other community services" sector. The former is highly intuitive, but the latter is not: it stems directly from the data in the ADB MRIOT, but there may be errors for this relatively aggregate sector for a small economy like Nepal, so we do not place any particular stress on this result.

Table 4.3: Backward Global Value Chain Participation by Sector—Intra-Asia (% of gross exports, baseline and counterfactuals)

Sector	Baseline	Scenario 1	Scenario 2
Agriculture, hunting, forestry, and fishing	7.984	8.160	8.129
Mining and quarrying	6.998	7.195	7.141
Food, beverages, and tobacco	13.902	14.217	14.138
Textiles and textile products	12.185	12.530	12.500
Leather, leather products, and footwear	15.745	16.069	16.053
Wood and products of wood and cork	11.290	11.449	11.447
Pulp, paper, paper products, printing, and publishing	12.236	12.461	12.393
Coke, refined petroleum, and nuclear fuel	26.888	27.198	27.103
Chemicals and chemical products	18.999	19.144	19.023
Rubber and plastics	14.676	14.725	14.683
Other nonmetallic minerals	19.890	20.208	19.991
Basic metals and fabricated metals	18.639	18.844	18.717
Machinery, n.e.c.	15.766	16.020	15.840
Electrical and optical equipment	19.043	19.178	19.003
Transport equipment	18.598	18.929	18.775
Manufacturing, n.e.c.; recycling	14.757	15.042	15.015
Electricity, gas, and water supply	12.409	12.759	12.584
Construction	23.500	23.880	23.458
Sale, maintenance, and repair of motor vehicles and motorcycles; retail sale of fuel	9.197	10.121	9.687
Wholesale trade and commission trade, except of motor vehicles and motorcycles	11.053	11.633	11.656
Retail trade, except of motor vehicles and motorcycles; repair of household goods	8.656	9.662	9.166
Hotels and restaurants	12.874	13.448	13.100
Inland transport	11.571	11.884	11.740
Water transport	25.088	25.722	25.769
Air transport	22.478	23.131	22.767
Other supporting and auxiliary transport activities; activities of travel agencies	9.526	9.976	9.730
Post and telecommunications	**11.774**	**12.765**	**12.538**
Financial intermediation	**9.203**	**10.235**	**9.845**
Real estate activities	**3.400**	**3.658**	**3.694**
Renting of M&Eq and other business activities	**10.801**	**11.579**	**11.014**

continued on next page

Table 4.3 continued

Sector	Baseline	Scenario 1	Scenario 2
Public administration and defense; compulsory social security	10.777	11.162	11.265
Education	6.145	6.546	6.341
Health and social work	15.431	15.699	15.420
Other community, social, and personal services	**5.944**	**6.579**	**6.359**
Private households with employed persons	7.039	7.410	7.170

M&Eq = machinery and equipment, n.e.c. = not elsewhere classified.

Notes: Boldface indicates sectors subject to a change in trade costs. In Scenario 1 (Trade Liberalization), all economies reduce international iceberg trade costs in digitally delivered services by 10% but leave intranational trade costs unchanged. In Scenario 2 (Deregulation), all economies reduce international and intranational iceberg trade costs in digitally delivered services by 10%. Sector definitions are based on ADB Multi-Regional Input–Output Tables.

Source: Author's calculations.

Table 4.4: Counterfactual Changes in Intra-Asian Exports by Economy (% of baseline)

Economy	Scenario 1	Scenario 2
Bangladesh	1.356	-2.950
Bhutan	2.478	-3.150
Brunei Darussalam	1.961	-3.078
Cambodia	-0.360	-3.258
China, People's Republic of	2.148	-3.101
Hong Kong, China	19.466	1.209
India	4.081	-3.098
Indonesia	2.663	-2.626
Japan	1.113	-4.102
Kazakhstan	3.981	-3.096
Korea, Republic of	2.746	-2.743
Kyrgyz Republic	3.431	1.911
Lao People's Democratic Republic	2.239	-3.801
Malaysia	4.251	-2.351
Maldives	2.104	-3.660
Mongolia	1.892	-1.321
Nepal	24.852	-3.292

continued on next page

Table 4.4 *continued*

Economy	Scenario 1	Scenario 2
Pakistan	6.465	-3.396
Philippines	5.356	-3.702
Singapore	2.826	-0.836
Sri Lanka	4.133	-4.473
Taipei,China	1.283	-3.653
Thailand	1.725	-2.292
Viet Nam	-0.353	-3.770

Notes: In Scenario 1 (Trade Liberalization), all economies reduce international iceberg trade costs in digitally delivered services by 10% but leave intranational trade costs unchanged. In Scenario 2 (Deregulation), all economies reduce international and intranational iceberg trade costs in digitally delivered services by 10%.

Source: Author's calculations.

Under Scenario 2, results are more mixed due to the substitution logic. Total exports decrease in some economies, while smaller increases are recorded in those where digitally delivered sectors play a large role in total exports, like Hong Kong, China. That noted, the position for changes in real income is largely the opposite of what is seen in the trade data: deregulation tends to have larger (positive) real income effects than trade liberalization, as is standard in the literature.

We can also look at GVC integration at the economy level. Focusing again first on forward integration, Table 4.5 shows results. Changes are generally positive but small for economies. The reason for these modest results is that economy-level results aggregate over all sectors, whereas changes in trade patterns primarily affect the sectors where trade costs were assumed to change. As such, the initial importance of those sectors in total exports is determinative of changes in total forward linkages. Changes at a disaggregated level tend to be more substantial, especially in digitally delivered sectors, but also in those other sectors that use those services intensively as inputs.

Table 4.6 presents results for backward linkages. Results are comparable to those for forward linkages: in most cases, economies see an increase in backward linkages in both scenarios relative to the baseline, although there are some cases where the opposite is true. Changes are relatively modest, because the larger sector changes discussed in this section are only part of each economy's overall trade patterns, so sector patterns of specialization influence the final result. As with forward linkages, however, the overall picture is that trade liberalization and deregulation affecting digitally delivered sectors can boost GVC integration in the region, albeit with differences in nature and extent across economies.

Table 4.5: Forward Global Value Chain Participation by Economy—Intra-Asia (% of gross exports, baseline and counterfactuals)

Economy	Baseline	Scenario 1	Scenario 2
Bangladesh	15.368	15.679	15.439
Bhutan	10.839	11.240	10.910
Brunei Darussalam	27.443	27.369	27.529
Cambodia	11.821	12.012	11.988
China, People's Republic of	17.087	17.373	17.494
Hong Kong, China	16.265	16.896	16.239
India	15.989	15.496	16.137
Indonesia	21.987	21.982	22.135
Japan	21.122	21.435	21.516
Kazakhstan	21.608	21.300	21.552
Korea, Republic of	16.725	16.769	16.857
Kyrgyz Republic	10.891	11.439	12.992
Lao People's Democratic Republic	30.102	30.182	30.381
Malaysia	27.038	26.581	26.886
Maldives	12.991	13.418	13.138
Mongolia	17.482	17.426	17.500
Nepal	10.489	10.57	10.487
Pakistan	20.563	20.604	20.454
Philippines	14.407	15.193	14.813
Singapore	14.537	14.260	14.492
Sri Lanka	13.643	13.660	13.710
Taipei,China	18.110	18.206	18.237
Thailand	13.749	13.819	13.969
Viet Nam	10.624	10.719	10.699

Notes: In Scenario 1 (Trade Liberalization), all economies reduce international iceberg trade costs in digitally delivered services by 10% but leave intranational trade costs unchanged. In Scenario 2 (Deregulation), all economies reduce international and intranational iceberg trade costs in digitally delivered services by 10%.

Source: Author's calculations.

Table 4.6: Backward Global Value Chain Participation by Economy
(% of gross exports, baseline and counterfactuals)

Economy	Baseline	Scenario 1	Scenario 2
Bangladesh	19.997	19.630	20.074
Bhutan	15.956	16.030	16.133
Brunei Darussalam	10.119	10.614	10.306
Cambodia	21.658	21.688	21.543
China, People's Republic of	9.281	9.461	9.386
Hong Kong, China	23.684	22.923	24.123
India	13.753	13.387	13.791
Indonesia	10.583	10.687	10.622
Japan	13.921	13.906	13.903
Kazakhstan	9.339	10.195	9.717
Korea, Republic of	24.064	24.323	24.300
Kyrgyz Republic	19.987	20.041	19.204
Lao People's Democratic Republic	8.106	8.180	8.022
Malaysia	16.935	17.407	17.214
Maldives	28.229	28.395	28.459
Mongolia	19.242	20.346	19.864
Nepal	18.063	16.441	18.029
Pakistan	7.907	7.686	7.932
Philippines	21.328	20.436	20.989
Singapore	33.446	33.608	33.708
Sri Lanka	11.660	11.933	11.895
Taipei,China	27.138	27.122	27.140
Thailand	20.280	20.453	20.209
Viet Nam	27.216	27.623	27.238

Notes: In Scenario 1 (Trade Liberalization), all economies reduce international iceberg trade costs in digitally delivered services by 10% but leave intranational trade costs unchanged. In Scenario 2 (Deregulation), all economies reduce international and intranational iceberg trade costs in digitally delivered services by 10%.

Source: Author's calculations.

4.4   Conclusion and Policy Implications

This chapter has shown that digitally delivered services are an important part of the trade landscape in Asia. Available evidence also suggests that trade costs, including those due to regulatory heterogeneity, are a significant determinant of the observed pattern of trade and GVC integration across economies.

In light of these realities, it is not surprising that a "thought experiment" in which trade costs are reduced for digitally delivered sectors, either through trade liberalization (foreign partners only) or deregulation (all partners, including domestic trade), typically has a substantial impact on the regional economy. Generally speaking, deregulation has a larger impact on real incomes than trade liberalization because it affects price in the internal market more strongly: reducing internal trade costs through deregulation increases consumption possibilities more strongly than only when deregulation involves external partners. By contrast, trade effects are stronger for trade liberalization, because there is no switch to increased domestic sourcing (which reduces trade) but rather a shift away from the domestic market. Both policy approaches therefore have significant economic effects.

In addition, the experiment shows that a reduction in trade costs of digitally delivered services can have spillover effects on other sectors. While impacts on forward GVC integration are not large in absolute terms, they are significant when set against the slow pattern of change set out in section 4.2: trade liberalization and deregulation have clear potential to promote increased use of digitally delivered services as inputs into the production and export of other goods and services, which cements their already important role in regional GVCs.

A significant area for future research is to attempt to relate policy restrictiveness as measured by the DSTRI to bilateral trade flows and trade costs. Identification is challenging, because the DSTRI primarily varies across economies rather than within economies across time periods. But expanding the thought experiment approach to relate it more closely to concrete policy changes would be an important piece of value added.

Turning to the policy implications, the analysis here points to three major conclusions. First, from a welfare perspective, it is important to consider nondiscriminatory policy changes in addition to trade policy reforms. While both are important from a purely trade flow perspective, changes in real income tend to be dominated by reforms that also influence conditions in the domestic market. This result is highly intuitive: most economies source the bulk of their inputs domestically, and sell the bulk of their output there, in the sectors identified as digitally enabled. The price implications are maximized when domestic reforms occur, not just international. So, efforts to liberalize the policy environment should ensure that nondiscriminatory measures are also addressed.

Second, Asian economies have the scope to conduct policy reforms on the basis of regional models. The data show substantial variation within the region in policy stances, ranging from relatively liberal to relatively restricted. Reducing trade costs can therefore help put the focus on moving toward policy regimes more like those seen in the Asian markets with the least restrictions, such as Japan, the Republic of Korea, and Malaysia. A stock of good practices in the region could be shared through existing channels such as the Association of Southeast Asian Nations and the Asia-Pacific Economic Cooperation.

Finally, the evidence shows that liberalizing the policy environment for digitally delivered services can have spillover effects to other sectors, including through GVC linkages. As a result, ongoing policy discussions on GVC deepening in the region, as well as trade policy linkages more broadly, need to consider the digital dimension. Trade agreements are increasingly devoting specific text to digital issues, but a case exists for ensuring that schedules of specific commitments are similarly ambitious in the sectors identified here as digitally delivered. New generation trade agreements involving Asian economies, such as the Comprehensive and Progressive Agreement for Trans-Pacific Partnership and the Regional Comprehensive Economic Partnership, will be evaluated in part based on their ability to extend GVC linkages, including through supporting the application of digital technologies. Using trade agreements to reduce regulatory heterogeneity as well as liberalizing underlying policies could be a fruitful avenue for future regional integration efforts.

Bibliography

Aichele, R., and I. Heiland. 2018. Where Is the Value Added? Trade Liberalization and Production Networks. *Journal of International Economics*. 115 (C). pp. 130–144.

Anderson, J., and E. Van Wincoop. 2003. Gravity with Gravitas: A Solution to the Border Puzzle. *American Economic Review*. 93 (1). pp. 170–192.

———. 2004. Trade Costs. *Journal of Economic Literature*. 42 (3). pp. 691–751.

Baldwin, R. 2011. Trade and Industrialization after Globalization's Second Unbundling: How Building and Joining a Supply Chain Are Different and Why It Matters. *NBER Working Paper*. No. 17716. Cambridge, MA: National Bureau of Economic Research.

Caliendo, L., and F. Parro. 2015. Estimates of the Trade and Welfare Effects of NAFTA. *Review of Economic Studies*. 82 (1). pp. 1–44.

Dee, P. 2005. A Compendium of Barriers to Services Trade. *Working Paper*. Canberra: Asia-Pacific School of Economics and Government.

Dekle, R., J. Eaton, and S. Kortum. 2007. Unbalanced Trade. *American Economic Review* 97 (2). pp. 351–355.

Eaton, J., and S. Kortum. 2002. Technology, Geography, and Trade. *Econometrica*. 70 (5). pp. 1741–1779.

Egger, P., and M. Larch. 2008. Interdependent Preferential Trade Agreement Memberships: An Empirical Analysis. *Journal of International Economics*. 76 (2). 384–399.

Egger, P., M. Larch, S. Nigai, and Y. Yotov. 2018. Trade Costs in the Global Economy: Measurement, Aggregation, and Decomposition. *WTO Working Paper*. ERSD-2021-2. Geneva: World Trade Organization.

Ferracane, M., H. Lee-Makiyama, and E. van der Marel. 2018. *Digital Trade Restrictiveness Index*. Brussels: European Centre for International Political Economy.

Heid, B., M. Larch, and Y. Yotov. 2021. Estimating the Effects of Non-Discriminatory Trade Policies Within Structural Gravity Models. *Canadian Journal of Economics*. 54 (1). pp. 376–409.

Johnson, R. and G. Noguera. 2012. Accounting for Intermediates: Production Sharing and Trade in Value Added. *Journal of International Economics*. 86 (2). pp. 224–236.

Koopman, R., Z. Wang, and S. J. Wei. 2014. Tracing Value-Added and Double Counting in Gross Exports. *American Economic Review*. 104 (2). pp. 459–494.

Liberatore, A. Forthcoming. Statistics on Digital Trade in Services. *Statistics Working Paper*. Paris: Organisation for Economic Co-operation and Development.

Nordas, H. 2016. Services Trade Restrictiveness Index (STRI): The Trade Effect of Regulatory Differences. *Trade Policy Paper*. No. 189. Paris: Organisation for Economic Co-operation and Development.

Ottaviano, G. 2015. European Integration and the Gains from Trade. In H. Badinger and V. Nitsch, eds. *Routledge Handbook of the Economics of European Integration*. London: Routledge.

Santos Silva, J. and S. Tenreyro. 2006. The Log of Gravity. *Review of Economics and Statistics*. 88 (4). pp. 641–658.

Shepherd, B. 2019. Productivity and Trade Growth in Services: How Services Helped Power Factory Asia. In M. Helble and B. Shepherd, eds. *Leveraging Services for Development: Prospects and Policies*. Manila: Asian Development Bank Institute.

Wang, Z., S. J. Wei, and K. Zhu. 2013 (Revised 2018). Quantifying International Production Sharing at the Bilateral and Sector Levels. *NBER Working Paper*. No. 19677. Cambridge, MA: National Bureau of Economic Research.

Appendix A4.1: A Quantitative Trade Model with Global Value Chain Linkages

Trade policy analysis has traditionally used computable general equilibrium (CGE) models to examine the economy-wide impacts of reform. This section takes a different approach, drawing on the literature on "new quantitative trade models" (Ottaviano 2015). The new generation of models incorporates insights from standard trade theory, such as Ricardian technology differences and trade flows governed by structural gravity equations. But it incorporates the full general equilibrium approach of earlier CGE literature, in the sense that macroeconomic constraints are respected, relative prices matter, and sectors exhibit input–output relationships. Model outputs are familiar from the literature, but a key contribution of the model in this chapter is that it makes it possible to identify global value chain (GVC) linkages at a disaggregated level, with the same Wang, Wei, and Zhu (2013) approach used in this chapter. In other words, a trade policy change maps both counterfactual changes in trade and welfare and counterfactual changes in, for example, forward GVC integration. The model is therefore ideally suited to examining the GVC implications of policy changes that affect digital trade.

A.   Consumption Side

The consumption side of the model comes from Caliendo and Parro (2015). A measure Ln of representative households in n economies (subscript) maximize Cobb Douglas utility by consuming final goods in j sectors (superscript), with consumption shares α_n^j summing to unity.

$$(1)\, u(C_n) = \prod_{j=1}^{J} (C_n^j)^{\alpha_n^j}$$

B.   Production Side

The production side of the model also comes from Caliendo and Parro (2015) via Aichele and Heiland (2018), which can be seen as a multisector generalization of Eaton and Kortum (2002). As in Aichele and Heiland (2018), there is provision for different shares in intermediate and final consumption. Each sector produces a continuum of intermediate goods $\omega^j \in [0,1]$. Each intermediate good uses labor and composite intermediate goods from all sectors. Intermediate goods producers have production technology as follows:

$$(2)\ q_n^j(\omega^j) = z_n^j(\omega^j)[l_n(\omega^j)]^{\beta_n^j} \prod_{k=1}^{J} [m_n^{k,j}(\omega^j)]^{\gamma_n^{k,j}}$$

where $z_n^j(\omega^j)$ is the efficiency of producing intermediate good ω^j in economy n; $l_n(\omega^j)$ is labor; $m_n^{k,j}(\omega^j)$ are the composite intermediate goods from sector k used for the production of intermediate good ω^j; and β_n^j is the cost share of labor and $(1 - \beta_n^j)\gamma_n^{k,j}$ is the cost share of intermediates from sector k used in the production of intermediate good ω^j, with $\Sigma_{k=1}^{J}\gamma_n^{k,j} = 1$.

Production of intermediate goods exhibits constant returns to scale with perfect competition, so firms price at marginal cost. The cost of an input bundle can therefore be written as follows:

$$(3)\ c_n^j = Y_n^j w_n^{\beta_n^j} \left(\prod_{k=1}^{J} (P_n^{km})^{\gamma_n^{k,j}} \right)^{1-\beta_n^j}$$

where P_n^{km} is the price of a composite intermediate good from sector k; w is the wage; and Y_n^j is a constant.

Producers of composite intermediate goods in economy n and sector j supply their output at minimum cost by purchasing intermediates from the lowest cost suppliers across economies, similar to the mechanism in the single sector model of Eaton and Kortum (2002).

Composite intermediate goods from sector j are used in the production of intermediate good ω^k in amount $m_n^{j,k}(\omega^k)$ in all sectors k, as well as final goods in consumption C_n^j. The composite intermediate is produced using constant elasticity of substitution (CES) technology:

$$(4)\ Q_n^j = \left[\int r_n^j(\omega^j)^{1-\frac{1}{\sigma^j}} d\omega^j \right]^{\frac{\sigma^j}{\sigma^j-1}}$$

where r is demand from the lowest cost supplier, and σ is the elasticity of substitution across intermediate goods within a sector.
Solving the producer's problem gives an expression for demand:

$$(5)\ r_n^j(\omega^j) = \left(\frac{p_n(\omega^j)}{P_n^j} \right)^{-\sigma^j} Q_n^j$$

where $p_n(\omega^j)$ is the lowest price of a given intermediate good across economies; and $P_n^j = \left[\int p_n(\omega^j)^{1-\sigma^j} d\omega^j \right]^{\frac{1}{1-\sigma^j}}$ is the CES price index.

C.   Trade Costs and Equilibrium

Trade costs consist of tariff and nontariff measures as components as in Aichele and Heiland (2018), in the standard iceberg formulation for imports by economy n from economy i, with trade costs potentially differing by end use (intermediate, m, or final, f):

$$(6) \; \kappa_{ni}^{jv} = \left(1 + t_{ni}^{jv}\right) * \tilde{t}_{ni}^{jv}, v \ni (m, f)$$

where t is the ad valorem tariff, and $\tilde{t}$ is nontariff-measure-related trade costs, including potentially policy measures but also geographic and historical factors that drive a wedge between producer prices in the exporting economy and consumer prices in the importing economy (Anderson and Van Wincoop 2003). Unlike in Caliendo and Parro (2015), we assume that all sectors are tradable. This assumption accords with the reality in our data, where sectors are sufficiently aggregated that trade always takes place, at least to some degree.

With this definition of trade costs, the price of a given intermediate good in economy n is

$$(7) \; p_n^j(\omega^j) = \min_i \frac{c_i^j \, \kappa_{ni}^{jm}}{z_i^j(\omega^j)}$$

As in Eaton and Kortum (2002), the efficiency of producing ω^j in economy n is the realization of a Fréchet distribution with location parameter $\lambda_n^j \geq 0$ and shape parameter $\theta^j > \sigma^j - 1$. The intermediate price index can therefore be rewritten as follows:

$$(8) \; P_n^{jm} = A^j \left[\sum_{i=1}^{N} \lambda_i^j \left(c_i^j \kappa_{ni}^{jm}\right)^{-\theta^j} \right]^{-\frac{1}{\theta^j}}$$

where A^j is a constant.

Then from the utility function, prices are

$$(9) \; P_n^f = \prod_{j=1}^{N} \left(\frac{P_n^{jf}}{\alpha_n^j}\right)^{\alpha_n^j}$$

Bringing together these ingredients gives a relationship for bilateral trade at the sector level that follows the general form of structural gravity, but developed in an explicitly multisector framework and with different relations for intermediate and final consumption:

$$(10) \; \pi_{ni}^{jv} = \frac{X_{ni}^{jv}}{X_n^{jv}} = \frac{\lambda_i^j \left[c_i^j \kappa_{ni}^{jv}\right]^{-\theta^j}}{\sum_{h=1}^{N} \lambda_h^j \left[c_h^j \kappa_{nh}^{jv}\right]^{-\theta^j}}$$

For analytical purposes, a key feature of the gravity model in equation 10 is that the unit costs term depends through equation 3 on trade costs in all sectors and economies. This result is an extension of the multilateral resistance reasoning in Anderson and Van Wincoop (2003) to the case of cross-sector linkages.

Goods market equilibrium is defined as follows, where Y is the gross value of production:

$$(11) \quad Y_n^j = \sum_{i=1}^{N} \frac{\pi_{in}^{jm}}{1 + t_{in}^{jm}} X_i^{jm} + \sum_{i=1}^{N} \frac{\pi_{in}^{jf}}{1 + t_{in}^{jf}} X_i^{jf}$$

with

$$X_n^{jm} = \sum_{k=1}^{J} \frac{\pi_{in}^{jm}}{1 + t_{in}^{jm}} \gamma_h^{j,k} (1 - \beta_h^k) Y_h^k$$

$$(12) \quad X_n^{jf} = \alpha_n^j I_n$$

National income is the sum of labor income, tariff rebates, and the exogenous trade deficit:

$$(12) \quad I_n = w_n L_n + R_n + D_n$$

The model is then closed by setting income equal to expenditure:

$$(13) \quad \sum_{j=1}^{J} X_n^{jm} \sum_{i=1}^{N} \frac{\pi_{ni}^{jm}}{1 + t_{ni}^{jm}} + \sum_{j=1}^{J} X_n^{jf} \sum_{i=1}^{N} \frac{\pi_{ni}^{jf}}{1 + t_{ni}^{jf}} - D_n = \sum_{j=1}^{J} Y_n^j$$

where I represents final absorption as the sum of labor income, tariff revenue, and the trade deficit; R is tariff revenue, and trade deficits sum to zero globally and to an exogenous constant nationally. So aggregate trade deficits are exogenous, but sector deficits are endogenous.

Caliendo and Parro (2015) show that the system defined by equations 3, 8, 10, 11, and 13 can be solved for equilibrium wages and prices, given tariffs and structural parameters.

1. Counterfactual Simulation

Using exact hat algebra (Dekle, Eaton, and Kortum 2007), it is simpler to solve the model in relative changes than in levels. This process is equivalent to performing a counterfactual simulation in which a baseline variable v is shocked to a counterfactual value v', and the relative change is defined as $\hat{v} = \frac{v'}{v}$. Aichele and Heiland (2018) show that counterfactual changes in input costs are given by

$$(14)\ \hat{c}_n^j = \hat{w}_n^{\beta_n^j}\left(\prod_{k=1}^{J}\hat{p}_n^{km}\gamma_n^{k,j}\right)^{1-\beta_n^j}$$

The change in the price index is

$$(15)\ \hat{P}_n^{jv} = \left[\prod_{i=1}^{N}\pi_{ni}^{jv}\left[\hat{\kappa}_{ni}^{jv}\hat{c}_i^j\right]^{-\theta^j}\right]^{-\frac{1}{\theta^j}}$$

The change in the bilateral trade share is

$$(16)\ \hat{\pi}_{ni}^{jv} = \left[\frac{\hat{\kappa}_{ni}^{jv}\hat{c}_i^j}{\hat{P}_n^{jv}}\right]^{-\theta^j}$$

Counterfactual intermediate goods and final goods expenditure are given by

$$(17)\ X_n^{jm'} = \sum_{k=1}^{N}\gamma_n^{j,k}\left(1-\beta_n^k\right)\left(\sum_{i=1}^{N}X_i^{km'}\frac{\pi_{in}^{km'}}{1+t_{in}^{km'}} + X_i^{kf'}\frac{\pi_{in}^{kf'}}{1+t_{in}^{kf'}}\right)$$

with

$$(18)\ X_n^{jf'} = \alpha_n^j I_n'$$

$$(19)\ I_n' = \hat{w}_n w_n L_n + \sum_{j=1}^{J}X_n^{jm'}\left(1-F_n^{jm'}\right) + \sum_{j=1}^{J}X_n^{jf'}\left(1-F_n^{jf'}\right) + D_n$$

The trade balance condition requires

$$(20)\ \sum_{j=1}^{J}F_n^{jm'}X_n^{jm'} + \sum_{j=1}^{J}F_n^{jf'}X_n^{jf'} - D_n = \sum_{j=1}^{J}\sum_{i=1}^{N}X_i^{jm'}\frac{\pi_{in}^{jm'}}{1+t_{in}^{jm'}} + \sum_{j=1}^{J}\sum_{i=1}^{N}X_i^{jf'}\frac{\pi_{in}^{jf'}}{1+t_{in}^{jf'}}$$

The change in welfare is given by the change in real income:

$$(21)\ \hat{W}_n = \frac{\hat{I}_n}{\prod_{j=1}^{J}\left(\hat{P}_n^{jf}\right)^{\alpha_n^j}}$$

The relative change in trade costs is given by the definition of the counterfactual simulation, and in our specification can cover nontariff measures and tariffs. Solving the model using exact hat algebra makes it possible to conduct the counterfactual experiment without having data on productivity, and importantly, without trade costs data other than those being simulated. Because of the multiplicative form of iceberg trade costs, solution in relative changes means that trade cost components, such as geographic and historical factors, which are constant in the baseline and counterfactual, simply cancel out. The parameters β_n^j (cost share of labor), $(1 - \beta_n^j)\gamma_n^{k,j}$ (cost share of intermediates), and α_n^j (share of each sector in final demand) can be calibrated directly from the baseline data, as can value added $(w_n L_n)$. Egger et al. (2018) provide updated estimates of the trade elasticity θ^j at the same level of disaggregation used in our data.

Caliendo and Parro (2015) develop an iterative procedure for solving the model, which we follow here in the modified version developed by Aichele and Heiland (2018).

2.   *Trade in Value Added*

We follow Aichele and Heiland (2018) in extending the Caliendo and Parro (2015) framework to consider value-added trade, which helps identify the proportion of gross value trade that is considered to take place within GVCs. We differ from them, however, in the concept of value-added trade. They use Johnson and Noguera (2012) and Koopman, Wang, and Wei (2014), but as Wang, Wei, and Zhu (2013) point out, the measures derived in those papers only provide consistent results at an aggregate level. We are interested in a bilateral and sector disaggregation, so we follow the same basic approach of Aichele and Heiland (2018), but then apply the key result from Wang, Wei, and Zhu (2013) when it comes time to decompose gross value trade into its value-added components.

Given the model setup described in the previous subsection, Aichele and Heiland (2018) derive input–output coefficients as follows:

$$(22)\ \left(1 + t_{ih}^{km}\right)a_{ih}^{k,j} = \pi_{ih}^{km}\left(1 - \beta_h^j\right)\gamma_h^{k,j}$$

where a is the input–output coefficient; and $\left(1 - \beta_h^j\right)\gamma_h^{k,j}$ is the cost share of intermediates from sector k.

Equation (20) makes clear that if the model dataset includes a baseline input–output table (A), as is necessary, then it is straightforward to calculate a counterfactual input–output matrix (A′), using the outputs of the counterfactual solution defined above.

Wang, Wei, and Zhu (2013) show that gross exports can then be fully and consistently decomposed into value-added components at the bilateral level as follows (with sector superscripts suppressed for readability):

$$(23)\ \pi^{j}_{ni} = DVA + FVA + PDC$$

$$DVA = \left(V^{i}B^{ii}\right)' * Y^{ni} + \left(V^{i}L^{ii}\right)' * \left(A^{ni}B^{nn}Y^{nn}\right)$$

$$+\left(V^{i}L^{ii}\right)' * \left[A^{ni}\sum_{h\neq n,i}^{N}B^{hn}Y^{hh} + A^{ni}B^{nn}\sum_{h\neq n,i}^{N}Y^{hn} + A^{ni}\sum_{h\neq n,i}^{N}B^{hn}\sum_{k\neq n,i}^{N}Y^{kh}\right]$$

$$+\left(V^{i}L^{ii}\right)' * \left[A^{ni}B^{nn}Y^{in} + A^{ni}\sum_{h\neq n,i}^{N}B^{hn}Y^{ih} + A^{ni}B^{in}Y^{ii}\right]$$

$$FVA = \left(V^{n}B^{in}\right)' * Y^{ni} + \left[\left(\sum_{h\neq n,i}^{N}V^{h}B^{ih}\right)' * Y^{ni}\right]$$

$$+\left(V^{n}B^{in}\right)' * \left(A^{ni}L^{nn}Y^{nn}\right) + \left(\sum_{h\neq n,i}^{N}V^{h}B^{ih}\right)' * \left(A^{ni}L^{nn}Y^{nn}\right)$$

$$PDC = \left(V^{i}L^{ii}\right)' * \left(A^{ni}B^{in}\sum_{h\neq n,i}^{N}Y^{hi}\right) + \left(V^{i}L^{ii}\sum_{h\neq n,i}^{N}A^{hi}B^{ih}\right)' * \left(A^{ni}X^{n}\right)$$

$$+\left(V^{n}B^{in}\right)' * \left(A^{ni}L^{nn}E^{n*}\right) + \left(\sum_{h\neq n,i}^{N}V^{h}B^{ih}\right)' * \left(A^{ni}L^{nn}E^{n*}\right)$$

where E is exports to economy n from economy i, with a star indicating an economy total across all other partners; Y is final demand for economy i's output in economy n; and DVA is domestic value added, FVA is foreign value added, and PDC is pure double counting. A is an input-output matrix, with superscripts used to define submatrices by economy pair. B is the global Leontief inverse based on A, with superscripts again indicating submatrices. V is the matrix of value-added shares, calculated directly from A. Y is the matrix of final demand. X is the vector of gross output by economy. L is the local Leontief inverse, defined as follows for the three-economy case (n, i, and k):

$$(24)\ L = \begin{bmatrix} B^{nn}_{11} & B^{nn}_{12} & 0 & 0 & 0 & 0 \\ B^{nn}_{21} & B^{nn}_{22} & 0 & 0 & 0 & 0 \\ 0 & 0 & B^{ii}_{11} & B^{ii}_{12} & 0 & 0 \\ 0 & 0 & B^{ii}_{21} & B^{ii}_{22} & 0 & 0 \\ 0 & 0 & 0 & 0 & B^{kk}_{11} & B^{kk}_{12} \\ 0 & 0 & 0 & 0 & B^{kk}_{21} & B^{kk}_{22} \end{bmatrix}$$

The above presentation is at the economy-pair level for simplicity, but Wang, Wei, and Zhu (2013) show that it can be extended to the sector level. The decomposition can therefore show DVA, FVA, and PDC in, for example, the People's Republic of China's exports of electrical equipment to the United States.

The sum of FVA and PDC is typically understood as a measure of production sharing, and we adopt that interpretation here.

Our approach to analyzing value-added trade is straightforward. As per Wang, Wei, and Zhu (2013), the decomposition for the baseline case can be calculated directly from the observed input–output table. We then use A' as calculated above to conduct a second decomposition for the counterfactual input–output table. The difference between the two shows the extent of changes in GVC trade as a result of the change in trade costs assumed for the counterfactual.

5

DATA-RELATED RESTRICTIONS AND DIGITAL SERVICES TRADE: COMPARING ASIA WITH THE REST OF THE WORLD

Erik van der Marel

5.1   Introduction

Cross-border trade in services has steadily expanded over the last 2 decades and now represents more than 20% of global trade. Digital services trade is growing in importance, and its share of cross-border trade in services is dependent on digital infrastructure as the channel for the transmission of information over the internet (WTO 2019). Yet, as governments increasingly constrain this information—or, more specifically, data—trade in digital services is affected (Ferracane and van der Marel 2021). The focus of this chapter is to analyze what specific data-related policies produce a trade-reducing effect on cross-border trade in digital services, with a specific emphasis on Asia.

Data-related policies are defined in this chapter as regulatory measures that restrict the flow of electronic data between economies. We concentrate on three types: (i) data localization policies, (ii) local storage requirements, and (iii) conditional flow regimes. As these policies inhibit the free flow of data across borders, they also hamper trade in digital services, given that it relies on the transmission of data across economies. According to our definition of digital services, economies currently imposing data localization requirements alone already are involved in about 15% of global digital services trade, with Asian economies taking a rising share (Figure 5.1). Restricting the movement of data across borders impedes the ability of firms to source and send data where its value is best used, hindering their chances of exploiting comparative advantage in digital services.

The three policy measures raise costs for firms to conduct business across borders by either mandating to keep data within a certain territory or by imposing additional requirements on data transferred abroad. Previous work has demonstrated that higher restrictiveness in these three measures is significantly associated with decreasing performance of firm productivity (Ferracane et al. 2018) and cross-border trade in services (Ferracane and van der Marel 2021). This chapter follows these two studies by investigating which of the three data-related policy measures inhibit cross-border trade in digital services. Given that the identification strategy of both studies required the three policy measures to be aggregated, this chapter improves on this by carving out the specifics and the trade effect of each policy measure individually and analyzing the effect on digital services only.

This chapter extends the identification strategy to consider the Asian region too. Many economies in Asia have applied data-related restrictions in recent years. As Asia's involvement in global digital services trade has grown over the last 2 decades, recent data-related restrictions applied in the region have also grown and have most likely impeded the potential to benefit from digital services trade. Yet, the region is large and includes economies with very different characteristics. To tease out the extent to which data-related policies across the globe have reduced trade in Asian economies, the empirical approach in this chapter employs an interaction term consisting of economies in the region. This way, the results illustrate whether much of the adverse trade impact following data-related restrictions across the globe indeed takes place in Asia.

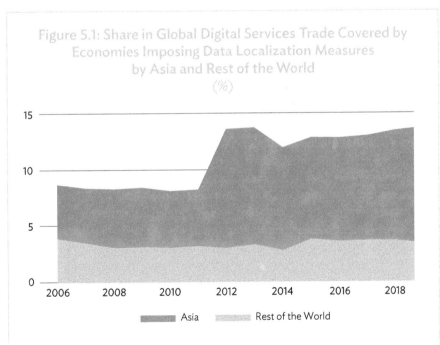

Figure 5.1: Share in Global Digital Services Trade Covered by Economies Imposing Data Localization Measures by Asia and Rest of the World (%)

Notes: Digital services trade covers imports and exports of digital and digital-enabled services as defined in column 4 of Table 5.2. Data localization policies cover those for which an initial 1 and 0.5 was assigned to economies.

Source: Author's calculations.

The analysis is carried out by adopting a difference-in-difference (DID) approach. More specifically, we first interact our economy-wide variable assigning unity each time an economy enacts a data restriction in a given year, with another variable that indicates whether a sector is classified as a digital service. This interaction term differentiates the group of digital sectors that are proportionately more affected by the implementation of data-related policies economies impose during the period covered by the analysis. In the other group, the non-digital services, no economy-wide policy "treatment" is observable. We classify the treatment sectors as digital-intense on the basis of a sector's usage of software over labor: services measuring greater usage of software compared with labor are, in our view, more reliant on the cross-border flow of data across borders, such as cloud computing, and therefore more sensitive to changes in data-related policies.

In a second step, we interact this economy-sector variable with another dummy giving unity to Asian economies. This allows us to determine whether the average negative trade impact caused by economies imposing data-related restrictions is also happening in Asia. There is reason to believe that the region experiences much of the trade fall following the application of data-related restrictions across the globe. Several Asian economies have applied stricter data regulations in recent years, such as the People's Republic of China (PRC) and Indonesia. This chapter therefore tries to tease out whether (i) the imposition of data-related policies in Asia could have a negative trade impact similar to the rest of the world, and (ii) if so, which of the three data-related policies are primarily responsible for this potential effect.

The baseline results show that digital services imports do indeed decline in economies that implement data-related restrictions (exports are covered in section 5.4.3). This outcome is particularly strong for data localization and local storage requirements. Our findings also suggest that the imposition of a conditional flow regime is more complex as it does not necessarily have a significant negative trade impact. The results are different when including Asia in extended baseline regressions. Although Asian economies also appear to suffer a decline in digital services trade when strict data localization rules are applied, this is not the case for local storage requirements. Instead, strict rules as part of a conditional flow regime seem to be more burdensome for digital services trade in Asia, contrary to the rest of the world.

The next section discusses the three data-related policies in greater detail and explains how to quantify them. After that, the chapter presents an empirical strategy with the baseline and extended baseline specification considering Asia, before reporting the results of the regressions and finally discussing policy implications of the findings.

5.2   Data-Related Policies

The data-related policies this chapter covers are (i) data localization policies, (ii) local storage requirements, and (iii) conditional flow regimes. As these policies inhibit the free flow of data across borders, they also affect trade in digital services, given that these rely on the transmission of data between economies. Previous research has established either theoretically or empirically the triangular relationship between cross-border data flows, digital services trade, and data-related policies. Manyika et al. (2016), for instance, claim that the contribution of cross-border data flows to GDP has overtaken that of flows in goods during the current wave of globalization. Recent work by Goldfarb and Trefler (2018) discusses the potential theoretical implications of data-related policies, such as data localization, on international trade and how that connects to existing trade models.

This chapter follows up on the empirical work by Ferracane and van der Marel (2021), which studies the proportionate trade impact of data-related policies in digital services sectors. Ferracane and van der Marel examine this by constructing a composite indicator that interacts an index of regulatory restrictiveness in data with a measure of sector-level digital or data intensity. As such, this work applies a weighted approach of a self-developed index of data policy restrictiveness, with a measure of data intensity for each services sector covered. This index contains a long series of specific regulatory policies in data, including restrictions related to both cross-border and domestic data usage. The results show that, whereas cross-border restrictions had a negative and significant impact on digital services trade, rules governing domestic processing did not.

The empirical study in this chapter will disentangle which of the cross-border restrictions covered by the data restrictiveness index are driving the negative trade result. Restrictions related to the cross-border flow of data include the three categories of interest. This policy categorization follows Ferracane (2017) and Ferracane, Lee-Makiyama, and van der Marel (2018). Note that data localization policies can entail a summary label covering various policies that ban the transfer of data abroad or can include a requirement for local processing.

5.2.1   Cross-Border Data Flow Restrictions

More specifically, bans on the transfer of data across borders and local processing requirements are the measures with the most restrictive effect on cross-border data flows. In case of a ban on the transfer of data or a local processing requirement, a firm needs to either build data centers within the implementing jurisdiction or switch to local service providers. This increases costs if the domestic service providers are less efficient than foreign ones. The difference between transfer bans and local processing requirements is quite subtle. In a transfer ban, the firm is not allowed to even send a copy of the data cross-border. Where a local processing requirement is in place, the firm can still send a copy of the data abroad—which can be important for communication between a subsidiary and its parent and, in general, for exchange of information within the group. In both cases, however, the main data processing activities need to be done in the imposing jurisdiction.

The second category covers local storage requirements. These measures require a firm to keep copies of certain data within the economy. Local storage requirements often apply to specific data such as accounts or bookkeeping. As long as the copy of the data remains within the national territory, the firm can operate as usual.

The third category of trade cost-enhancing measures related to cross-border flow of data is the case of a conditional flow regime. Measures under this regime forbid transfer of the data abroad unless certain conditions are fulfilled. If the conditions are stringent, the measure can easily result in a ban to transfer. The conditions can apply either to the recipient economy (e.g., some jurisdictions require that data can be transferred only to economies with an "adequate" protection) or to the firm (e.g., a condition might consist in the need to request the data subject to consent to the cross-border transfer of their data).

Contrary to Ferracane and van der Marel (2021), in this study, these policy categories are not lumped together and developed in a composite index measuring aggregate data restrictiveness. Instead, only a value of 1 is applied in case economies impose one of the three policy restrictions. However, to add nuance, given that not all economies have an equally strict applied set of data-related restrictions, we also assign a 0.5 in case economies impose less strict rules. An example is when economies apply data restriction only to one or a subset of sectors or type of data—and not the entire economy. As part of our empirical strategy, these 0.5 scoring will be transformed into either a 0 or 1 to allow for a DID method to assess their effect on digital services trade.

5.2.2   Asia's Part in Global Data Restrictions

Asia's share in the total number of data-related restrictions globally is presented in Figure 5.2. The proportion of data localization measures occupied by Asian economies is larger than the rest of the world, representing a share of about 70%. Other economies besides the PRC and Indonesia also apply data localization policies.

In similar manner, Figure 5.2 also points to the number of economies in Asia and the rest of the world that apply local storage requirements and rules related to a conditional flow regime. The figure illustrates that Asia's share in local storage requirements is relatively small. Finally, conditional flow regimes are a lot more frequent, as shown in Figure 5.2. Many economies across the globe apply this type of data-related policy restriction. Yet, Asia's global share remains modest, in part because many European and Latin American economies apply rules related to conditional flow regimes. Note however that in Asia, policies on conditional flow are greater in number than those for data localization (Table 5.1).

Even as data restrictiveness is not measured in levels, as developed with the data policy index in Ferracane and van der Marel (2021), we nonetheless can construct a global level for data restrictiveness and a separate one for the Asian region. Figure 5.3, using their weights and applying these to the updated set of the three measures deployed in this chapter, shows the development of the level of data restrictiveness over time, globally and for Asia. Notice that in both indexes, a second layer of weights is applied on the basis of an economy's GDP (in constant United States [US] dollars) to account for some economies being larger than others. Asia's development of restrictiveness level seems more severe than for the world as a whole. In large part, this is driven by the PRC's larger economic weight in Asia.

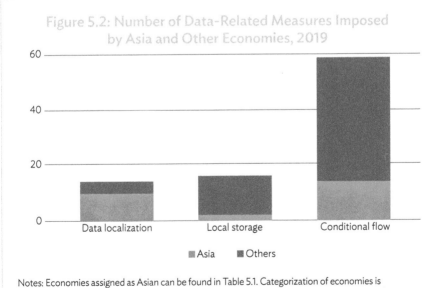

Figure 5.2: Number of Data-Related Measures Imposed by Asia and Other Economies, 2019

Notes: Economies assigned as Asian can be found in Table 5.1. Categorization of economies is performed on the basis of values assigned with an initial 0.5, meaning that economies also apply a partial restriction on the three types of data-related restrictions.

Source: Author's calculations.

Table 5.1: Economies Applying Data Restrictions

Data Localization	Local Storage	Conditional Flow Regime	
Australia[a]	Belgium	Argentina	Korea, Republic of[a]
Canada	Bulgaria	Australia[a]	Latvia
China, People's Rep. of[a]	Denmark	Austria	Lithuania
India[a]	Finland	Belgium	Luxembourg
Indonesia[a]	Germany	Brazil	Malaysia[a]
Korea, Republic of[a]	Greece	Brunei Darussalam[a]	Malta
Nigeria	India[a]	Bulgaria	Netherlands
Pakistan[a]	Italy	Canada	New Zealand[a]
Russian Federation	Netherlands	Chile	Nigeria
Taipei,China[a]	New Zealand[a]	China, People's Rep. of[a]	Norway
Thailand[a]	Poland	Colombia	Pakistan[a]
Türkiye	Romania	Costa Rica	Paraguay
Viet Nam[a]	Russian Federation	Croatia	Peru
	Sweden	Cyprus	Philippines[a]
	United Kingdom	Czech Republic	Poland
	United States	Denmark	Portugal
		Estonia	Romania
		Finland	Russian Federation
		France	Singapore[a]
		Germany	Slovakia
		Greece	Slovenia
		Hungary	South Africa
		Iceland	Spain
		India[a]	Sweden
		Indonesia[a]	Switzerland
		Ireland	Taipei,China[a]
		Israel	Thailand[a]
		Italy	Türkiye
		Japan[a]	United Kingdom

Note: Categorization of economies is performed on the basis of values assigned with an initial 0.5, meaning that economies also apply a partial restriction with respect to the three types of data-related restrictions.

[a] Asian economies.

Source: Author's compilation.

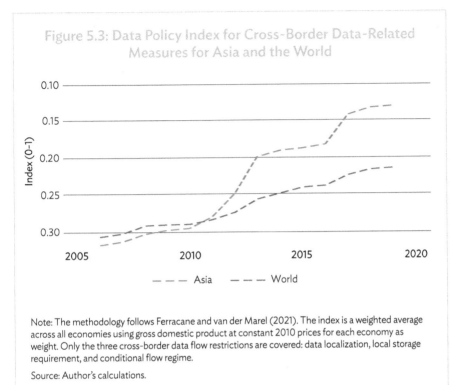

Figure 5.3: Data Policy Index for Cross-Border Data-Related Measures for Asia and the World

Note: The methodology follows Ferracane and van der Marel (2021). The index is a weighted average across all economies using gross domestic product at constant 2010 prices for each economy as weight. Only the three cross-border data flow restrictions are covered: data localization, local storage requirement, and conditional flow regime.

Source: Author's calculations.

5.3 Empirical Strategy

The DID approach in the empirical strategy regresses the outcome variable against a set of dummies that separates two groups for two time periods. One group is the treatment group, the other is the control. As with a standard DID analysis, the treatment group is exposed to a "treatment" in the second period, whereas the control group is not subjected to the treatment at any point. In a later stage, a third group of Asian economies undergoes the treatment.

In this chapter, the outcome variable is services trade. It is regressed on the treatment group of software-intense sectors for the period after economies have implemented their data-related policies. More specifically, a dummy variable is assigned to software-intense sectors starting from the year that economies imposed one of the three data restrictions presented in Table 5.1. The untreated control group, comprising non-software-intense sectors, is given a zero during the entire regression period. The DID approach is therefore composed of two levels of "differences": one that distinguishes between software-intense and non-software-intense services sectors (or digital services); and another that differentiates between pre- and post-year of implementation (known in the baseline as YIMP).

In more formal terms, we regress the following baseline specification:

$$ln(\text{SM})_{cst} = \varPhi + \theta D_{cst} \bullet \text{Software intense}_s \geq \text{YIMPL}_{ct-1} + \delta_{st} + \gamma_{ct} + \varepsilon_{cst} \quad (5.1)$$

In equation (5.1), the response variable is the logarithm (ln) of cross-border imports of services (SM) in economy c, for services sector s in time t. Data are taken from the World Trade Organization (WTO)–United Nations Conference on Trade and Development (UNCTAD)–International Trade Centre (ITC) annual trade in services dataset and the WTO–Organisation for Economic Co-operation and Development (OECD) BaTIS dataset for robustness checks. Then, the term D_{cst} denotes the dummy variable that is of interest. It captures any difference in services imports between software-intense and non-software-intense services before and after the year of implementation of an economy's data restriction denoted with YIMP_{ct}.

We also apply fixed effects that capture all other aggregate factors that otherwise would cause shifts in services trade over time, even in the presence of other regulatory changes. They are specified at sector-year, δ_{st}, and economy-year, γ_{ct}. The former group of fixed effects controls for sector-specific conditions, such as other sector intensities besides software. Examples are skill- and capital-intensities that affect production structures in sectors. They also cover services policy changes over the years specific to sectors. The latter set of fixed effects controls for economy-wide trends over time that are specific to an economy, such as macroeconomic conditions.[1] Sector fixed effects are applied at the 2-digit aggregate, given that the trade data are reported at this level. Finally, ε_{cst} is the residual term. Regressions are estimated with robust standard errors clustered by economy-sector-year and are performed over 2006–2019, the years for which we have policy data after taking a 1-year lag.

As said, our source of services trade is the WTO–UNCTAD–ITC annual dataset, which covers exports and imports of total commercial services. This database covers 222 entities and includes economies and regional aggregations

---

[1] Note that fixed effects by economy-sector would take out any variation across software-intense and non-software-intense sectors between economies imposing data-related restrictions and those who do not. We therefore do not apply these set of fixed effects. In case we did, we would only pick up total import developments of economies imposing data-related restrictions, compared to all other economies, given that no distinction could be made between an economy's sector trade patterns. Appendix Figure A5.1.1 presents an example for economies imposing data localization: they exhibit higher trade growth of total imports. Applying economy-sector fixed effects would measure this trend only. Using sector-year fixed effects, we are able to capture the fact that economies applying data localization policies experienced a decline in software-intensive imports compared to all other non-software-intense services imports over time, as illustrated in Appendix Figure A5.1.2.

or economic groupings during 2005–2020 at the two-digit level. The data are in line with the sixth edition of the International Monetary Fund's Balance of Payments and International Investment Position Manual (BPM6), as well as the 2010 edition of the Manual on Statistics of International Trade in Services (MSITS 2010). Compared with the BPM5 classification, major changes for the Balance of Payments classification for services have been introduced with regard to financial intermediation services, insurance services, intellectual property, and manufacturing and maintenance services, many of which we use in our empirical specification.

This chapter also uses a second source of service trade from the WTO–OECD BaTIS dataset. BaTIS stands for Balanced Trade in Services and is an experimental dataset containing a complete, consistent, and balanced matrix of international trade in services. Trade data cover 2005–2020, for over 200 reporters and partners, and 12 categories from the Extended Balance of Payments Services classification 2010 besides total services. In the data file, one can find reported values—trade data as reported by the relevant statistical authorities—as found in the WTO–UNCTAD–ITC database; final values, which include the reported data and all the estimations and adjustment procedures used to ensure complete consistency of the dataset; and balanced values, which are the reconciled trade value of reported exports and mirror imports. We choose final values as a midway of manipulated data given the reported values are already covered by the first annual dataset. See Fortanier et al. (2017) for details.

5.3.1   Software Intensities

Software intensities are measured using information on software usage by sector of the US. Specifically, this chapter takes the 2011 Census ICT Survey, which reports survey data at detailed four-digit North American Industry Classification System (NAICS) sector level. The data record how much each industry and services sector spend (in millions of US dollars) on information and communication technology (ICT) hardware equipment and computer software.

The survey reports two types of software expenditure: capitalized and non-capitalized. We select both because the two components together proxy the degree to which sectors are digital-intense and reliant on the transmission of data over the internet. Capitalized expenditure is closer to the concept of intensities for factors of production such as capital and labor, as developed in the previous literature (e.g., Chor 2011; Romalis 2004). Non-capitalized expenditure relates more to the input support of firms and enters in the production function as intermediate services. Capitalized expenditure is consisting of longer-term investments made in computer software. It excludes purchases and payroll for developing software, software licensing and services, and maintenance agreements for software, which are all components that are measured as non-capitalized purchases.

The year 2010 is selected for computing software intensities. Choosing this year avoids the risk of being endogenous to the trade data as it lies in the middle of the time period. Software expenditure is divided over labor, for which we also use data from 2010. The labor data are sourced from the US Bureau of Labor Statistics (BLS). These software intensities are therefore similar to the ones computed in Ferracane and van der Marel (2021). For our DID analysis, all we need is an indicator that assigns unity to a services sector classified as software intense. In doing so, we determine whether a sector adheres to this condition when it shows a software-over-labor ratio higher than the sample median. Sectors showing a ratio below this threshold are assigned a zero.

Intensities are computed at four-digit NAICS level and then concorded into two-digit BPM6, from where the median is computed. Because no concordance table exists between NAICS and BPM6, a self-constructed matrix is used. Numbers are aggregated at two-digit BPM6 level by taking the simple average. Note that one sector—royalties and license fees and intellectual property—forms a mismatch between the two classification tables. This category is neither reported in the US Census nor in the US BLS database. Nonetheless, it is an important sector as it covers, among other items, patents, trademarks, and copyrights—all activities that are digital-intense and for which the trade data record high volumes of services exports. For this reason, this chapter uses a self-constructed concordance table to incorporate this sector.[2]

Table 5.2 reports the sectors classified as software-intense and separates between two types of digital services. One category is digital services, which are data-reliant sectors that show extremely high software-over-labor ratios. The table also shows sectors exhibiting high software intensities, but which typically are not part of what the policy literature classifies as pure data sectors. We call these digital-enabled services. Even though data and digitalization penetrate all parts of the economy, not all services classify as data or digital sectors. This separation follows broadly the Organisation for Economic Co-operation and Development (OECD)–World Trade Organization (WTO)–International Monetary Fund (IMF) Handbook on Measuring Digital Trade, which breaks down digital trade into two categories: ICT and ICT-enabled services. The ICT-enabled services can cover many sectors, not just digital services such as health and education. To account for this distinction, we include a second column, digital-enabled services, that expands the core list of digital services but excludes types of services that are not necessarily digital (yet).

---

[2] The concordance table between four-digit NAICS and two-digit BPM6 can be obtained upon request. Admittedly, the inclusion of intellectual property or royalties and license fees as a service is a balance of payments decision, and there is some debate about whether this is truly a service. In addition, for some economies, this may also reflect tax and transfer pricing as drivers of observable trade in this sector. However, since this sector is included in all publicly available data sources that record trade in services, we prefer to include it. Nonetheless, in our regression we have also dropped this sector entirely as additional (unreported) robustness checks. Results do not alter apart from slight coefficient size changes. Results are available and can be obtained upon request.

Table 5.2: Sectors Classified as Software-Intensive (Over Labor)

Code	Sector Description	Digital	Digital-Enabled
SI1	Telecommunication	•	•
SI2	Computer	•	•
SI3	Information	•	•
SF	Insurance	•	•
SG	Financial	•	•
SH	Intellectual property		•
SJ1	Research and development		•
SJ2	Professional and management		•
SJ3	Technology, trade-related, and other		•
SB	Maintenance and repair		
SD	Travel		
SE	Construction		
SC1	Sea transport		
SC2	Air transport		
SC3	Other transport		
SC4	Postal and courier		
SK1	Audiovisual and related		
SK2	Personal, cultural, and recreation		

Source: Author's compilation.

Digital services tabulated in the third column of Table 5.2 cover telecommunications, computer services, and information services, and form natural contenders of data, given that these sectors are highly digital. Information services involve activities such as data processing and web search, all of which are high users of software. This column includes financial and insurance services, which are also assessed as greater consumers of software than labor and rely on cross-border data flows. The two sectors are broadly considered as very digital-intense, given that over the years internet technologies have brought massive changes to the financial services industry.[3] The next column expands the list of digital sectors with services that are also commonly understood as

---

[3] Another non-ICT sector that is software-intense is retail. However, neither the US Census nor the BPM6 classification shows a separate entry for retail or wholesale distribution services, which is the reason why this sector is omitted in our analysis of intensities and is not covered in our regression analysis.

digital-intense and are not always pure digital services even as they rely on the cross-border flow of data and the internet and do show a software-over-labor ratio above the median or mean. These are mostly business services.[4]

5.3.2   Extended Baseline for Asia

We extend the baseline specification to consider additional effects for the Asian region. As has been explained, much of the global policy action related to data restrictions took place in Asian economies. By extending the baseline regressions, we can uncover whether the changes in data-related policies of the region really resulted in the negative trade effect in digital services observed at global level in previous empirical works. In other words, the aim is to find out whether Asian economies have experienced a differential effect of a reduction in imports after data-related policies are changed. The way in which we apply this extended baseline is to interact the variable of interest D_{cst} with another dummy called $ASIA_c$, which assigns unity for each Asian economy. It means that these economies are interacted with the DID dummy that signifies the group of digital sectors, starting from the year each policy was implemented.

In more formal terms, we augment the baseline specification with a triple interaction term as follows:

$$ln(SM)_{cst} = \Phi + \theta D_{cst} \bullet \text{Software intense}_s \geq YIMP_{ct-1} * ASIA_c + \delta_{st} + \gamma_{ct} + \varepsilon_{cst}$$

$$(5.2)$$

As stated in equation (5.2), we cover for the Asian region by the term $ASIA_c$. This is a dummy for the 16 Asian economies in the 64 economies covered by the dataset. The Asian economies covered are duly noted in Table 5.1.[5] Together this group is therefore separately interacted with our DID dummy, in addition to the average effect for all economies as a control variable. Typically, the interaction term now comprises three terms for which all components should be controlled for, including the Asian region. Yet, given that the Asian economies themselves are subsumed in the economy-year fixed effects, no separate control variable for these economies can be included. All other terms in the equation remain unchanged and follow the baseline specification stated in equation (5.1).

The interpretation of the Asian dummy becomes somewhat different than the baseline specification. That is, given the interaction variable with Asian economies, a significant result on this triple interaction term confirms whether

---

[4]   Note that the BaTIS dataset follows exactly the same sector division but at slightly more aggregate level.

[5]   Asian economies were selected in consultation with ADB staff.

any differential effect is apparent for the Asian region compared with the baseline interaction term for all economies. As always, the result of the baseline coefficient becomes somewhat less informative regardless of its significance. Therefore, we also put for every regression a Wald test of joint significance using the result of the F-statistic.[6] For each regression, the p-values are reported for this F-statistic. Keeping in mind a threshold of 0.05, a p-value exceeding this means that the null hypothesis of a joint significance can be rejected. If not, the baseline coefficient result is jointly significant with the Asian interaction dummy.

5.4   Results

Results of the baseline and extended regressions are reported from Table 5.3 onward. Table 5.3 shows the regression results by taking the three data-related restrictions together and checking whether the aggregate assessment is consistent with findings in the literature. That is, we create a separate dummy variable each time an economy implements at least one of the three data-related policies. We call this variable CB, denoting cross-border data restrictions. Following our DID equations (5.1) and (5.2), this variable is then interacted with the list of digital services sectors, called DS, following Table 5.2. In the next step, we interact this term with the Asia dummy, called Asia, that singles out the region and, in effect, therefore creates a triple interaction term. Notice that for columns (1) and (2) in Table 5.3, we put a score of 0 for those economies that have implemented data restrictions initially assigned a 0.5, whereas in columns (3) and (4), we give these partial restrictions a full score of 1 to check results.

The coefficient results from the baseline regression presented in column (1) confirms our prior that any of the implemented data-related restrictions are associated with lower levels of digital services imports. This result echoes the empirical findings in Ferracane and van der Marel (2021) even as our study lacks their use of a restrictiveness index. Instead, we simply employ a dummy variable following the requirement for a DID specification. The fact that, in both cases, results are negative and significant is reassuring even if our coefficient size is smaller than in previous work. This lower coefficient size is unsurprising given the nature of the explanatory variables. In economic terms, it implies an average negative trade effect in digital services of about 15% for economies implementing any of these three data-related restrictions compared with economies that do not implement them.

---

[6] A significant result on the Wald test of joint significance means that both variables, i.e., the baseline and the extended one, are both significant and therefore retain their predictive power and should be added in the regression.

Table 5.3: Baseline and Extended Difference-in-Difference Regression for Any Data-Related Restrictions

	(1)	(2)	(3)	(4)
	ln(SM)			
	0.5 > 0		0.5 > 1	
CB * DS	-0.138***	-0.090*	-0.097	-0.044
	(0.003)	(0.050)	(0.115)	(0.478)
CB * DS * Asia		-0.614***		-0.325***
		(0.000)		(0.000)
FE Economy-Year	Yes	Yes	Yes	Yes
FE Sector-Year	Yes	Yes	Yes	Yes
Observations	11,454	11,454	11,454	11,454
Adjusted R-squared	0.774	0.775	0.774	0.775
p-values F-stat		0.000		0.000

CB = cross-border data restrictions, DS = digital services sector, FE = fixed effects, ln = natural logarithm, SM = cross-border imports of services.

Notes: * $p<0.10$, ** $p<0.05$, *** $p<0.01$; p-values in parentheses.

Source: Author's calculations.

Next, we report the results from the extended regression in column (2). It now becomes clear that the differential impact for Asia becomes highly significant with a negative coefficient sign, whereas the control variable for the average effect remains only weakly significant, though still negative. The size of the coefficient results could be interpreted as Asian economies exhibit a higher-than-average effect compared with the rest of the world, given its higher value compared with columns (1) and (2). However, one needs to be careful with such inference given that, in principle, there is no reason why certain groups of economies would be innately more sensitive to data-related restrictions than others. Instead, the coefficient result should be interpreted as indicating that much of the global trade adjustment in digital services due to data-related restrictions occurs in Asia, as the differential effect on the significant triple interaction suggests. Note that the null hypothesis of a joint significance cannot be rejected.

Results for Asia retain their negative significance when fully incorporating the partial scores for the data restrictions, as reported in the last column. The average effect for the rest of the world loses its significance entirely in both columns (3) and (4). This may mean that, unlike in Asia, moderate data-related restrictions have no trade-reducing associations in the rest of the world, although the p-values suggest the two variables are still jointly significant. One potential explanation is that the enabling environment at the economy-sector level may compensate for this effect in other economies, which in Asia is not the case—a factor that is only controlled for at the economy and sector individually.[7] However, using the alternative dataset from BaTIS shows in Table 5.4 that, when assigning a full score for economies having these partial data restrictions, the coefficient results for the average effect do come out as negative and significant in column (3) but not in column (4), although with a joint significance.

Table 5.4: Baseline and Extended Difference-in-Difference Regression for Any Data-Related Restrictions Using BaTIS Database

	(1)	(2)	(3)	(4)
	\multicolumn{4}{c}{ln(SM)}			
	0.5 > 0		0.5 > 1	
CB * DS	-0.142***	-0.098*	-0.185**	-0.118
	(0.009)	(0.072)	(0.014)	(0.119)
CB * DS * Asia		-0.436***		-0.361***
		(0.000)		(0.000)
FE Economy-Year	Yes	Yes	Yes	Yes
FE Sector-Year	Yes	Yes	Yes	Yes
Observations	8,569	8,569	8,569	8,569
Adjusted R-squared	0.782	0.783	0.782	0.783
p-values F-stat		0.000		0.000

BaTIS = WTO–OECD Balanced Trade in Services dataset, CB = cross-border data restrictions, DS = digital services sector, FE = fixed effects, ln = natural logarithm, OECD = Organisation for Economic Co-operation and Development, SM = border imports of services, WTO = World Trade Organization.

Notes: * p<0.10, ** p<0.05, *** p<0.01; p-values in parentheses.

Source: Author's calculations.

[7] For instance, some economies may have developed a strong digital infrastructure with sophisticated internet connection or constructed data centers that help develop trade in digital services sectors —something that is hard to control for at the economy-sector level. By similar token, economies may still suffer from high restriction in digital sectors themselves such as telecommunications, an issue we control for as part of our robustness checks.

5.4.1 Specific Data Restrictions

Tables 5.5 and 5.6 report the results for the three specific data restrictions. They are labeled in the two tables as follows: data localization as DL; local storage requirement as LS; and conditional flow regimes as CF. Table 5.5 reports the results for using the WTO–UNCTAD–ITC annual trade in services dataset, Table 5.6 reports the results for BaTIS.

The results in Table 5.5 show that the average effect for data localization policies disappears but becomes highly significant for the Asian region, both when entered alone and when entered together with all the other variables in column (4). The reverse appears the case for local storage requirements in column (2). This variable remains significant for the average effect across all economies but becomes insignificant when interacting with the Asia dummy. Note that the joint significance is nearly rejected. This suggests that the trade-reducing impact of economies imposing local storage requirements may not be as great in Asia as elsewhere in the world. This is not the case for the restrictions related to a conditional flow regime, where results show a negative coefficient for the triple interaction term for Asia when entered alone in column (3) and when putting together with the other restrictions in column (4). Interestingly, the average effect for conditional flow regimes stays significant in the last column, albeit weakly.

Table 5.5: Extended Difference-in-Difference Regression for the Three Data-Related Restrictions Separately

	(1)	(2)	(3)	(4)	(5)	(6)	(7)	(8)
			ln(SM)				ln(SM)	
			0.5 > 0				0.5 > 1	
DL * DS	-0.069			-0.006	0.128			0.104
	(0.704)			(0.978)	(0.115)			(0.202)
DL * DS * Asia	-0.873***			-0.931***	-0.580***			-0.578***
	(0.000)			(0.000)	(0.000)			(0.000)
LS * DS		-0.213**		-0.239**		-0.099**		-0.157***
		(0.013)		(0.015)		(0.024)		(0.001)
LS * DS * Asia		0.061		-0.050		0.047		0.136
		(0.883)		(0.905)		(0.704)		(0.302)
CF * DS			-0.022	-0.082*			-0.019	-0.080
			(0.618)	(0.075)			(0.708)	(0.148)
CF * DS * Asia			-0.480***	-0.369***			-0.352***	-0.072
			(0.000)	(0.000)			(0.000)	(0.400)

continued on next page

Table 5.5 continued

	(1)	(2)	(3)	(4)	(5)	(6)	(7)	(8)
	ln(SM)				ln(SM)			
	0.5 > 0				0.5 > 1			
FE Economy-Year	Yes	Yes	Yes	Yes	Yes	Yes	Yes	Yes
FE Sector-Year	Yes	Yes	Yes	Yes	Yes	Yes	Yes	Yes
Observations	11,454	11,454	11,454	11,454	11,454	11,454	11,454	11,454
Adjusted R-squared	0.775	0.774	0.775	0.776	0.775	0.774	0.775	0.775
p-values F-stat	0.000	0.042	0.000	0.000	0.000	0.076	0.000	0.000

CF = conditional flow regimes, DL = data localization, DS = digital services sector, FE = fixed effects, ln = natural logarithm, LS = local storage requirements, SM = cross-border imports of services.

Notes: * $p<0.10$, ** $p<0.05$, *** $p<0.01$; p-values in parentheses.

Source: Author's calculations.

Table 5.6: Extended Difference-in-Difference Regression for the Three Data-Related Restrictions Separately Using BaTIS Database

	(1)	(2)	(3)	(4)	(5)	(6)	(7)	(8)
	ln(SM)				ln(SM)			
	0.5 > 0				0.5 > 1			
DL * DS	0.024 (0.915)			0.118 (0.601)	0.171* (0.056)			0.120 (0.171)
DL * DS * Asia	-0.434* (0.089)			-0.505* (0.053)	-0.642*** (0.000)			-0.600*** (0.000)
LS * DS		-0.307*** (0.002)		-0.350*** (0.002)		-0.210*** (0.000)		-0.279*** (0.000)
LS * DS * Asia		0.296 (0.595)		0.207 (0.713)		0.171 (0.108)		0.152 (0.218)
CF * DS			-0.067 (0.200)	-0.098* (0.072)			-0.094 (0.110)	-0.151** (0.023)
CF * DS * Asia			-0.546*** (0.000)	-0.463*** (0.000)			-0.483*** (0.000)	-0.200* (0.053)
FE Economy-Year	Yes	Yes	Yes	Yes	Yes	Yes	Yes	Yes
FE Sector-Year	Yes	Yes	Yes	Yes	Yes	Yes	Yes	Yes
Observations	8,569	8,569	8,569	8,569	8,569	8,569	8,569	8,569

continued on next page

Table 5.6 *continued*

	(1)	(2)	(3)	(4)	(5)	(6)	(7)	(8)
	ln(SM)				ln(SM)			
	0.5 > 0				0.5 > 1			
Adjusted R-squared	0.782	0.782	0.783	0.783	0.783	0.782	0.783	0.784
p-values F-stat	0.008	0.008	0.000	0.000	0.000	0.001	0.000	0.000

BaTIS = WTO–OECD Balanced Trade in Services dataset, CF = conditional flow regimes, DL = data localization, DS = digital services sector, FE = fixed effects, ln = natural logarithm, LS = local storage requirements, OECD = Organisation for Economic Co-operation and Development, SM = cross-border imports of services, WTO = World Trade Organization.

Notes: * $p<0.10$, ** $p<0.05$, *** $p<0.01$; p-values in parentheses.

Source: Author's calculations.

These results are largely similar when leveling up all partial restrictions into a full score and when using the BaTIS dataset. Columns (5)–(8) in Table 5.5 report coefficient results that largely match the first four columns, although the coefficient sizes of all significant results are lower. Moreover, the significant and negative results for the conditional flow restrictions disappear when entered in combination with the other two restrictions in the last column. This is the case for both the average effect and the Asian triple effect. Looking at Table 5.6, use of BaTIS data shows the results for data localization measures for the Asian interaction term now come out as weakly significant. Otherwise, all other results are similar to those reported in Table 5.4. This measure of data localization again becomes strongly significant when assigning a full score for the partial data restrictions, and the same applies for the conditional flow restrictions in column (8).

5.4.2   Digital-Enabled Services

We repeat the last set of regressions by expanding the list of sectors with digital-enabled services. As explained, these sectors include intellectual property, research and development services, professional and management activities, and other business services. These sectors are found to have relatively high software-over-labor ratios and heavily rely on cross-border flows of data too. In turn, these four additional sectors are therefore also likely to be sensitive to regulatory changes in the free flow of data. When reporting results, the list of digital-enabled services is now denoted with DEnS instead of DS.

Results for digital-enabled services are reported in Table 5.7 using the WTO–UNCTAD–ITC annual trade in services dataset and in Table 5.8 using the BaTIS. The results in Table 5.7 show that, again, the variable measuring data localization comes out as strongly negative and significant for the Asian interaction term. This variable stays significant when entered with all other policy measures in column (4). The results for both data storage requirement and conditional flow restrictions remain largely insignificant for the Asian economies with an F-statistic rejected or almost rejected. For restrictions related to conditional flow regimes, these policies are not negatively associated with trade for the expanded list of digital-enabled services in Asia, contrary to the results for the narrow list in Table 5.5. However, when assigning the partial restrictions into full scoring, results for this policy become significant again for Asia in column (7). The full scoring method provides negative and strongly significant results for Asia for the local storage requirements, although surprisingly positive coefficient results are recorded for the average effects.

Using BaTIS, the results in Table 5.8 show a more consistent pattern across the two scoring systems for the partial measures. That is, data localization measures come out with a negative and significant coefficient result for the Asian triple interaction term, with also a stable coefficient size. Similarly, the negative and significant result for local storage requirement is consistent for the non-Asian variable across columns (2), (4), (6), and (8). Also, the interaction term for Asia regarding conditional flow restrictions remains intact across the reporting columns but loses its significance once entered with the other policy restrictions as reported in the last column. A further surprising result is the positive and weakly significant result found for local storage requirement for digital-enabled services, although this is only the case when partial scores are set to 1 instead of 0. One likely explanation is that some overscoring takes place that, in the regressions, picks up a mere trade expansion of economies in which otherwise only limited restrictions apply in reality.

Table 5.7: Extended Difference-in-Difference Regression for the Three Data-Related Restrictions Separately for Digital-Enabled Services

	(1)	(2)	(3)	(4)	(5)	(6)	(7)	(8)
	ln(SM)					ln(SM)		
	0.5 > 0					0.5 > 1		
DL * DEnS	-0.042			0.086	0.129			0.134
	(0.836)			(0.697)	(0.114)			(0.105)
DL * DEnS * Asia	-1.046***			-1.148***	-0.538***			-0.568***
	(0.000)			(0.000)	(0.000)			(0.000)
LS * DEnS		-0.159		-0.230**		0.092**		0.045
		(0.102)		(0.034)		(0.029)		(0.306)
LS * DEnS * Asia		0.039		0.121		-0.442***		-0.342***
		(0.935)		(0.801)		(0.000)		(0.003)

continued on next page

Table 5.7 continued

	(1)	(2)	(3)	(4)	(5)	(6)	(7)	(8)
			ln(SM)				ln(SM)	
			0.5 > 0				0.5 > 1	
CF * DEnS			0.116**	0.061			0.141***	0.044
			(0.011)	(0.190)			(0.006)	(0.432)
CF * DEnS * Asia			-0.094	0.014			-0.226***	0.099
			(0.362)	(0.894)			(0.002)	(0.291)
FE Economy-Year	Yes	Yes	Yes	Yes	Yes	Yes	Yes	Yes
FE Sector-Year	Yes	Yes	Yes	Yes	Yes	Yes	Yes	Yes
Observations	11,454	11,454	11,454	11,454	11,454	11,454	11,454	11,454
Adjusted R-squared	0.776	0.774	0.774	0.776	0.775	0.774	0.775	0.775
p-values F-stat	0.000	0.256	0.031	0.000	0.000	0.000	0.000	0.000

CF = conditional flow regimes, DEns = digital-enabled services, DL = data localization, DS = digital services sector, FE = fixed effects, ln = natural logarithm, LS = local storage requirements, SM = cross-border imports of services.

Notes: * p<0.10, ** p<0.05, *** p<0.01; p-values in parentheses.

Source: Author's calculations.

Table 5.8: Extended Difference-in-Difference Regression for the Three Data-Related Restrictions Separately for Digital-Enabled Services Using BaTIS Database

	(1)	(2)	(3)	(4)	(5)	(6)	(7)	(8)
			ln(SM)				ln(SM)	
			0.5 > 0				0.5 > 1	
DL * DEnS	0.110			0.281	0.209**			0.178*
	(0.643)			(0.256)	(0.030)			(0.065)
DL * DEnS * Asia	-0.543**			-0.716**	-0.537***			-0.522***
	(0.047)			(0.012)	(0.000)			(0.000)
LS * DEnS		-0.366***		-0.452***		-0.171***		-0.227***
		(0.000)		(0.000)		(0.000)		(0.000)
LS * DEnS * Asia		0.539		0.538		0.201*		0.238**
		(0.362)		(0.366)		(0.054)		(0.044)
CF * DEnS			-0.032	-0.062			-0.012	-0.041
			(0.548)	(0.253)			(0.841)	(0.542)
CF * DEnS * Asia			-0.302***	-0.208*			-0.293***	-0.098
			(0.008)	(0.079)			(0.000)	(0.366)

continued on next page

Table 5.8 *continued*

	(1)	(2)	(3)	(4)	(5)	(6)	(7)	(8)
	ln(SM)				ln(SM)			
	0.5 > 0				0.5 > 1			
FE Economy-Year	Yes	Yes	Yes	Yes	Yes	Yes	Yes	Yes
FE Sector-Year	Yes	Yes	Yes	Yes	Yes	Yes	Yes	Yes
Observations	8,569	8,569	8,569	8,569	8,569	8,569	8,569	8,569
Adjusted R-squared	0.783	0.782	0.782	0.783	0.783	0.782	0.782	0.783
p-values F-stat	0.009	0.001	0.020	0.000	0.000	0.001	0.001	0.000

BaTIS = WTO–OECD Balanced Trade in Services dataset, CF = conditional flow regimes, DEns = digital-enabled services, DL = data localization, DS = digital services sector, FE = fixed effects, ln = natural logarithm, LS = local storage requirements, OECD = Organisation for Economic Co-operation and Development, SM = cross-border imports of services, WTO = World Trade Organization.

Notes: * $p<0.10$, ** $p<0.05$, *** $p<0.01$; p-values in parentheses.

Source: Author's calculations.

5.4.3   Exports

A further check is to see whether the reported results also hold as true for exports as they do for imports. Even as conceptually the relationship between data-related restrictions and exports is weaker than for imports, it is a natural question to ask if there is a two-way effect in digital services trade. That question becomes even more acute in a global context, where about half of total international trade, and increasingly also digital services trade, is characterized by global value chains (World Bank 2020). In other words, the increase in exports experienced within global value chains correlates positively with the extent to which economies are able to source imports. Given that digital services markets are becoming increasingly global, and that supply chain trade takes place within services sectors (Heuser and Mattoo 2017; De Backer and Miroudot 2013), interest in the impacts on exports is warranted.

Results for the same set of baseline regressions but for exports, ln(SX), are reported in Tables 5.9 for digital services and in Table 5.10 for digital-enabled services. Table 5.9 shows that the coefficient result for data localization restrictions comes out with a negative sign but is only significant when entered with the other three policy variables in both column (4) and column (8) for the Asian interaction term.[8] A further result is that the coefficient for local storage

---

[8]   Note that the two variables in column 1 and column 4 are still jointly significant, although in column 4 above a p-value threshold of 0.05.

requirement is positive when partial restrictions are fully accounted, which again may be a result from overshooting the measured regulatory burden in case of assigning a full score. Also, their joint significance is largely rejected, similar to the result in column (2). Next, restrictions for a conditional flow regime give a negative and significant coefficient result on the average effect variable, and a nonsignificant one in column (3) and column (7). Results for digital-enabled services in Table 5.10 are in line; however, they show a stronger negative result for both data localization measures for the average effect and local storage requirement for Asia, but not for the results on conditional flow regimes.

Table 5.9: Extended Difference-in-Difference Regression for the Three Data-Related Restrictions Separately for Digital Services Using Exports

	(1)	(2)	(3)	(4)	(5)	(6)	(7)	(8)
	ln(SX)				ln(SX)			
	0.5 > 0				0.5 > 1			
DL*DS	-0.105 (0.600)			-0.135 (0.540)	-0.102 (0.255)			-0.040 (0.664)
DL*DS*Asia	-0.372 (0.125)			-0.519** (0.047)	-0.061 (0.591)			-0.395*** (0.003)
LS*DS		-0.136 (0.164)		-0.020 (0.862)		0.053 (0.307)		0.115** (0.035)
LS*DS*Asia		0.805 (0.151)		0.366 (0.520)		-0.155 (0.345)		-0.443** (0.014)
CF*DS			-0.318*** (0.000)	-0.362*** (0.000)			-0.360*** (0.000)	-0.475*** (0.000)
CF*DS*Asia			-0.141 (0.211)	-0.057 (0.616)			0.045 (0.589)	0.381*** (0.000)
FE Economy-Year	Yes	Yes	Yes	Yes	Yes	Yes	Yes	Yes
FE Sector-Year	Yes	Yes	Yes	Yes	Yes	Yes	Yes	Yes
Observations	11,209	11,209	11,209	11,209	11,209	11,209	11,209	11,209
Adjusted R-squared	0.733	0.733	0.734	0.734	0.733	0.733	0.734	0.734
p-values F-stat	0.004	0.178	0.000	0.000	0.076	0.450	0.000	0.000

CF = conditional flow regimes, DL = data localization, DS = digital services sector, FE = fixed effects, ln = natural logarithm, LS = local storage requirements, SX = cross-border exports of services.

Notes: * $p<0.10$, ** $p<0.05$, *** $p<0.01$; p-values in parentheses.

Source: Author's calculations.

Table 5.10: Extended Difference-in-Difference Regression for the Three Data-Related Restrictions Separately for Digital-Enabled Services Using Exports

	(1)	(2)	(3)	(4)	(5)	(6)	(7)	(8)
	ln(SX)				ln(SX)			
	0.5 > 0				0.5 > 1			
DL * DEnS	-0.639***			-0.943***	-0.171*			-0.074
	(0.001)			(0.000)	(0.062)			(0.435)
DL * DEnS * Asia	-0.456*			-0.198	-0.099			-0.345**
	(0.057)			(0.475)	(0.399)			(0.013)
LS * DEnS		0.199**		0.449***		0.547***		0.572***
		(0.044)		(0.000)		(0.000)		(0.000)
LS * DEnS * Asia		0.828		0.447		-0.486***		-0.594***
		(0.138)		(0.430)		(0.001)		(0.000)
CF * DEnS			-0.018	-0.096*			0.037	-0.135**
			(0.738)	(0.082)			(0.541)	(0.044)
CF * DEnS * Asia			-0.089	0.044			0.050	0.504***
			(0.450)	(0.713)			(0.560)	(0.000)
FE Economy-Year	Yes	Yes	Yes	Yes	Yes	Yes	Yes	Yes
FE Sector-Year	Yes	Yes	Yes	Yes	Yes	Yes	Yes	Yes
Observations	11,209	11,209	11,209	11,209	11,209	11,209	11,209	11,209
Adjusted R-squared	0.734	0.733	0.733	0.735	0.733	0.735	0.733	0.736
p-values F-stat	0.000	0.025	0.690	0.000	0.001	0.000	0.671	0.000

CF = conditional flow regimes, DEns = digital-enabled services, DL = data localization, DS = digital services sector, FE = fixed effects, ln = natural logarithm, LS = local storage requirements, SX = cross-border exports of services.

Notes: * p<0.10, ** p<0.05, *** p<0.01; p-values in parentheses.

Source: Author's calculations.

5.4.4 People's Republic of China

Having a large market, and therefore being a relatively large trader in the Asian region, inclusion of the PRC could drive much of the significant results obtained in the baseline regressions. Therefore, we perform regressions by excluding the PRC from our sample to check at whether the baseline results remain stable and are not skewed into a negative direction just because the economy is included.

In doing so, the baseline regression results reported in Tables 5.3 and 5.5 are repeated and reported in Tables 5.11 and 5.12—i.e., for the aggregate dummy capturing all three types of data policies together and for separating them, respectively. The coefficient outcomes show that excluding the PRC from the sample does not affect the results, which remain stable and statistically significant compared with the initial baseline regression. This is true when using the annual dataset and when using the BaTIS dataset (output omitted). Similarly, the results remain stable when performing the regressions for digital-enabled services (output omitted).[9] A marginal difference, nonetheless, apparent in both tables is that, when the PRC is excluded, the coefficient sizes are somewhat bigger. One potential explanation is that other economies are much smaller and therefore have a higher dependency on global markets, which explains their economic effects as captured by the coefficient size.

Table 5.11: Baseline and Extended Difference-in-Difference Regression for Any Data-Related Restrictions, Excluding the PRC

	(1)	(2)	(3)	(4)
	ln(SM)			
	0.5 > 0		0.5 > 1	
CB * DS	-0.121***	-0.089*	-0.083	-0.044
	(0.008)	(0.054)	(0.180)	(0.482)
CB * DS * Asia		-0.505***		-0.258***
		(0.000)		(0.000)
FE Economy-Year	Yes	Yes	Yes	Yes
FE Sector-Year	Yes	Yes	Yes	Yes
Observations	11,352	11,352	11,352	11,352
Adjusted R-squared	0.772	0.773	0.772	0.773
p-values F-stat		0.000		0.000

CB = cross-border data restrictions, DS = digital services sector, FE = fixed effects, ln = natural logarithm, PRC = People's Republic of China, SM = cross-border imports of services.

Notes: * p<0.10, ** p<0.05, *** p<0.01; p-values in parentheses.

Source: Author's calculations.

---

[9] Regressions results are omitted to save space and preserve conciseness but are available upon request. A further remark for the results for digital-enabled services is that the positive coefficient results come out as having weaker statistical significance when the PRC is excluded.

Table 5.12: Extended Difference-in-Difference Regression for the Three Data-Related Restrictions Separately, Excluding the PRC

	(1)	(2)	(3)	(4)	(5)	(6)	(7)	(8)
	ln(SM)				ln(SM)			
	0.5 > 0				0.5 > 1			
DL * DS	-0.070			-0.005	0.127			0.104
	(0.702)			(0.981)	(0.115)			(0.200)
DL * DS * Asia	-0.739***			-0.888***	-0.501***			-0.502***
	(0.001)			(0.000)	(0.000)			(0.000)
LS * DS		-0.226***		-0.239**		-0.115***		-0.156***
		(0.008)		(0.015)		(0.009)		(0.001)
LS * DS * Asia		0.058		-0.047		0.046		0.115
		(0.889)		(0.911)		(0.711)		(0.384)
CF * DS			-0.036	-0.081*			-0.038	-0.080
			(0.417)	(0.078)			(0.460)	(0.149)
CF * DS * Asia			-0.347***	-0.368***			-0.286***	-0.065
			(0.000)	(0.000)			(0.000)	(0.457)
FE Economy-Year	Yes	Yes	Yes	Yes	Yes	Yes	Yes	Yes
FE Sector-Year	Yes	Yes	Yes	Yes	Yes	Yes	Yes	Yes
Observations	11,352	11,352	11,352	11,352	11,352	11,352	11,352	11,352
Adjusted R-squared	0.773	0.772	0.773	0.773	0.773	0.772	0.773	0.773
p-values F-stat	0.000	0.028	0.000	0.000	0.000	0.031	0.000	0.000

CF = conditional flow regimes, DL = data localization, DS = digital services sector, FE = fixed effects, ln = natural logarithm, LS = local storage requirements, PRC = People's Republic of China, SM = cross-border imports of services.

Notes: * p<0.10, ** p<0.05, *** p<0.01; p-values in parentheses.

Source: Author's calculations.

5.5   Conclusion

This chapter finds that Asian economies are more impacted than the rest of the world by the negative and significant association between data-related policy restrictions and global trade in digital services.

It comes to this conclusion through a difference-in-difference approach, in which Asian economies are singled out through the use of an interaction term and then assessed as a separate entity. As such, the significant results for the Asian region should be interpreted against the global benchmark. Our question is, does the Asian region show any differential impact when it comes to the data-related restrictions it implements on digital services trade? This was assessed for three specific data-related restrictions: data localization, local storage requirement, and strict conditional flow regime. Two definitions of digital and data-reliant services, one narrow in scope and one broad, were employed.

The differential effect in Asia regarding data-related restrictions are—at the very minimum using our baseline specification—particularly true for data localization and strict conditional flow regimes enacted in Asian economies. The results remain stable when using an alternative source of trade in services, when expanding the scope of digital services to digital-enabled services, and when assigning partial restrictions for a full score. The results of local storage requirement for the Asian region are less clear. At times, no significant coefficient results were found, and the results were not consistent for the Asian region across the different specifications and robustness checks. Moreover, as far as the variation in the data allows, the results are not mainly driven by one economy, even as the PRC has the highest number of restrictions.

The Asian region is a dynamic area where digital activity continues to accelerate. The PRC, as a particularly large market, has great potential for expansion of its digital services sectors, given that the success of many digital services depends on scale. Asia, therefore, retains a huge potential to catalyze the digital services trade as a driving force for economic growth, along with structural transformation under a fast-evolving digital economy. Rationalizing and lowering data flow restrictions, although having to be vetted against multiple policy objectives at the same time, will contribute to garnering greater trade performances in digital services, as this chapter demonstrates.

Bibliography

Arnold, J., B. Javorcik, and A. Mattoo. 2011. The Productivity Effects of Services Liberalization: Evidence from the Czech Republic. *Journal of International Economics*. 85 (1). pp. 136–146.

Arnold, J., B. Javorcik, M. Lipscomb, and A. Mattoo. 2015. Services Reform and Manufacturing Performance: Evidence from India. *The Economic Journal*. 126 (590). pp. 1–39.

Bauer, M., H. Lee-Makiyama, E. van der Marel, and B. Verschelde. 2016. A Methodology to Estimate the Costs of Data Regulation. *International Economics*. 146 (2). pp. 12–39.

Borchert, I., B. Gootiiz, J. Magdeleine, J. Marchetti, A. Mattoo, E. Rubio, and E. Shannon. 2019. Applied Services Trade Policy: A Guide to the Services Trade

Policy Database and Services Trade Restrictions Index. *WTO Staff Working Paper*. ERSD-2019-14. Geneva: World Trade Organization.

Bourlès, R., G. Cette, J. Lopez, J. Mairesse, and N. Nicoletti. 2013. Do Product Market Regulations in Upstream Sectors Curb Productivity Growth? Panel Data Evidence for OECD Countries. *The Review of Economics and Statistics*. 95 (5). pp. 1750–1768.

Chor, D. 2011. Unpacking Sources of Comparative Advantage: A Quantitative Approach. *Journal of International Economics*. 82 (2). pp. 152–167.

Cory, N., and L. Dascoli. 2021. *How Barriers to Cross-Border Data Flows Are Spreading Globally, What They Cost, and How to Address Them*. Information Technology & Innovation Foundation. https://itif.org/publications/2021/07/19/how-barriers-cross-border-data-flows-are-spreading-globally-what-they-cost/.

De Backer, K., and S. Miroudot. 2013. Mapping Global Value Chains. *OECD Trade Policy Papers*. No. 159. Paris: Organisation for Economic Co-operation and Development.

Ferracane, M. F. 2017. Restrictions on Cross-Border Data Flows: A Taxonomy. *ECIPE Working Paper*. No. 2017/1. Brussels: European Centre for International Political Economy.

Ferracane, M. F., and E. van der Marel. 2021. Do Data Flows Restrictions Inhibit Trade in Services? *Review of World Economics*. 57. pp. 727–776.

Ferracane, M. F., J. Kren, and E. van der Marel. 2018. Do Data Policy Restrictions Impact the Productivity Performance of Firms? *ECIPE Working Paper*. No. 2018/1. Brussels: European Centre for International Political Economy.

Ferracane, M. F., H. Lee-Makiyama, and E. van der Marel. 2018. *Digital Trade Restrictiveness Index*. Brussels: European Centre for International Political Economy.

Fortanier, F., A. Liberatore, A. Maurer, G. Pilgrim, and L. Thomson. 2017. The OECD-WTO Balanced Trade in Services Database. *OECD-WTO Working Paper*. November. Paris: Organisation for Economic Co-operation and Development.

Goldfarb, A., and D. Trefler. 2018. AI and International Trade. *NBER Working Paper Series*. No. 24254. Cambridge MA: National Bureau of Economic Research.

Heuser, C., and A. Mattoo. 2017. Services Trade and Global Value Chains. *World Bank Policy Research Working Paper*. No. 8126. Washington, DC: World Bank.

Manyika, J., S. Lund, J. Bughin, J. Woetzel, K. Stamenov, and D. Dhingra. 2016. *Digital Globalization: The New Era of Global Flows*. Washington, DC: McKinsey and Company.

Mattoo, A., and J. P. Meltzer. 2018. International Data Flows and Privacy: The Conflict and Its Resolution. *Policy Research Working Paper*. No. 8431. Washington, DC: World Bank.

Organisation for Economic Co-operation and Development (OECD) and World Trade Organization (WTO). 2017. Services Trade Policies and Their Contribution to Connectivity and Development. In *Aid for Trade at a Glance 2017: Promoting Trade, Inclusiveness and Connectivity for Sustainable Development.* Geneva and Paris: WTO and OECD Publishing.

OECD–WTO–International Monetary Fund (IMF). 2020. *Handbook on Measuring Digital Trade: Version 1.* https://www.oecd.org/sdd/its/Handbook-on-Measuring-Digital-Trade-Version-1.pdf.

Riker, D. 2015. The Impact of Restrictions on Mode 3 International Supply of Services. *Journal of International and Global Economic Studies.* 8 (1). pp. 1–20.

Romalis, J. 2004. Factor Proportions and the Structure of Commodity Trade. *American Economic Review.* 91 (1). pp. 67–97.

Shepherd, B., and E. van der Marel. 2013. Services Trade, Regulation, and Regional Integration: Evidence from Sectoral Data. *The World Economy.* 36 (11). pp. 1393–1405.

World Bank. 2020. *World Development Report 2020: Trading for Development in an Age of Global Value Chains.* Washington, DC.

World Trade Organization (WTO). 2019. *World Trade Report 2019: The Future of Services Trade.* Geneva.

Appendix A5.1: Import Growth of Economies Imposing Data Localization Policies

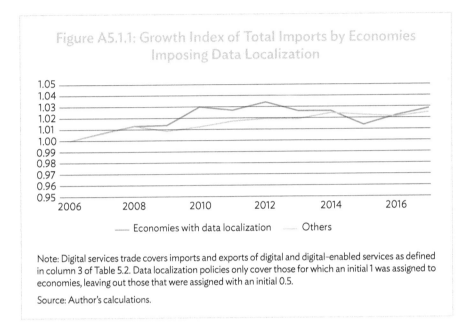

Figure A5.1.1: Growth Index of Total Imports by Economies Imposing Data Localization

—— Economies with data localization   —— Others

Note: Digital services trade covers imports and exports of digital and digital-enabled services as defined in column 3 of Table 5.2. Data localization policies only cover those for which an initial 1 was assigned to economies, leaving out those that were assigned with an initial 0.5.

Source: Author's calculations.

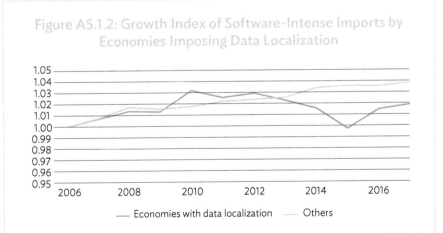

Figure A5.1.2: Growth Index of Software-Intense Imports by Economies Imposing Data Localization

—— Economies with data localization   —— Others

Note: Digital services trade covers imports and exports of digital and digital-enabled services as defined in column 3 of Table 5.2. Data localization policies only cover those for which an initial 1 was assigned to economies, leaving out those that were assigned with an initial 0.5.

Source: Author's calculations.

6 | DIGITAL SERVICES TRADE AND TRADE AGREEMENTS

Henry Gao

Trade agreements have become the main forum for the regulation of digital services trade issues over the past decade. This chapter provides a comprehensive examination of the regulation of digital services trade in trade agreements, first reviewing the rules in the World Trade Organization (WTO), then comparing the approaches between the United States (US), the People's Republic of China (PRC), and the European Union (EU), and explaining the reasons for their deep differences. This chapter further analyzes such provisions in trade agreements in Asia and the Pacific, which has become one of the most dynamic regions in terms of new regulations on digital trade issues, with a mix of digital services trade chapters in regional and bilateral free trade agreements. By drawing lessons from existing agreements, the chapter also illustrates how economies in the region may further develop digital services trade.

6.1 Regulation of Digital Services in the World Trade Organization[1]

Pending eventual negotiations of new disciplines in the WTO, the main obligations for the regulation of digital trade or e-commerce[2] under the WTO legal framework can be found in the General Agreement on Trade in Services (GATS) and in the GATS Reference Paper on Telecommunications (reference paper). The reference paper sets out the basic rights for access to and the use of public telecommunications networks and services by services suppliers, including e-commerce suppliers (WTO 1994). The general principle is that services

---

[1] This section is largely based on Gao (2017).

[2] E-commerce and digital trade are often used interchangeably. But, as noted at the outset of this chapter, the Organisation for Economic Co-operation and Development's definition of e-commerce (which covers only digitally ordered trade) differs from the WTO definition, which also covers digital delivery of services. Therefore, the term e-commerce is sometimes used in this chapter to refer only to e-commerce for goods. The chapter otherwise refers to e-commerce for services (e-services) or more often to digital services trade including data flows.

suppliers shall be able to access and use public telecommunications networks and services on reasonable and nondiscriminatory terms and conditions. This principle is elaborated to strike a delicate balance between users' rights (para. 5 lit. b and c) and regulators' rights (para. 5 lit. e-g).[3] Another key discipline to consider on regulating trade in digital services is the WTO Moratorium on Customs Duties on Electronic Transmissions (Box 6.1).

Box 6.1: The Evolution of Digital Services in the World Trade Organization

World Trade Organization (WTO) members adopted a Declaration on Global Electronic Commerce at the 2nd WTO Ministerial Conference (MC) in May 1998. The declaration focused on the establishment of a comprehensive work program on "all trade-related issues relating to global electronic commerce," and a WTO moratorium on customs duties on electronic transmissions (WTO 1998).

World Trade Organization Work Programme on Electronic Commerce

Under the WTO Work Programme on Electronic Commerce, adopted by the General Council in September 1998, "electronic commerce" covers "the production, distribution, marketing, sale or delivery of goods and services by electronic means" (WTO 1998). Its scope also includes "issues relating to the development of the infrastructure for electronic commerce." Responsibilities are divided among different WTO bodies required to report progress to the General Council on a regular basis.

- **The Council for Trade in Services** is responsible for examining the treatment of e-commerce in the General Agreement of Trade in Services (GATS) legal framework, including horizontal issues such as the scope and classification of sectors, access to and use of public telecommunications transport networks and services, and the application of core unconditional obligations (most favored nation, transparency) and discretionary negotiated commitments (market access, national treatment, domestic regulations).
- The **Council for Trade in Goods** is tasked with examining aspects of e-commerce relevant to the provisions of the General Agreement on Tariffs and Trade (GATT) 1994, the agreements covered under Annex 1A of the WTO Agreement, and the approved work program, which include tariff-related issues, and nontariff issues such as rules of origin, customs valuation, and import licensing and standards.
- The **Council for Trade-Related Aspects of Intellectual Property Rights** deals with intellectual property issues arising in connection with e-commerce (protection and enforcement of copyright and trademarks, access to technology).
- The **Committee on Trade and Development** reviews and reports on the development implications of e-commerce, taking into account the economic, financial, and development needs of developing countries.

continued on next page

---

[3] Gao (2008) presents a detailed discussion on this principle.

Box 6.1 *continued*

- The **General Council** is responsible for the review of any crosscutting trade-related issues and all aspects of the work program concerning the imposition of customs duties on electronic transmissions.

Moratorium on Customs Duties

The "practice of not imposing customs duties on electronic transmissions" has been extended repeatedly since 1998, with the latest extension in June 2022 at MC 12 that will remain in effect until the next WTO ministerial conference or until 31 March 2024 should MC 13 be postponed beyond that date.[a] This moratorium nevertheless left a few questions unanswered.

- Does the term "electronic transmissions" refer only to the medium of e-commerce, or to the content of the transmission as well, i.e., the underlying product or service being transmitted?
- If it refers to the medium of transmission only, could other digital products supplied via traditional mediums, such as books, music, or videos on CDs, be subject to customs duties?
- Does the prohibition apply only to customs duties, or does it extend to other fees or charges imposed on the digital products?
- Does the moratorium apply only to imports or also to exports?

Although contested, the moratorium is widely cited by the global services business community as having been fundamental in support of innovation and growth in digital services, and some WTO members have made commitments in regional trade agreements to ban customs duties on e-transmissions.

Notwithstanding the ambitious agenda in the work program, WTO members were unable to reach any decisions on new substantive disciplines on e-commerce (WTO 2013). This changed at the 11th Ministerial Conference in December 2017, when 71 members led by three co-conveners—Australia, Japan, and Singapore—made a joint statement to "initiate exploratory work together toward future WTO negotiations" on e-commerce. The plurilateral negotiations started formally in January 2019 and at the time of writing, 86 members are participating.

[a] WTO. MC12 Briefing Note: E-commerce. https://www.wto.org/english/thewto_e/minist_e/mc12_e/briefing_notes_e/bfecom_e.htm#.YwyWcHYykv8 (accessed 30 August 2022).

Source: Gao (2017).

Beyond the rules in the telecoms reference paper, the issues involved in the regulation of digital trade in the WTO fall largely into three areas: classifications, obligations, and exemptions.

This chapter presents a preview of three main approaches, each embodied by the regulatory experiences of the US, the EU, and the PRC, and each focusing on different aspects of digital services trade. With these models in mind, attention then shifts specifically to Asia and the Pacific, with a comprehensive mapping of 53 free trade agreements (FTAs) in the region that include chapters on digital trade issues. Lessons are drawn over gaps identified in these agreements, as well as on how economies in Asia and the Pacific may improve their digital trade chapters to better harness opportunities for digital services trade.

6.1.1   Classifications

Internet activities can be classified as goods or services (Wunsch-Vincent and Hold 2012). The distinction is not merely theoretical; it has profound practical implications. If internet activities are treated as goods, they could be subject first and foremost to customs duties, as well as most favored nation (MFN), national treatment, and an entire set of nontariff disciplines such as those on rules of origin, import licensing, customs valuation, and so on. On the other hand, if they are treated as services, the members would be unable to regulate them through border measures such as tariffs, but would have significant leeway in imposing domestic regulations. While some activities such as the online delivery of books and audiovisual products could arguably be classified as goods, according to the technology-neutrality principle,[4] most activities carried through the internet share more similarities with services trade. For example, many e-commerce activities such as online shopping and gaming are intangible and non-storable like services. Similarly, many e-commerce activities such as online search and e-mail involve joint inputs from suppliers and consumers, and so are tailored to the needs of specific consumers like other services.

Focusing on services, the GATS takes a different regulatory stance to the General Agreement on Tariffs and Trade (GATT), which applies a uniform set of rules to most products. According to the GATS "positive listing" approach, WTO members only assume obligations with respect to sectors they have included in their schedule of specific commitments.[5] Therefore, to determine whether a given e-commerce activity is covered, one has to determine which sector or subsector such activity falls under and then examine the respective schedules.

Services are classified under the GATS according to the Services Sectoral Classification List, which puts all services into 12 sectors and 160 subsectors (WTO 1991). While this system does a good job in classifying most other services sectors, it has not been so useful in classifying e-commerce activities. To start with, the classification list is outdated as it is based on the United Nations Provisional

---

[4]   As noted by the WTO Secretariat, "the GATS is technologically neutral in the sense that it does not contain any provisions that distinguish between the different technological means through which a service may be supplied" (WTO 1999).

[5]   WTO. General Agreement on Trade in Services. Article XVI: Market Access. https://www.wto.org/english/tratop_e/serv_e/gatsintr_e.htm.

Central Product Classification (CPCprov).[6] The CPCprov was published in 1990, when the internet was still in its infancy and many e-commerce activities, such as search engines, did not even exist. It does not provide direct reference to many e-commerce activities common today. Instead, they are often scattered across sectors. For example, search engine services can arguably be classified under either telecommunication services or computer and related services. Paradoxically, some classifications under the Services Sectoral Classification List also overlap with each other. For example, under the list, online info processing and data processing share the same code under CPCprov, but info processing is grouped under telecommunication services and data processing under computer services.

To better capture the reality of e-commerce activities, the classification system needs to be reviewed and revamped.[7] Different approaches should be taken, depending on the nature of the services. On the one hand, e-commerce activities supplied through traditional channels before the advent of the internet should be grouped under the original sector as per the technology-neutrality principle, unless online delivery has changed their nature.[8] Thus, online banking services should be classified under banking services, and online universities should be classified under educational services, and so on. On the other hand, the classification of services that only emerged with the birth of the internet is trickier. Given that the latest version of the Central Product Classification (CPC) includes many such services, it is tempting to simply replace the reference to the CPCprov codes in the Services Sectoral Classification List with the corresponding codes in the new version. However, this approach is undesirable. First, as the Services Sectoral Classification List is not mandatory, not every WTO member uses it or includes explicit reference to the CPC codes in its schedule.[9] Second, even where the CPC is used, the schedule cannot be simply updated with the new CPC versions. This is because the CPC often reshuffles the code numbers around when the versions are updated, thus the same code numbers under different versions

---

[6] United Nations. 1991. Provisional Central Product Classification. *Statistical Papers*. Series M. No. 77. New York. http://unstats.un.org/unsd/CR/Registry/regcst.asp?Cl=9&Lg=1.

[7] Tuthill and Roy (2012) provide an overview of the classification issues for e-commerce.

[8] Peng (2016) discusses the application of the technology-neutrality principle to e-commerce activities.

[9] Notably, the US does not use the CPC code in its classification, see WTO (1994). However, while the US schedule makes no explicit references to CPC numbers, it corresponds closely with the GATT Secretariat's list (USITC 1998). This issue was also debated in the US-Gambling case (WTO 2005).

might refer to entirely different services.[10] Third, as cases like US-Gambling have shown, WTO members have found it challenging to understand even their own commitments (WTO 2005). Thus, they will not accept a comprehensive update of the schedules without careful scrutiny.

Because of these difficulties, even an update of the schedules based on the latest CPC version probably cannot be achieved without major negotiation efforts. In addition, as many e-commerce activities are closely linked, it is probably better to take a cluster approach in the review and deal with them together.[11]

6.1.2   Obligations

A WTO member may choose among different levels of liberalization even for services covered in its schedule. It may do so by inscribing commitments ranging from "none" (which means "no limitation" or "fully liberalized") to "unbound" (which means "no commitment") in the market access and national treatment columns (WTO 2001). Thus, determining a member's specific obligations with respect to e-commerce activities requires examining the specific wording of that member's schedule.

Other than general rules such as the MFN principle, most substantive obligations under the GATS only apply when a member schedules relevant commitments. The member may choose the level of market access[12] and/or national treatment[13] it is willing to offer for each sector included in its schedule. Moreover, such scheduled commitments are also subject to sector- or mode-specific limitations. This regulatory framework creates several problems for e-commerce activities.

First is ambiguity in sectoral coverage. Even though a member may choose which sectors to include in its schedule, ambiguities could still arise due to imperfections in the classification system. A good example is the US-Gambling dispute. In this dispute, the US included in its schedule a subsector entitled

---

[10] A good example is the classification of data processing services (CPC 843) under CPCprov and CPC Ver.1, which is discussed in Gao (2012).

[11] The cluster approach was proposed by the US and the EU in 2000 (WTO 2000a, 2000b). This approach grew out of an initial proposal by the Dominican Republic, El Salvador, and Honduras for an annex on tourism in the GATS described in Raghavan (2000).

[12] GATS Article XVI.1 states, "With respect to market access through the modes of supply identified in Article I, each Member shall accord services and service suppliers of any other Member treatment no less favourable than that provided for under the terms, limitations and conditions agreed and specified in its Schedule."

[13] GATS Article XVII.1 states, "In the sectors inscribed in its Schedule, and subject to any conditions and qualifications set out therein, each Member shall accord to services and service suppliers of any other Member, in respect of all measures affecting the supply of services, treatment no less favourable than that it accords to its own like services and service suppliers."

"Other Recreational Services (except sporting)." While the US argued that "sporting" includes gambling services, the WTO Panel disagreed and ruled that sporting does not include gambling services and so should be included in the US commitments (WTO 2005). While this problem could arise in any services sector, e-commerce activities are particularly prone to interpretive ambiguities because of the classification difficulties mentioned earlier.

The second problem is confusion on modes of supply. Under the GATS, services could be supplied in four modes: (i) cross-border supply, (ii) consumption abroad, (iii) commercial presence, and (iv) movement of natural persons.[14] For e-commerce activities, it is quite difficult to tell if a service is supplied through mode 1 or 2 given that the service is provided in cyberspace (WTO 1998; Wunsch-Vincent and Hold 2012). Further complications could arise when the service supplier is located in another WTO member but maintains a server in the home economy of the consumer. In such cases, it could be argued that mode 3 should apply. As a member may have different levels of commitments depending on the mode of supply, confusion over the mode of supply could create illogical consequences.

To address these problems, it would benefit WTO members to agree on a set of scheduling guidelines for e-commerce activities. This would help clarify the meaning of schedules and avoid future complications. A set of principles on a minimum regulatory standard for e-commerce activities should also be formulated. The GATS Reference Paper on Telecommunications (WTO 1996) provides a good model given the close links between the two sectors.[15]

6.1.3   Exceptions

Legitimate policy reasons may lead WTO members to deviate from their trade obligations. Such deviations are permitted by both the GATT and the GATS through "General Exceptions" clauses.[16] However, as illustrated by the record of WTO disputes, the preferred exceptions under each agreement are rather different. The most commonly cited exceptions under the GATT, are the ones to

---

[14] GATS Article 1.2 states, "For the purposes of this Agreement, trade in services is defined as the supply of a service: (a) from the territory of one Member into the territory of any other Member; (b) in the territory of one Member to the service consumer of any other Member; (c) by a service supplier of one Member, through commercial presence in the territory of any other Member; and (d) by a service supplier of one Member, through presence of natural persons of a Member in the territory of any other Member."

[15] Kariyawasam (2012) gives an example on how the reference paper can be revised to apply to internet networks.

[16] GATT 1994 Article XX and GATS Article XIV.

protect public health and the environment.[17] Under the GATS, the most frequently invoked clause has been the public morals exception in Article XIV(a).[18]

Interestingly, in two cases concerning internet services, i.e., *US–Gambling* and *China–Publications and Audiovisual Products,* respondents cited the public morals exception to defend their measures. In their rulings, the panels and the Appellate Body give national authorities wide discretion in defining both the boundaries and depth of the exception, but this could lead to bizarre results (WTO 2005, 2010). For example, in *China–Publications and Audiovisual Products,* the Appellate Body encouraged the PRC government to conduct censorship itself as, from the perspective of WTO law, this could supposedly be less trade-restrictive than outsourcing censorship to private firms.[19]

A good way to prevent the potential abuse of the exception is to adopt some universal benchmark on what may qualify as public morals, so that fundamental human rights, such as those enshrined in the Universal Declaration of Human Rights,[20] will not be harmed under the guise of protection of public morals. As the core competence of the WTO is in trade, it is ill-equipped for this task. Instead, members should consider adopting a mechanism similar to the one that exists under the Sanitary and Phytosanitary (SPS) Agreement—that is, having the standards formulated by another international organization[21] with competence

---

[17] GATT 1994 Article XX(b) and (g). Article XX(b) was invoked in disputes such as the *European Communities—Measures Affecting Asbestos and Asbestos-Containing Products* (DS135); *Brazil—Measures Affecting Imports of Retreaded Tyres* (DS332); *European Communities—Measures Prohibiting the Importation and Marketing of Seal Products* (DS400, DS401); *United States—Measures Affecting the Production and Sale of Clove Cigarettes* (DS406); and *Indonesia—Importation of Horticultural Products, Animals and Animal Products* (DS477, DS478). Article XX(g) was invoked in disputes such as *United States—Standards for Reformulated and Conventional Gasoline* (DS2); *China—Measures Related to the Exportation of Various Raw Materials* (DS394, DS395, DS398); and *Measures Related to the Exportation of Rare Earths, Tungsten and Molybdenum* (DS431, DS432, DS433).

[18] GATS Article XIV(a) has been invoked in disputes such as *US–Gambling* (WTO 2005) and *China–Publications and Audiovisual Products* (WTO 2010).

[19] In this case, the US proposed that, instead of having the importing firms conduct the content review of imported publications, the PRC government shall be given sole responsibility for conducting content review. Both the Panel and the Appellate Body agreed that these are reasonably available alternatives (WTO 2010). Delimatsis (2012) includes a discussion on the Panel and Appellate Body decisions on *China—Publications and Audiovisual Products.*

[20] United Nations. Universal Declaration of Human Rights (1948). https://www.ohchr.org/en/resources/educators/human-rights-education-training/universal-declaration-of-human-rights-1948.

[21] The WTO Agreement on the Application of Sanitary and Phytosanitary Measures (SPS Agreement), Annex A, para. 3, refers explicitly to the SPS standards, guidelines, and recommendations made by various international organizations such as the Codex Alimentarius Commission, the International Office of Epizootics, and the Secretariat of the International Plant Protection Convention.

on public morals issue, and making it mandatory for the WTO to consult them when disputes arise.[22]

Due to its unique nature, e-commerce activities pose special challenges to the GATS regulatory framework on all three issues. While the GATS, in its current form, is not well suited to the regulation of e-commerce, it can keep up with the regulatory task. However, to make this happen, new approaches are needed for dealing with e-commerce activities, especially on key issues such as classifications, obligations, and exceptions.

In this regard, the WTO can learn from the approaches taken in the various FTAs, which are discussed in the next section.

6.2   Regulation of Digital Services Trade: Three Models[23]

Any framework for digital trade regulation would involve three groups of players: the individual, who provides the raw data and uses the processed data; the firm, which processes raw inputs from the consumer, and usually controls such data; and the state, which monitors and regulates the data used by the first two groups. Their different interests often result in conflicting priorities, with the individual advocating privacy protection, the firm promoting unhindered data flow, and the state focusing on the security implications.

While all regulators would agree on the need to strike a balance between the clashing interests of different stakeholders, their approaches often differ in practice. Some jurisdictions prioritize the need to safeguard the privacy of users. A good example in this regard is the General Data Protection Regulation (GDPR) of the EU, which recognizes "[t]he protection of natural persons in relation to the processing of personal data" as "a fundamental right."[24] On the other hand, some jurisdictions put the commercial interests of firms first. In the US, this is reflected in the 1996 Telecommunication Act, which notes that it is "the policy of the United

---

[22] SPS Agreement Article 11.2 gives the right to dispute settlement panels to consult the relevant international organizations on scientific or technical issues; whereas, SPS Agreement Article 12.3 requires the SPS Committee to "maintain close contact with the relevant international organizations in the field of sanitary and phytosanitary protection ... with the objective of securing the best available scientific and technical advice for the administration of this Agreement."

[23] This section is largely based on Gao (2021).

[24] Regulation (EU) 2016/679 of the European Parliament and of the Council of 27 April 2016 on the protection of natural persons with regard to the processing of personal data and on the free movement of such data, and repealing Directive 95/46/EC (General Data Protection Regulation), OJ L 119, 04.05.2016; cor. OJ L 127, 23.5.2018, Recital 1.

States … to preserve … free market … unfettered by Federal or State regulation."[25] In contrast, national security concerns are often cited to justify restrictions on cross-border data flows, though to varying degrees in different economies. A recent example is the PRC's 2017 Cybersecurity Law, which imposed several restrictions aiming to "safeguard cybersecurity, protect cyberspace sovereignty, and national security."[26] These divergent approaches are also reflected in the trade agreements concluded by the three main players.

6.2.1 United States

As the world's largest economy and, until recently, the largest trader, the US is a highly competitive exporter in both agricultural and industrial goods and services. It has been promoting free trade and dismantling barriers in its trade agreements. This approach is also carried over into the digital age, with US trade agreements pioneering the inclusion of digital trade issues with an expansive set of obligations.

In particular, two provisions have become essential parts of the digital trade chapters in US trade agreements, with the recently concluded US–Mexico–Canada Agreement (USMCA) as the most prominent example: the first provision is the guarantee on free cross-border flow of data by stating that "no Party shall prohibit or restrict the cross-border transfer of information, including personal information, by electronic means" (Article 19.11); and the second is the prohibition of data localization requirements by stipulating that "no Party shall require a covered person to use or locate computing facilities in that Party's territory as a condition for conducting business in that territory" (Article 19.12).[27]

Both provisions provide strong protection of the interests of the firm, deeming restrictions on cross-border flow of data and various localization requirements as obstacles to conducting business across national boundaries.

As will be seen from the experiences of the PRC and the EU, two of the most frequent reasons used by governments to regulate data are protection of privacy or national security. In both of these areas, however, the US has taken somewhat different approaches in its trade agreements.

On privacy protection, US trade agreements only require parties to adopt their own legal framework for data protection, which could take many different legal

---

[25] Telecommunication Act of 1996, 47 U.S.C. 230(b)(2). https://www.law.cornell.edu/uscode/text/47/230 (accessed 20 February 2020).

[26] Cybersecurity Law of the People's Republic of China [*Zhonghua Renmin Gongheguo Wangluo Anquan Fa*], as adopted at the 24th Session of the Standing Committee of the Twelfth National People's Congress of the People's Republic of China on 7 November 2016, Art. 1.

[27] Office of the United States Trade Representative. Agreement between the United States of America, the United Mexican States, and Canada 7/1/20 Text. https://ustr.gov/trade-agreements/free-trade-agreements/united-states-mexico-canada-agreement/agreement-between.

approaches, including "comprehensive privacy, personal information or personal data protection laws, sector-specific laws covering privacy, or laws that provide for the enforcement of voluntary undertakings by enterprises relating to privacy" (USMCA footnote 4). This is very different from the EU approach, where trade partners are required to adopt GDPR-equivalent clauses. While the US agreements also call for parties to "take into account principles and guidelines of relevant international bodies" (USMCA Article 19.8.2), the examples only include the Asia-Pacific Economic Cooperation (APEC) Privacy Framework and the Organisation for Economic Co-operation and Development Recommendation of the Council concerning Guidelines Governing the Protection of Privacy and Transborder Flows of Personal Data (2013), which are regarded as providing minimum levels of data protection or "first generation" data privacy standards (Greenleaf 2018).

The US trade agreements seem to be relatively more concerned with making sure that the commercial interests of firms are not hurt by over-restrictive privacy regimes. Take for example the clause on personal information protection under the USMCA, which covers six paragraphs. One of these contains substantive obligations to adopt or maintain legal framework on personal information protection (Article 19.8.2), while three are aimed at minimizing the regulatory burden for businesses. The first among the three calls the parties to ensure that "any restrictions on cross-border flows of personal information are necessary and proportionate to the risks presented" (Article 19.8.3), which are apparently modeled after the necessity test and proportionality principle under the WTO. The second requires parties to "endeavor to adopt nondiscriminatory practices in protecting users of digital trade from personal information protection violations occurring within its jurisdiction," which also draws from the nondiscrimination principle of the WTO, especially the national treatment obligation. Last, while the agreement recognizes the varying legal approaches parties might take on personal information protection, it also encourages them to develop "mechanisms to promote compatibility between these different regimes." Again, trade lawyers would recognize in these provisions vestiges of rules on mutual recognition, harmonization, and equivalence under various WTO agreements.

On security, the US trade agreements focus on "threats to cybersecurity [that] undermine confidence in digital trade"—i.e., "malicious intrusions or dissemination of malicious code that affect electronic networks" (USMCA Article 19.15). Put differently, the US approach mainly focuses on cybersecurity risks facing the private sector, which is quite different from the PRC approach that focuses on perceived threats to national security. At the same time, the US approach also tries to minimize disruptions to the operations of firms, by calling parties to adopt "risk-based approaches that rely on consensus-based standards and risk management best practices to identify and protect against cybersecurity risks" (USMCA Article

19.15). The risk-based approach is carried over from the regulatory framework under the WTO, especially under the agreements on technical barriers to trade and sanitary and phytosanitary measures. By placing restrictions on the regulatory measures that governments might adopt, such an approach provides better protection for firms' businesses. Similarly, the reference to "consensus-based standards" also reflects practices in the US that were codified in the Cybersecurity Enhancement Act of 2014.[28] The act calls for the National Institute for Standards and Technology under the Commerce Department to "facilitate and support the development of a voluntary, consensus-based, industry-led set of standards, guidelines, best practices, methodologies, procedures, and processes to cost effectively reduce cyber risks to critical infrastructure."[29] Under the act, US cybersecurity standards are developed as a partnership between the government and the private sector, which serves to reduce the cybersecurity risks for the firms.

Many other provisions in the USMCA are also designed to help develop digital trade. This is done by either removing regulatory barriers, such as the provision on nondiscriminatory treatment of digital products, or providing an enabling framework for digital trade such as through provisions on the domestic electronic transaction legal framework, recognition of the legal validity of electronic signatures or electronic authentication methods, the acceptance of electronic documents as the legal equivalent of their paper versions, and open government data. The most interesting provision, though, is the provision on principles on access to and use of the internet for digital trade (USMCA Article 19.10). This clause is mainly designed to deal with the risks that market players who own or control key infrastructures could abuse their power by unreasonably denying their business users access to their infrastructures, making it impossible for these users to conduct e-commerce activities. To deal with this problem, the agreements provide consumers (including business users) with the freedom of access to the internet and to use it for e-commerce, subject only to network management and network safety restrictions. This provision apparently grew out of the net neutrality principle from the domestic telecom regulatory framework in the US. In a way, it supports digital companies' businesses in the economies in which they operate, so that they would not be held hostage by the network-throttling practices often found in some of the economies.

6.2.2   People's Republic of China

For the PRC, the key to data regulation is data security. Such a regulatory approach, dubbed "data regulation with Chinese characteristics" in Gao (2019),

---

[28] Text—S.1353—113th Congress (2013–2014): Cybersecurity Enhancement Act of 2014. 2013. https://www.congress.gov/bill/113th-congress/senate-bill/1353/text (accessed 15 June 2021).

[29] Sec. 101. Public–Private Collaboration on Cybersecurity.

is the result of an evolution spanning 25 years. The evolving approach closely traces the development of the internet sector in the PRC. In the early days of the internet, regulations focused on computer and internet hardware, requiring all connections to go through official gateways sanctioned by the government. As the internet gradually expanded with the proliferation of software and apps catered to popular uses, the government moved on to regulate the software and started to require software used for internet access to be sanctioned by the government. As cyberspace became an indispensable part of everyday life and began to permeate every sector from socializing, shopping, to entertainment and education, the government shifted focus to the regulation of content and now data, especially with the rise of big data and artificial intelligence. Moreover, data regulation has now been elevated to the level of national security with the introduction of the Cybersecurity Law in 2016. The agency responsible for content regulation, the Cyberspace Administration of China, mainly focuses on making sure that the cyberspace is secure.

At the international level, the PRC has traditionally taken a cautious approach to provisions on digital trade in trade agreements. Until recently, it did not even include e-commerce chapters in its regional trade agreements (RTAs). This changed only with its FTAs with the Republic of Korea and Australia, both signed in 2015. Nonetheless, the provisions in these two FTAs remain rather modest, as they mainly address issues related to trade facilitation, such as moratoriums on customs duties on electronic transmission, recognition of electronic authentication and electronic signature, protection of personal information in e-commerce, paperless trading, domestic legal frameworks governing electronic transactions, and the need to provide consumers using electronic commerce with protection on the same level as traditional forms of commerce.

A major breakthrough was made in the Regional Comprehensive Economic Partnership (RCEP) Agreement, which the PRC signed with other 14 economies in the region in November 2020. Under the chapter on e-commerce, the PRC and all other RCEP members agreed to not "require a covered person to use or locate computing facilities in that Party's territory as a condition for conducting business in that Party's territory" (Article 12.14), or "prevent cross-border transfer of information by electronic means where such activity is for the conduct of the business of a covered person" (Article 12.15).[30]

Agreeing to the twin provisions on data flow and data localization under the RCEP is a notable evolution in the PRC's approach. In practice, it is important to keep in mind that both provisions are overshadowed by national security concerns allowing members to adopt "any measure that it considers necessary

---

[30] Association of Southeast Asian Nations (ASEAN) Secretariat. Legal Text of the RCEP Agreement. https://rcepsec.org/legal-text/.

for the protection of its essential security interests." Such security measures "shall not be disputed by other Parties," and will not be subject to legal challenge.[31]

Another exception to these two obligations is "any measure ... that [the implementing Party] considers necessary to achieve a legitimate public policy objective." The necessity test is not the one found in the general exceptions clause under GATT Art. XX, but is the one under the security exceptions clause under GATT Art. XXI—i.e., what the party taking such measure "considers necessary." This approach is further confirmed by the footnotes to the two provisions on data flow and data localization, which "affirm that the necessity behind the implementation of such legitimate public policy shall be decided by the implementing Party."

What then, could such "legitimate public policy objective" entail? Like most other economies, this could include laws for the protection of privacy or personal information. Yet, the PRC approach to privacy protection also comes with its own limitations. To start, privacy protection is a rather new concept in the PRC law. Privacy was first recognized as a civil right under the Tort Liability Law in 2009. This was duly incorporated into PRC's Civil Code enacted in 2020, which has a separate chapter on privacy and personal information protection as part of the volume on personality rights.[32] According to Art. 1035 of the Civil Code, the processing of personal information shall be based on the consent of the data subject, "except if there are different requirements under laws or administrative regulations," which envisages the cases where laws do not require the consent of the data subject.

In addition, government agencies in charge of cybersecurity monitoring and management and their staff are required to keep confidential any personal or privacy information they obtain in the discharge of their duty. The PRC's new Personal Information Protection Law also confirms that data processors do not need to obtain the consent of the data subject when discharging official duty and responsibility (Article 13.3) (Box 6.2).

At the same time, it should also be noted that many of these features are not unique to the PRC and are found in other privacy laws, such as the GDPR.[33]

---

[31] RCEP chapter on e-commerce is carved out from the normal dispute settlement procedure.

[32] Chapter 6, Volume 4 of The State Council of the PRC. See Civil Code of the People's Republic of China. http://english.www.gov.cn/archive/lawsregulations/202012/31/content_WS5fedad98c6d0f72576943005.html.

[33] For example, Article 6 of the GDPR.

Box 6.2: The New Personal Information Protection Law of the People's Republic of China

The People's Republic of China (PRC) Personal Information Protection Law (PIPL) was adopted at the 13th National People's Congress on 20 August 2021 and took effect that November. The PIPL provides significant enhancement to the PRC's privacy protection regime. For example, besides the existing principles of lawfulness, fairness, and necessity, the new law adds a principle of good faith for the processing of personal information (Article 5). This is not just an abstract principle, but is reflected in the addition of new rules such as the prohibition of artificial intelligence powering differentiation pricing, a practice long complained by consumers (Article 24). The law also explicitly spells out specific consumer rights, such as the right to refuse to consent or to withdraw consent already given (Article 15), along with a corresponding provision banning data processors from refusing to provide products or services unless such consent is essential for such products or services (Article 16). The biggest impact of the law is on the big platform companies, which are subject to additional obligations such as the establishment of independent bodies composed of mainly outsiders to monitor their protection of personal information (Article 58). This is, in some ways, similar to the regulation of the "gatekeepers" under the European Union's proposed Digital Markets Act.[a] In addition, the provision on data portability could also constrain big platform companies' capacity to keep the consumers' data as their own and reduce their competitive advantage (Article 45). The new law echoes the PRC's commitments in the Regional Comprehensive Economic Partnership by explicitly allowing cross-border data transfer, as per commitments under international agreements (Article 38). This could open the door for further international collaboration such as the participation in the Asia-Pacific Economic Cooperation (APEC) cross-border privacy rules system.[b]

[a] Article 2, Proposal for a Regulation of the European Parliament and of the Council on Contestable and Fair Markets in the Digital Sector (Digital Markets Act). https://eur-lex.europa.eu/legal-content/EN/TXT/PDF/?uri=CELEX:52020PC0842&from=en.

[b] APEC. What Is the Cross-Border Privacy Rules System? https://www.apec.org/About-Us/About-APEC/Fact-Sheets/What-is-the-Cross-Border-Privacy-Rules-System.

Source: Author.

While it is common to have personal information protection laws as exceptions to the twin provisions on data flow and data localization, the exceptions under the PRC data regulation regime cover not only personal data and "important data," a highly important concept that is poorly defined (Gao 2021). In addition, the newly enacted Data Security Law adds another concept of "national core data." This is defined as "data-related to national security, the lifeline of the national economy, people's livelihood and major public interests" and will be subject to "a more stringent management system." It is likely that the scope of the new category of "national core data" will be narrower than "important data," but it is unclear how much narrower it will be.

6.2.3   European Union

The EU has, as its main concern, the privacy of the individual. This started with the Data Protection Directive in 1995, which prohibits the transfer of personal data to non-EU economies, unless they have privacy protection standards deemed adequate (Gao 2021). The directive was replaced by the GDPR in 2018 (Aaronson and Leblond 2018).

Despite having a name that suggests a broader reach, the GDPR applies only to personal data, which is defined as "any information relating to an identified or identifiable natural person ('data subject')" (Article 4.1). It regulates the behavior of the data controller and processor, which are respectively defined as the one who "determines the purposes and means of the processing of personal data" and "processes personal data on behalf of the controller" (Articles 4.7 and 4.8). Under the GDPR, the processing of personal data is only allowed with the "explicit" consent of the data subject and a few other specifically enumerated reasons (Articles 49.1.a and 6.1), under a set of principles that specifies the scope and manner of such processing (Mattoo and Meltzer 2018). Transfer of personal data to third economies is allowed only on the basis of an adequacy decision or appropriate safeguards (Articles 45 and 46).

Since its introduction, the GDPR has become the gold standard of privacy protection. Encouraged by its success, senior EU officials started to advocate for "technological sovereignty" (Burwell and Propp 2020; European Commission 2019b; Scott 2019). This concept is closely linked with "digital sovereignty," which was elaborated in the European Commission's "Communication on a European Strategy for Data" unveiled in February 2020 (European Commission 2020). Many commentators have pointed out that the new data strategy is designed to "counter the strong position of US and Chinese digital companies in the European market" (Burwell and Propp 2020) and remedy "the key European disadvantage" of "the lack of significant European digital corporations with global influence" (Hobbs 2020). The new data strategy aims to create "a single European data space" so that "by 2030, the EU share of the data economy—data stored, processed and put to valuable use in Europe—at least corresponds to its economic weight, not by *fiat* but by choice" (European Commission 2020).

This quest for digital sovereignty started out as a defensive move to fend off the encroachment into EU cyberspace by big firms from the outside. By combining the powers of its huge market and regulatory apparatus, the EU is trying to reclaim digital sovereignty, not only from other economies, but more importantly, from the digital giants.

The data strategy can be seen as part of a broader EU plan to establish "strategic autonomy." The concept started as an idea from a 1994 white paper on defense published by France (Government of France 1994). Gradually, however, it was accepted by the big three member states: Germany, France, and Italy (Franke and Varma 2019). The concept was adopted by the European Union in 2016 when it unveiled its Global Strategy, which was supposed to "nurture[s] the ambition of strategic autonomy" (European Commission 2016). With the election of Donald Trump as US president and amid Brexit (the United Kingdom leaving the European Union), the concept started to take off among EU member states (Franke and Varma 2019). While there was some ambiguity on the exact content of the concept, the bigger member states typically perceived it as referring to decision-making autonomy (Franke and Varma 2019). This was recently validated in the February 2021 trade strategy paper, which refined it as a concept of "open strategic autonomy" emphasizing "the EU's ability to make its own choices and shape the world around it through leadership and engagement, reflecting its strategic interests and values," with a priority area being the digital agenda (European Economic and Social Committee 2021).

On data flow, the EU takes a bifurcated approach. Nonpersonal data are supposed to flow freely under its Framework for the Free Flow of Non-Personal Data,[34] while cross-border flows of personal data are subject to stringent requirements under the GDPR, despite its explicit recognition that "[f]lows of personal data to and from countries outside the Union and international organizations are necessary for the expansion of international trade and international cooperation."[35] Due to high compliance costs (as noted by Irwin 2021), however, the GDPR has proven to be "challenging especially for the small and medium-sized enterprises."[36] Schechner and Drozdiak (2018) report that to stay away from potential legal challenges, many US websites blocked access by EU customers before the GDPR went into effect, and these remained unavailable in the EU months after (South 2018).

In addition to its negative impact on cross-border data flow, the GDPR also creates pressure toward data localization, especially after the decision of the Court of Justice of the European Union in Data Protection Commissioner v. Facebook Ireland, Maximillian Schrems (Schrems II).[37] However, as Chander (2020) eloquently argues, data localization not only will not "solve the policy objectives identified in Schrems II, it will create "its own policy problems." The data localization requirements for nonpersonal data were banned by the Framework for

---

[34] Framework for the Free Flow of Non-Personal Data in the European Union of the European Parliament and of the Council of 14 November 2018, Regulation 2018/1807.

[35] GDPR, Recital 101.

[36] Communication from the Commission to the European Parliament and the Council. Data protection as a pillar of citizens' empowerment and the EU's approach to the digital transition—two years of application of the General Data Protection Regulation. SWD(2020) 115 final. Brussels. 24 June 2020.

[37] Case C-311/18, ECLI:EU:C:2020:559 (16 July 2020).

the Free Flow of Non-Personal Data, which mandated EU member states to repeal their data localization laws by 30 May 2021. In contrast, however, the GDPR does not include such a prohibition. On the contrary, data localization requirements for personal data are quite common among EU countries (Burwell and Propp 2020), with most covering special categories of sensitive data like health-related personal data or financial services data (Cory 2017). On the latter point, it is worth noting that the EU approach again diverges from the current US approach. When the US negotiated the Comprehensive and Progressive Agreement for Trans-Pacific Partnership (CPTPP), it carved out the entire financial services sector from the scope of its e-commerce chapter, including prohibition of data localization requirements.[38] However, the new USMCA explicitly brought the financial services sector under the ban by stating that data localization should not be required "so long as the Party's financial regulatory authorities, for regulatory and supervisory purposes, have immediate, direct, complete, and ongoing access to information processed or stored on computing facilities that the covered person uses or locates outside the Party's territory."[39] It will be interesting to see whether the EU approach shifts closer to the US approach in the future.

In its RTAs, the EU has not been able to include substantive language on data issues until recently. This was due to the internal differences between the two director-generals (DGs) with overlapping jurisdictions on the issue, i.e., DG for Trade, which favors free trade for the sector, and DG for Justice, which has concerns over personal information protection (Aaronson 2019). Thus, notwithstanding its strong interest in privacy protection, the EU position in existing FTAs has been rather modest, which usually requires parties to adopt their own laws for personal data protection to help maintain consumer trust and confidence in electronic commerce.[40] In February 2018, however, the two DGs were finally able to reach a compromise, which included, on the one hand, horizontal clauses on free flow of all data and ban on localization requirements, while on the other, affirming the EU's right to regulate by making clear that it shall not be subject to investor–state arbitration.[41] Despite this development, the EU still seems to prefer handling data flow issues through bilateral "adequacy" recognitions, which so far have been granted to only a dozen countries.[42] In many of its latest FTAs,

---

[38] Comprehensive and Progressive Agreement for Trans-Pacific Partnership (CPTPP), Art. 14.1.

[39] USMCA, Art. 17.18.2.

[40] USMCA, Art. 17.18.2.

[41] USMCA, Art. 17.18.2, at 262.

[42] So far, the EU has granted adequacy recognitions to Andorra, Argentina, Canada (commercial organizations), Faroe Islands, Guernsey, Isle of Man, Israel, Japan, Jersey, New Zealand, Switzerland, and Uruguay. See European Commission. Adequacy Decisions. https://ec.europa.eu/info/law/law-topic/data-protection/international-dimension-data-protection/adequacy-decisions_en.

data flow issues were left out in the main text, with a separate adequacy decision adopted. An example is its Economic Partnership Agreement (EPA) with Japan (European Commission 2019a). In that case, the adequacy decision was adopted separately from the EPA, which does not include commitments on free flow of data.[43] The recent FTA with Viet Nam lacks not only provisions on data flow and localization, but also any plan for an adequacy decision.

6.2.4   Why the Differences?

The diverging approaches among the three major players are not randomly chosen. Instead, they reflect deeper differences in their respective commercial interests and regulatory approaches within each jurisdiction.

First, the global e-commerce market is largely dominated by the PRC and the US. Among the 10 biggest digital trade firms in the world, six are American and four are Chinese.[44] Of course, this does not necessarily mean that they must share the same position. Upon closer examination, one can see that US firms on the list tend to be pure digital services firms. Firms like Facebook, Google, and Netflix do not sell physical products, but only provide digitalized services such as online search, social network, or content services. In contrast, two of the top three Chinese firms—Alibaba and JD.com—sell mainly physical goods. This is why the US focuses on the "digital" side, while the PRC focuses on the traditional "trade" side when it comes to digital trade, as the author has argued in another paper (Gao 2018).

It can be said that the PRC also has giant pure digital firms like Baidu and Tencent, which are often referred to as the Google and the Facebook of the PRC. However, because they serve the domestic market almost exclusively and most of their facilities and operations are based in the PRC, they do not share the demands for free cross-border data flow as their US counterparts, which have data centers in strategic locations around the world.

As for the EU, with no major players in the game, some view their restrictive privacy rules as a form of "digital protectionism" to fend off the invasion of American and Chinese firms (Aaronson 2019).

The second influence is their different domestic regulatory approaches. In the US, the development of the sector has long benefited from its "permissive legal framework" (Chander 2013), which aims to reduce government regulation

---

[43] According to Art. 8.81 of the EPA, "The Parties shall reassess within three years of the date of entry into force of this Agreement the need for inclusion of provisions on the free flow of data into this Agreement."

[44] Wikipedia. List of Largest Internet Companies. https://en.wikipedia.org/wiki/List_of_largest_internet_companies (accessed 20 February 2020).

of the internet to a minimum and relies heavily on self-regulation in the sector. Such policy is even codified in the law, with the Telecommunication Act of 1996 explicitly stating that it is "the policy of the United States ... to preserve the vibrant and competitive free market that presently exists for the internet and other interactive computer services, unfettered by Federal or State regulation."[45] Therefore, it is no surprise that the US wishes to push for deregulation and the free flow of information at the international level, a long-standing policy that can be traced back to the Framework for Global Electronic Commerce announced by the Clinton administration in 1997 (Aaronson and Leblond 2018). At the same time, the US does not have a comprehensive privacy protection framework. Instead, it relies on a patchwork of sector-specific laws, which provides privacy protection for consumers of a variety of sectors such as credit reports and video rental (Chander 2013). This is complemented by case-by-case enforcement actions by the Federal Trade Commission, and self-regulation by firms themselves. This explains why, in its RTAs, the US does not mandate uniform rules on personal information protection but allows members to adopt their own domestic laws.

On the other hand, in the PRC, the internet has been subject to substantial government regulations, which not only dictate the hardware one must use to connect to international networks, but also the content that may be transmitted online (Gao 2019). Many foreign websites are either filtered or blocked in the PRC, which confirms its cautious position on free flow of data. Moreover, in 2017, the PRC also adopted the Cybersecurity Law, which requires operators of critical information infrastructure to store locally personal information they collected or generated in the PRC. Privacy protection is also weak in the PRC, as it was only incorporated into its legal system in 2009, along with exemptions for the government.

The EU, in contrast, has a long tradition of human rights protection, partly in response to the atrocities of World War II (Mattoo and Meltzer 2018). Coupled with the absence of major digital players wielding significant market power and the lack of a strong central government with overriding security concerns, this translates into a strong emphasis on privacy in the digital sphere. Moreover, the EU is also able to transcend the narrow mercantilist confines of the US (Schwartz and Peifer 2017), and recognize privacy not only as a consumer right, but also as a fundamental human right that is recognized in several fundamental EU instruments[46] and the constitutions of many member states.[47] Such a refreshing

---

[45] Telecommunication Act of 1996, 47 U.S.C. 230(b)(2). https://www.law.cornell.edu/uscode/text/47/230 (accessed 20 April 2018).

[46] For example, Art. 8 of the 8 Charter of Fundamental Rights of the European Union, 2000 O.J C 364/10; Convention for the Protection of Human Rights and Fundamental Freedoms, 4 November 1950, 312 U.N.T.S. 222, Art. 8.

[47] These include Germany, Greece, Hungary, Poland, and Spain (Matto and Meltzer 2018).

perspective is probably the biggest contribution that the EU has made to digital trade issues.

6.3   Trade Agreements in Developing Asia

The three models discussed in this chapter are not limited to the three jurisdictions. Instead, as illustrated by Ferracane and van der Marel (2021) in their recent comprehensive survey, these three models cover most of the economies around the world, including Asia and the Pacific.

To assess the state of play in Asia and the Pacific, this chapter maps the main agreements in the region. More specifically, the mapping covers all FTAs by the main players in the region with chapters on e-commerce or digital trade since 2000. The mapping also covers the mega-FTAs in Asia and the Pacific, i.e., the RCEP, CPTPP, USMCA, and the EU–Canada Comprehensive Economic and Trade Agreement, as well as the two stand-alone digital trade agreements: the Digital Economy Partnership Agreement and digital economy agreements. Using the CPTPP and USMCA as a benchmark, the mapping groups digital trade provisions in these trade agreements into four categories.

The components of the first category are the six provisions designed to create a facilitating environment for digital trade in general, such as the provisions on the elimination of customs duties on electronic transmission, nondiscriminatory treatment of digital product, domestic electronic transactions framework, electronic authentication and electronic signatures, and paperless trading provisions. These provisions provide the necessary regulatory and technological environment to enable the smooth functioning of digital trade, which also forms the bedrock for conducting digital services trade.

The second category consists of five provisions to minimize the commercial and regulatory burden for digital services trade providers, such as those on access to and use of the internet for electronic commerce, free flow of data, prohibition of data localization requirements, prohibition on forced transfer of source code, and open government data. These provisions focus on the most common regulatory and commercial obstacles facing digital services trade firms. By removing these obstacles, digital services will be able to flow more freely across economies, creating massive economies of scale with the data they amass across different markets.

The third category includes three provisions to protect the interests of consumers, such as those on online consumer protection, privacy and personal information protection, and unsolicited commercial electronic messages. By addressing the main concerns of consumers, these provisions enhance the trust of consumers in digital services trade and so indirectly boost the rate of take-up of digital services among consumers.

The last category includes four provisions to preserve the regulatory autonomy of the government, such as those on cybersecurity, exceptions, and cooperation. These provisions help governments to reserve the space necessary to deal with various social policy objectives even though they might ostensibly be inconsistent with various obligations under the digital trade chapter.

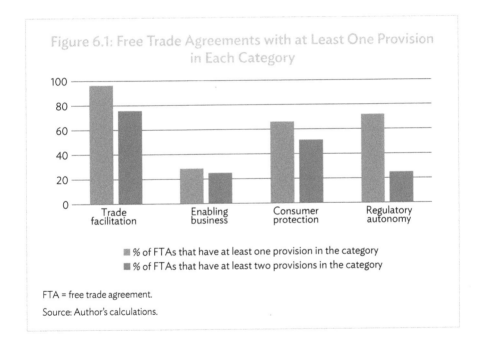

Figure 6.1: Free Trade Agreements with at Least One Provision in Each Category

% of FTAs that have at least one provision in the category
% of FTAs that have at least two provisions in the category

FTA = free trade agreement.
Source: Author's calculations.

Among the four types of provisions, the first is the most popular, with more than three-quarters of the surveyed FTAs including at least two provisions in this category (Figure 6.1). There are several possible reasons for this. The first is that many of these obligations are not entirely new, but repeats obligations in other international agreements, such as the UNCITRAL Model Law on Electronic Commerce (1996), the United Nations Convention on the Use of Electronic Communications in International Contracts, and the WTO Trade Facilitation Agreement. Moreover, as these provisions lay down the infrastructure necessary to facilitate digital trade and do not prescribe a specific regulatory approach on sensitive issues, they face the least resistance from the bureaucracy and governments generally welcome them. At the same time, even as these provisions can help developing economies foster trade in digital services, there could be problems in implementation. The first is that implementation of some provisions might require additional investment in hardware and software, which can be a challenge for some developing economies. Second, merely having the facilities might not be sufficient. Instead, the statutory requirements on documentary formalities might also need to be modified to account for the new ways of contracting and approval. As many developing economies lack the experience and expertise in this regard, they might need technical assistance from the relevant international agencies.

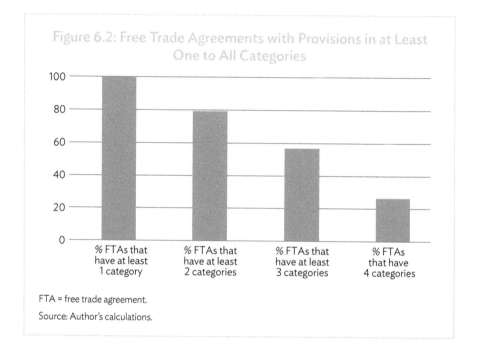

Figure 6.2: Free Trade Agreements with Provisions in at Least One to All Categories

FTA = free trade agreement.
Source: Author's calculations.

The second type of provision does facilitate digital services trade by taking down regulatory barriers that blocks or impedes trade flow. The problem, however, is that the primary beneficiaries of such measures tend to be overseas firms, which supply their services through the cross-border supply mode. This could raise a host of economic and social issues, such as crowding out domestic services suppliers and therefore taking away both sales and jobs, reduction of government revenues as the overseas services suppliers are unlikely to pay value-added taxes or income tax, suppressing the development of the local e-commerce suppliers, and raising the hurdles for regulatory enforcement actions as the online suppliers are much more difficult to regulate. Because of these issues, many developing economies are reluctant to agree to these provisions, which are included in only a quarter of surveyed FTAs (Figure 6.1). Again, here the issue is not just purely economic, the lack of regulatory capacity is also a major issue that regulators in many economies have to grapple with. On the other hand, without these policies, the digital giants would hesitate to enter the local market due to cybersecurity concerns (when data cannot flow freely) and additional costs (for building local servers). Thus, many developing economies also understand the need to agree to these provisions, at least as a welcoming signal to foreign digital firms. Two things need to be done to assuage the concerns of these developing economies. The first is to raise awareness on the basics of digital trade, especially those of data transfer, so that it is understood that even localization requirements might not entirely prevent many of the potential problems associated with the free flow of data. The second would be to help developing economies learn from the regulatory practices in other economies. One such example could be the practices that can operate at sufficient regulatory capacity even with the offshore storage of data, provided they have "immediate, direct, complete, and ongoing access to" such data (USMCA Art. 17.18).

The third type of provision does not directly contribute to the development of digital services trade. But by fostering a trustworthy environment for the consumers, they may also make indirect contributions to digital trade by easing the concerns of the consumers against digital trade. The problem, however, is that developing economies often lack domestic laws and regulations on many of the issues in this category to start with. This makes it harder for them to formulate relevant laws and regulations, and sometimes such regulations are implemented in a way that affects digital suppliers more than traditional suppliers, which could raise national treatment issues as traditional suppliers are typically domestic suppliers. This is also reflected in Figure 6.1, with only half of the surveyed FTAs including at least two provisions from this category. Again, technical assistance would greatly help developing economies as they enter this new regulatory field.

The fourth type of provision, by design, boosts the power of the government vis-a-vis the digital firms and so does not appear to be facilitative in nature. These provisions provide the government the maneuvering space necessary to keep digital services under tighter regulatory supervision, which is crucial for many developing economies, with the bulk of digital services trade being provided by foreign suppliers. This also explains the popularity of these provisions, with more than 70% of the surveyed FTAs including at least one provision in this category (Figure 6.1), and even more if general exceptions clauses in the other chapters are included. Overall, 26% of the surveyed FTAs include provisions in each of the four categories (Figure 6.2).

To foster the development of the sector, developing Asia will need to beef up the provisions in the second and third categories. Given the complexity of digital services trade, it would be unrealistic to assume that the mere inclusion of these provisions would boost trade levels. Instead, this needs to be coupled with other efforts, such as building up the necessary infrastructure for digital trade, and putting in place the appropriate regulatory environment to strike the right balance between risk control and market liberalization. Given that many of these economies do not have sufficient experience, it is probably a good idea to start with market liberalization at the regional level. This could be facilitated by mutual recognition agreements on services, which so far has been restricted to the rich economies. Economies with similar regulatory frameworks can develop such recognition arrangements at the bilateral and regional levels first, before expanding them to a wider level.

Bibliography

Aaronson, S. A. 2019. What Are We Talking about When We Talk about Digital Protectionism? *World Trade Review*. 18. pp. 541–577.

Aaronson, S. A., and P. Leblond. 2018. Another Digital Divide: The Rise of Data Realms and Its Implications for the WTO. *Journal of International Economic Law*. 21 (2). pp. 245–72. https://doi.org/10.1093/jiel/jgy019.

Burwell, F., and K. Propp. 2020. The European Union and the Search for Digital Sovereignty: Building 'Fortress Europe' or Preparing for a New World? *Research Reports*. June. Washington, DC: Atlantic Council.

Chaisse, J., H. Gao, and C. Lo, eds. 2017. *Paradigm Shift in International Economic Law Rule-Making: TPP as a New Model for Trade Agreements*. Singapore: Springer.

Chander, A. 2013. *The Electronic Silk Road: How the Web Binds the World Together in Commerce*. New Haven, CT: Yale University Press.

———. 2020. Is Data Localization a Solution for Schrems II? *Journal of International Economic Law*. 23 (3). pp. 771–784.

Cory, N. 2017. Cross-Border Data Flows: Where Are the Barriers, and What Do They Cost? May. Information Technology & Innovation Foundation. http://www2.itif.org/2017-cross-border-data-flows.pdf.

Delimatsis, P. 2012. The Puzzling Interaction of Trade and Public Morals in the Digital Era. In M. Burri and T. Cottier, eds. *Trade Governance in the Digital Age: World Trade Forum*. Cambridge: Cambridge University Press.

European Commission. 2016. *Shared Vision, Common Action: A Stronger Europe. A Global Strategy for the European Union's Foreign and Security Policy*. Brussels.

———. 2019a. European Commission Adopts Adequacy Decision on Japan, Creating the World's Largest Area of Safe Data Flows. *Press Corner.* 23 January. https://ec.europa.eu/commission/presscorner/detail/en/IP_19_421.

———. 2019b. Questions to the Commissioner-Designate Thierry Breton. https://ec.europa.eu/commission/commissioners/sites/comm-cwt2019/files/commissioner_ep_hearings/answers-ep-questionnaire-breton.pdf.

———. 2020. Communication from the Commission to the European Parliament, the Council, the European Economic and Social Committee and the Committee of the Regions. 19 February. https://ec.europa.eu/info/sites/info/files/communication-european-strategy-data-19feb2020_en.pdf.

European Economic and Social Committee. 2021. *Trade Policy Review—An Open, Sustainable and Assertive Trade Policy.* https://trade.ec.europa.eu/doclib/html/159438.htm.

Ferracane, M. F., and E. van der Marel. 2021. Regulating Personal Data: Data Models and Digital Services Trade. *Policy Research Working Paper.* 9596. Washington, DC: World Bank.

Franke, U., and T. Varma. 2019. Independence Play: Europe's Pursuit of Strategic Autonomy. *European Council on Foreign Relations.* 18 July. https://ecfr.eu/special/independence_play_europes_pursuit_of_strategic_autonomy/.

Gao, H. 2008. Commentary on Telecommunication Services. In R. Wolfrum and P.-T. Stoll, eds. *Max Planck Commentaries on World Trade Law.* Volume VI: WTO—Trade in Services. Leiden: Brill Publishers.

———. 2012. Googling for the Trade-Human Rights Nexus in China: Can the WTO Help? In M. Burri and T. Cottier, eds. *Trade Governance in the Digital Age: World Trade Forum.* Cambridge: Cambridge University Press.

———. 2017. The Regulation of Digital Trade in the TPP: New Trade Rules for the Digital Age. In J. Chaisse, H. Gao, and C. Lo, eds. *Paradigm Shift in International Economic Law Rule-Making: TPP as a New Model for Trade Agreements.* Singapore: Springer.

———. 2018. Digital or Trade? The Contrasting Approaches of China and US to Digital Trade. *Journal of International Economic Law.* 21 (2). June. pp. 297–321.

———. 2019. Data Regulation with Chinese Characteristics. *SMU Centre for AI & Data Governance Research Paper.* No. 2019/04. Singapore: Singapore Management University.

———. 2021. Data Regulation with Chinese Characteristics. In M. Burri, ed. *Big Data and Global Trade Law.* Cambridge: Cambridge University Press.

Government of France. 1994. Livre Blanc sur la Défense 1994 (1994 White Paper on Defense). http://www.livreblancdefenseetsecurite.gouv.fr/pdf/le-livre-blanc-sur-la-defense-1994.pdf.

Greenleaf, G. 2018. *The UN Should Adopt Data Protection Convention 108 as a Global Treaty: Submission on 'the Right to Privacy in the Digital Age' to the UN*

High Commission for Human Rights, to the Human Rights Council, and to the Special Rapporteur on the Right to Privacy. 8 April. https://www.ohchr.org/Documents/Issues/DigitalAge/ReportPrivacyinDigitalAge/GrahamGreenleafAMProfessorLawUNSWAustralia.pdf.

Hobbs, C. 2020. Europe's Digital Sovereignty: From Rulemaker to Superpower in the Age of US-China Rivalry. 30 July. European Council on Foreign Relations. https://ecfr.eu/publication/europe_digital_sovereignty_rulemaker_superpower_age_us_china_rivalry/.

Irwin, L. 2021. How Much Does GDPR Compliance Cost in 2021? IT Governance European Blog. June. https://www.itgovernance.eu/blog/en/how-much-does-gdpr-compliance-cost-in-2020.

Kariyawasam, R. 2012. Better Regulation of Digital Markets: A New Look at the Reference Paper. In M. Burri and T. Cottier, eds. *Trade Governance in the Digital Age: World Trade Forum.* Cambridge: Cambridge University Press.

Mattoo, A., and J. P. Meltzer. 2018. International Data Flows and Privacy: The Conflict and Its Resolution. *Journal of International Economic Law.* 21 (4). pp. 769–789.

Peng, S. Y. 2016. GATS and the Over-the-Top Services: A Legal Outlook. *Journal of World Trade.* 50 (1). pp. 21–46.

Raghavan, C. 2000. To Cluster or Not to Cluster (in GATS). *South-North Development Monitor.* 19 July. Pulau Pinang, Malaysia: Third World Network .

Schechner, S., and N. Drozdiak. 2018. U.S. Websites Go Dark in Europe as GDPR Data Rules Kick In. *Wall Street Journal.* 25 May 2018. https://www.wsj.com/articles/u-s-websites-go-dark-in-europe-as-gdpr-data-rules-kick-in-1527242038.

Schwartz, P. M., and K. N. Peifer. 2017. Transatlantic Data Privacy Law. *The Georgetown Law Journal.* 106 (115). pp. 117–179.

Scott, M. 2019. What's Driving Europe's New Aggressive Stance on Tech? *Politico.* 28 October. https://www.politico.com/news/2019/10/28/europe-technology-silicon-valley-059988.

South, J. 2018. More than 1,000 U.S. News Sites Are Still Unavailable in Europe, Two Months after GDPR Took Effect. *NiemanLab.* 7 August. https://www.niemanlab.org/2018/08/more-than-1000-u-s-news-sites-are-still-unavailable-in-europe-two-months-after-gdpr-took-effect/.

Tuthill, L., and M. Roy. 2012. GATS Classification Issues for Information and Communication Technology Services. In M. Burri and T. Cottier, eds. *Trade Governance in the Digital Age: World Trade Forum.* Cambridge: Cambridge University Press.

United States International Trade Commission (USITC). 1998. *US Schedule of Commitments under the General Agreement on Trade in Services (with explanatory materials prepared by the USITC, includes supplemental commitments and MFN exemptions on basic telecommunication services, finalized on 15 February 1997, and on financial services, finalized 13 December 1997)*. Investigation No. 332–354. August.

World Trade Organization (WTO). 1991. *Services Sectoral Classification List*. MTN. GNS/W/120. 10 July. Geneva.

———. 1994. *United States of America, Schedule of Specific Commitments*. GATS/SC/90. 15 April. Geneva.

———. 1996. *Negotiating Group on Basic Telecommunications, Telecommunications Services: Reference Paper*. 24 April. Geneva.

———. 1998. *Work Programme on Electronic Commerce (Adopted by the General Council on 25 September 1998)*. WT/L/274. 30 September. Geneva.

———. 1999. *Work Program on Electronic Commerce: Progress Report to the General Council (Adopted by the Council for Trade in Services on 19 July 1999)*. S/L/74. 27 July. Geneva.

———. 2000a. *Council for Trade in Services Special Session: Communication from the European Communities and Their Member States—The Cluster Approach*. S/CSS/W/3. 22 May. Geneva.

———. 2000b. *Council for Trade in Services Special Session: Communication from the United States—Framework for Negotiation*. S/CSS/W/4. 13 July. Geneva.

———. 2001. *Guidelines for the Scheduling of Specific Commitments under the GATS, Adopted by the Council for Trade in Services on 23 March 2001*. S/L/92. 28 March.

———. 2005. *United States—Measures Affecting the Cross-Border Supply of Gambling and Betting Services* (Report of the Appellate Body). WT/DS285/R. 7 April.

———. 2010. *China—Measures Affecting Trading Rights and Distribution Services for Certain Publications and Audiovisual Entertainment Products (Report of the Appellate Body)*. WT/DS363/AB/R. 19 January. Geneva.

———. 2013. *Work Programme on Electronic Commerce, Dedicated Discussion on Electronic Commerce Under the Auspices of the General Council: Report to the 21 November 2013 Meeting of the General Council*. WT/GC/W/676. 11 November. Geneva.

———. General Agreement on Trade in Services. https://www.wto.org/english/tratop_e/serv_e/gatsintr_e.htm.

———. MC12 Briefing Note: E-commerce. https://www.wto.org/english/thewto_e/minist_e/mc12_e/briefing_notes_e/bfecom_e.htm#.YwyWcHYykv8 (accessed 30 August 2022).

Wunsch-Vincent, S., and A. Hold. 2012. Towards Coherent Rules for Digital Trade: Building on Efforts in Multilateral versus Preferential Trade Negotiations. In M. Burri and T. Cottier, eds. *Trade Governance in the Digital Age: World Trade Forum*. Cambridge: Cambridge University Press.

DIGITAL TRADE AGREEMENTS AND SERVICES TRADE: THE CASE OF THE REPUBLIC OF KOREA

CHAPTER

7

Minjung Kim

7.1 Introduction

E-commerce is gaining a deep foothold as an issue in regional trade agreements, making progress despite some sluggishness in the World Trade Organization (WTO) program as e-commerce provisions are gradually introduced and rules and principles solidified to govern digital trade. A few landmark plurilateral agreements have recently made significant contributions to the development of the regional digital trade framework in Asia and the Pacific. The Comprehensive and Progressive Trans-Pacific Partnership (CPTPP) Agreement and the Digital Economy Partnership Agreement (DEPA) are among the most noteworthy. In scope and detail on digital trade, both are steps ahead of other foreign trade agreements (FTAs).

Over the years, the Republic of Korea (ROK) has pursued regional trade agreements (RTAs) to increase trade and investment. As of June 2022, it has concluded 23 agreements, including the Korea–Singapore Digital Partnership Agreement (DPA) signed in December 2021, and 18 had entered into force to liberalize bilateral trade with more than 50 partners all over the world. Most deal with a broad range of issues, covering even new trade issues like environmental protection, labor standards, and digital trade. As the digital economy evolves and the spectrum of e-commerce expands, the ROK has therefore forged a rules-based bilateral system to maintain better e-commerce relations with its trading partners.

The Regional Comprehensive Economic Partnership (RCEP), which entered into force in February 2022, was the ROK's 18th RTA and its first plurilateral agreement.[1] RCEP's provisions bring the ROK the broadest binding rules on e-commerce to date. The framework covers the most diverse set of issues than any other trade agreement the ROK has joined. That said, having taken the

---

[1] The RCEP agreement was concluded in October 2019 and signed on 15 November 2020. Its 15 members comprise the 10 Association of Southeast Asian Nations (ASEAN) economies, along with Australia, the People's Republic of China (PRC), Japan, the Republic of Korea (ROK), and New Zealand.

initiative to engage in global efforts to form a new digital trade order, the ROK is likely to confront and should be dealing with even more diverse and complicated issues in the coming years.

The ROK's DPA with Singapore is expected to enter into force soon. It will be the first DPA devoted exclusively to regulating digital trade issues. This pact aims to prevent and dismantle digital trade barriers and promote cooperation over high-technology and emerging regulatory issues. Above all, it is expected to renew the ROK's digital trade relations with Singapore. The ROK can continue to amend its FTAs one by one in a similar way as it did with Singapore—and, in fact, has done so in deciding to join the CPTPP and the DEPA. As the ROK pitches in digital trade negotiations with global trade partners, its bilateral digital trade relations will significantly improve and uncover new opportunities.

Nevertheless, tremendous challenges lie ahead for the ROK as it adopts agreements with an increasing number of partners. For example, in joining the CPTPP and the DEPA, the ROK will be placed under increased pressure to keep its domestic system consistent with the new agreements. Also, because domestic laws, regulations, and systems continue to reform in order to tackle socioeconomic issues arising from digital transformation, it may not be an easy task to ensure consistency all the time. As the ROK integrates deeper with other digital economies, as yet unknown monumental challenges may indeed emerge.

Building on the case of the ROK, this chapter explores major digital trade rules and developments in bilateral e-commerce negotiations. Section 7.2 explores recent advances in global digital trade rules and discusses fundamental regulatory issues, including an issue on the blurred boundary. Section 7.3 focuses on the ROK's FTAs and explains evolvement of digital trade rules and challenges for future negotiations. Section 7.4 concludes.

7.2 Recent Advances in Digital Trade Rules

7.2.1 Regional Trends: From Free Trade Agreements to Digital Economy Agreements

Rules on electronic commerce in RTAs have progressively extended and so helped form a basic framework for digital trade. According to a WTO study, e-commerce chapters appear in more than 180 RTAs. Provisions that feature most frequently concern customs duties on electronic transmission, personal information, consumer protection, paperless trading, e-authentication, and e-signature. The RTA provisions largely stipulate similar rules and procedures from agreement to agreement and over time have forged what can be considered principles and norms to regulate each digital trade issue.

The CPTPP and the United States (US)–Mexico–Canada Agreement (USMCA) notably extended the regulatory scope by adding a wide range of new issues. Both introduced detailed rules regarding cross-border data flow and privacy protection, consumer protections, and anticompetitive activities, which conventionally had not been included in e-commerce negotiations. While the USMCA "digital trade" chapter is significantly similar to the CPTPP "e-commerce" chapter, for many provisions, it carries stronger binding force.

Over the last few years, economies across Asia and the Pacific have negotiated new forms of digital trade agreements. The most representative examples are the DEPA between Singapore, New Zealand, and Chile (in force from January 2021), and the Singapore and Australia DEA (December 2020). As the terms "digital economy" in the titles of the agreements indicate, both cover extended issues, ranging from promoting e-business and paperless trading, to ensuring cross-border data flow and data protection, to fostering governance and cooperation in the areas of artificial intelligence, digital identity, and financial technology (fintech).

In particular, both agreements validate fundamental principles for digital trade that are already included in other FTAs. Dozens of provisions concern digital products and data. Most importantly, they prohibit the levy of customs duties on electronic data transmission, prevent domestic digital trade measures from being discriminatory or unnecessary, and prohibit location-based requirements to computing facilities.

Above all, they encourage wider cooperation across multiple levels of forum. The forms of cooperation typically suggested in the articles involve information exchange, sharing of best practices, and standards-setting. Bilateral or international regulatory cooperation and technical cooperation are also encouraged. Transparency is certainly among key obligations applied to reduce trade costs and barriers; notifications and dialogues are basic procedural requirements.

The content and main features of the frameworks in the DEPA and DEAs are summarized in Table 7.1. Although the DEPA and DEA provisions are not directly relevant to services, they may have some overreaching impact on services sectors and trade in digital services. The legal scope of the two agreements clearly excludes services trade, but the reality of digital transformation and digital economy is complicating the classification issue. This is discussed in section 7.2.2.

From a trade law perspective and long-term retrospective view, digital trade rulemaking has grown more comprehensive and intensified. Recurring provisions from agreement to agreement possibly reflect central issues in digital trade negotiations, and their changing details may generally indicate how regulations might evolve, even as the outcome of negotiations depends on numerous factors. Moreover, it became increasingly evident from the adoption of the DEPA and the

Table 7.1: Major Provisions for Digital Trade

Primary Objective	Subject Matter	Related Digital Trade Provisions	
Data free flow and protection	Digital products, information, or data	• Customs duties on digital products • Nondiscriminatory treatment of digital products • Personal information protection • Cross-border transfer of information by electronic means • Location of computing facilities	• Location of computing facilities for financial services • Source code • ICT products that use cryptography (technical barrier to trade)
Business facilitation and promotion	E-businesses, e-transactions, logistics	• Paperless trading • Domestic electronic transaction framework • Electronic invoicing • Electronic payment • Electronic authentication and electronic signature	• Logistics • Express shipments (trade facilitation)
Connectivity and interoperability	Infrastructure, cable connection	• Internet interconnection charge sharing • Submarine telecommunications cable system (telecommunication services)	• Standards and conformity assessment for digital trade (technical barrier to trade)
Confident and safe environment	Consumers' rights, spams, cybersecurity	• Cybersecurity cooperation • Online safety and security (competition) • Unsolicited commercial electronic messages	• Online consumer protection • Principles on access to and use of the internet
Cooperation	Emerging technology, governance issues	• Digital identities • Financial technology cooperation • Artificial intelligence	• Public domain • Data innovation • Open government data
	Inclusion development	• Small and medium-sized enterprises	• Digital inclusion

FTA = free trade agreement, ICT = information and communication technology.

Note: This table shows major provisions and is not comprehensive.

Source: Author's analysis based on official FTA text.

Singapore–Australia DEA, and affirmed by the Korea-Singapore DPA (not yet in force) and the United Kingdom–Singapore DEA (in force from 14 June 2022), that the regulatory development has moved toward establishing a self-contained system. This point is elaborated in section 7.2.3.

Last, a fundamental systemic problem is the blurred boundary of digital trade negotiations. This is a controversial issue in legal terms and is explained in section 7.2.4.

7.2.2   Digital Trade Negotiations and Digital Services

Digitalization and World Trade Organization Law

Digital transformation has changed how international trade is conducted in many ways. Numerous studies show the substantial growth in digitally enabled trade in goods and services over the past decades (González and Ferencz 2018). While trade in advanced information and communication technology (ICT) products supports the cross-border movement of information and data, services based on data flows, in turn, help coordinate efficiently value chains and international trade (González and Jouanjean 2017; Miroudot and Cadestin 2017). Digital connectivity also makes logistics, telecommunications, and international business administration faster and more efficient, and helps significantly enlarge global production and trade networks (Choi 2010; González and Ferencz 2018).

Several WTO agreements are pertinent to digital trade. The plurilateral Information Technology Agreement has freed information technology (IT) products trade. The General Agreement on Trade in Services (GATS) is the basis for openness in services trade and is closely related with electronic transmissions. Under it, WTO members have made specific commitments, through which each has chosen services sectors and modes of supply to allow freer trade. Due to the flexibility of the GATS, committed sector openness varies markedly from one member to another. For example, the European Union (EU) has put little limitations on market access for computer services but far-reaching limitations on trade in audiovisual services.[2] In contrast, the US committed to very few barriers in both sectors.

In reality, digitally enabled services are prominent in telecommunications services, computer services, audiovisuals, and financial services.[3] To regulate trade in digitally enabled services, should the GATS specific commitments be applied

---

[2] Burri (2020a) explains that the EU's specific commitments for computer services include consultancy services related to the installation of computer hardware, software implementation services, data processing services, database services, maintenance and repair, and other related services.

[3] Burri (2020b) analyzes that a number of data-related provisions in preferential trade agreements deal with data flows in financial services and telecommunication services.

even if negotiations had been based on a framework created in the pre-internet era? One approach to this question is the principle of technology neutrality—i.e., the GATS schedules should remain neutral to technological progress and innovation. Although the principle has garnered a lot of support, the classification issue gets more complicated as the Fourth Industrial Revolution matures, and it is generally considered that operation of the GATS does not sufficiently cover and address trade issues on digital services.

Digital Services in Digital Trade Negotiations

RTA negotiations on digital trade commonly exclude matters relating to services trade. Many FTA e-commerce chapters clearly mention that measures affecting services delivered or performed electronically are regulated by their relevant chapters on investment, cross-border supply of services, and financial services. Thus, e-commerce or digital trade provisions should not be interpreted as changing existing GATS and RTA commitments and exceptions.

Nevertheless, e-commerce or digital trade provisions in RTAs can indirectly and actually affect businesses in all sectors. In reality, the flow of data and information is essential for business administration in digital economy, and a large portion of RTAs' crosscutting provisions dealing with data flow and protection—customs moratorium, nondiscrimination, localization of commercial data, domestic privacy rules, as examples—are relevant to digital businesses such as electronic platforms, clouding services, and internet-based telecommunication services.

These rules generally go beyond WTO law. Rules that address data flow and privacy are new to the general trade law framework. Much of the literature notes that data flow is different from trade flow in many aspects, especially on how it connects global businesses and forms global value chains (Aaronson and Leblond 2018; Burri 2020b; Casalini and González 2019; Sen 2018).

In addition, most recently adopted digital economy (partnership) agreements include additional categories that were not typically included in e-commerce provisions of FTAs. Most aim at facilitating digitization of business and ensuring a confident and safe environment. These rules are fundamentally related to digital capacity and competitiveness, which create a need for cooperation and assistance.

The new trends are summarized in Table 7.1. To elaborate, scores of the provisions in the DEPA and DEAs can be classified into five broad categories according to their primary objectives: data free flow and protection, business facilitation, connectivity and interoperability, trust and safety, and cooperation. Each category and its major provisions are further explained in section 7.2.3.

7.2.3   Major Digital Trade Rules in Negotiation

Flow of Information and Data

The first category of the RTA provisions, as shown in Table 7.1, aims to regulate cross-border flows of information. An early form of data-related obligations is found in the Korea–US FTA's provision entitled "Cross-Border Information Flow."[4] It requires the parties to eliminate unnecessary hindrance to the cross-border flow of electronic information. Along with this, the provision implies two principles: first, it recognizes that the free flow of information across borders facilitates trade and, second, it considers protection of personal information important to ensuring the free flow of information. In short, the provision suggests that commercial information needs to flow freely because it facilitates digital trade while personal information needs to be protected to ensure trust and security in the business environment.

Over time, an increasing number of RTAs have included similar but more elaborated provisions.[5] Articles on cross-border transfers of information generally require that "information, including personal information" be permitted to move between economies so long as they are pertinent to business activities. At the same time, they recognize a government's discretion to regulate electronic transfers under legitimate public policy. In practice, it is difficult to clearly distinguish commercially purposed transfer of information from certain categories of information controlled or protected by the government for public safety and security. For example, it can be very hard to allow people's health or financial information to be transferred internationally even if its purpose is to conduct business.

Those RTAs eventually came to introduce separate provisions on personal information.[6] They generally obligate a government to adopt or maintain a national framework that protects e-commerce users' personal information. For the sake of e-business, protection of personal information is generally viewed as essential to strengthen consumer confidence in e-commerce. To avoid unnecessary trade barriers, the articles also require national systems to be nondiscriminatory and compatible with other systems.

International communities, including the Organisation for Economic Co-operation and Development (OECD) and the Asia-Pacific Economic Cooperation (APEC), have long sought to ensure personal information protection

---

[4] Korea–US FTA 15.8.

[5] For example, major RTA provisions addressing cross-border transfer of information include CPTPP 14.11, USMCA 19.11, US-Japan Digital Trade Agreement (USJDTA) 11, DEPA 4.3, and Australia–Singapore Digital Economy Agreement (ASDEA) 23.

[6] For example, major RTA provisions addressing protection of personal information include CPTPP 14.8, USMCA 19.8, USJDTA 15, DEPA 4.2, and ASDEA 17.

worldwide. Some RTAs, for example, the USMCA and the Singapore and Australia DEA, specifically link their provisions with the works of those international organizations, while other RTAs like the CPTPP and the DEPA generally require relevant international standards to be considered.

Facilitation and Promotion of E-business

The second category of RTA e-commerce provisions concerns the agenda dealing with e-businesses facilitation, like e-authentication, e-signature, e-payment, e-invoicing, and digital identity, and is closely related to improving efficiency in business administration and transactions. This agenda will increase general benefits from new technology and the digitization of commercial activities.

The relevant provisions encourage parties to confirm the validity of e-authentication, e-signature, e-invoicing, and e-payments used in business transactions. They aim to ensure that technologies and domestic systems supporting electronic transactions remain interoperable and compatible with other economies.

In those RTAs, the United Nations Commission on International Trade Law (UNCITRAL) Model Law is a recommended specific standard for e-commerce business, while paperless customs procedures, express shipments, and more efficient logistics are largely promoted.

The agenda of e-payment, logistics, and express shipment is clearly about services. In case of e-payment, for example, the GATS would mainly deal with issues of market access and national treatment in the finance sector, while digital trade rules largely talk about making bilateral or even international trade interoperable, efficient, safe, and conducted through secure e-payment systems.

Reliable and Secure Digital Economy

The third agenda deals with online consumer protection, cybersecurity, and principles on internet access and use. Relevant provisions tackle problems of anticompetition, market failures, and consumer protection. Their implementation will largely lead to an assurance that the online systems are reliable and secure and induce more participants to online markets and digital business activities.

To elaborate, most RTAs have provisions to protect consumers and consumer rights. Online consumer protection, along with personal information protection, are considered key to build a reliable and trusted digital economy.[7] Domestic systems to shield consumers from undesirable advertisements and spam messages need to be adopted and properly maintained.

---

[7] CPTPP 14.7, USMCA 19.7, USJDTA 14, DEPA 6.3, and ASDEA 15; CPTPP 14.4, USMCA 19.3, USJDTA 16, DEPA 6.2, and ASDEA 19.

Some RTAs apply principles on access to the internet and its use.[8] Those principles try to give consumers the right to choose services and applications available online, to choose end-use devices to connect to the network unless they are harmful, and to access information on the network management practices of internet service providers.

Another category of e-commerce provisions is devoted to the safety and security of the infrastructure. One of the most important issues in that regard is cybersecurity, and provisions demanding cybersecurity cooperation are being specified.[9] Several articles in the DEPA, for example, emphasize the importance of computer security incident responses, the mitigation of malicious intrusions and disseminations, and workforce development in cybersecurity. Still, many RTAs just mention cybersecurity as one of many areas for cooperation.[10]

New Issues and Cooperation

Last, digital economy (partnership) agreements have introduced various new issues and digital technologies on which parties are expected to cooperate. They include digital identities, artificial intelligence governance, data innovation, public domain, fintech, inclusion of small and medium-sized companies, and digital inclusion.

In addition, to ensure connectivity and interoperability of the digital economy, these agreements encourage parties to cooperate on maintaining a safe and stable submarine telecommunication cable system and on developing digital and technology standards in regional and international forums.

7.2.4   An Issue of Regulatory Scope: E-Commerce and Digital Products

In the digital economy, goods and services are increasingly convergent and varieties of products delivered both in electronic form and on a physical carrier are growing.[11] As González and Ferencz (2018) explain, digitalization is "pervasive" throughout goods and services sectors, and digital connectivity not only has increased trade in "more complex manufacturers and digitally deliverable services" but has also improved the bundling of goods and services in international trade. The author

---

[8] CPTPP 14.10, USMCA 19.10, DEPA 6.4, and ASDEA 20.

[9] CPTPP 14.16, USJDTA 19, DEPA 5.1, and ASDEA 34.

[10] The ROK's FTAs belong to this category. Korea–Colombia FTA 12.6, Korea–Central America FTA 14.7, and RCEP 12.13.

[11] New forms of transactions in digital economy are well illustrated in González and Jouanjean (2017).

notes that digital trade in goods is increasingly supported by services like logistics and a rise of "new complementarities between goods and services."

As a result, the boundary of what is e-commerce by the WTO definition is increasingly blurred. The WTO, at the outset of its e-commerce work programs, defined e-commerce as "production, distribution, marketing, sale or delivery of goods and services by electronic means" (WTO 1998). Although the meaning itself is not a legal definition, it is generally accepted in negotiations. Over time, e-commerce talks are apt to deepen the goods and services dichotomy, and crosscutting issues like data flow or privacy go beyond accepted definitions.

In fact, transactions that can involve both trade in goods and trade in services are difficult to classify.[12] For instance, are e-books goods or services? Are movie streaming services audiovisual services? If they are not services, are they part of e-commerce?

These questions are critical because the answers determine applicable trade rules and commitments undertaken in the multilateral and regional trade agreements. In other words, if electronically transmitted products are determined to be services, or in more accurate terms, cross-border delivery of services, their transactions must abide by the GATS commitments on sector-specific market access and national treatment commitments and horizontal obligations. If they are classified as goods, then most-favored-nation tariffs and dozens of the other WTO agreements are relevant.

In RTA negotiations, some e-commerce chapters have introduced the term "digital products,"[13] which is commonly defined as "computer programs, text, video, images, sound recordings, and other products that are digitally encoded and produced for commercial sale or distribution, regardless of whether they are fixed on a carrier medium or transmitted electronically."[14]

Accordingly, a digital product is a digitally encoded commercial product, and whether it is fixed on goods is irrelevant. Nevertheless, its meaning is not sufficiently clear. For example, there is an FTA that specifies "digital products" in terms of HS codes.[15] Other FTAs, in contrast, contain an array of exemplary digital services, including software, communication contents, or audiovisual contents. However, they explicitly exclude finance sectors from the scope of e-commerce, possibly in an attempt to avoid unintended trade liberalization as a result of

---

[12] The issue is prominent in audiovisual services sector (Peng 2016, 2020).

[13] In the ROK's case, FTAs with Singapore, the US, Canada, Peru, and Central America include a definition for digital products. Also, many FTAs involving the US or influenced by its role in digital trade rule-making have included the definition (Burri 2020a).

[14] Korea–Singapore FTA 14.1, Korea–Peru FTA 14.10, Korea–US FTA 15.9, Korea–Canada FTA 13.9, Korea–Central America FTA 14.9.

[15] Annex 14-A to Korea–Central America FTA.

application.[16] Some FTAs even prevent parties from giving their views on the issue in a case where there is a conflict as to the application of the term, which may imply that the economies had expected inherent problems during negotiations.[17]

Another point of discussion concerns the difference an FTA makes if it does not define digital products in its text.[18] Most e-commerce chapters of FTAs suspend application of customs duties on cross-border electronic transmission of digital products, and some FTAs even require nondiscriminatory treatment for digital products. However, if the agreement has no definition in its text, the ambiguity problem becomes even more serious.

With the emergence of new business and the growing complexity in the forms of digital trade, however, the ambiguity of classification may become less relevant as the international trade system embraces other controversial and more substantive issues of the digital economy (Peng 2020).

7.3   Digital Trade Negotiations: The Case of the Republic of Korea

Backed by knowledge on the general trend of regional digital trade negotiations in section 7.2, this section discusses the main features of digital trade negotiations for the Republic of Korea (ROK). Major e-commerce rules are selected from the ROK's FTAs, as shown in Table 7.2, and their main features and relevant legal issues are explained in sections 7.3.1 through 7.3.4. Then, those FTA rules are compared with the DEPA rules in section 7.3.5, and future challenges for the ROK's digital trade negotiations are discussed.

7.3.1   The Scope

Exclusion of Electronic Supply of Services

The e-commerce chapters of the ROK's FTAs typically exclude "services delivered electronically" from their legal scope. Some clearly state that measures affecting the supply of a service delivered or performed electronically be subject to the

---

[16] Korea–Singapore FTA 14.1, Korea–Central America FTA 14.9.

[17] Korea–US FTA 15.9 and its footnote 4; Korea–China FTA 13.3 and its footnote 1.

[18] In fact, many FTAs do not define the term "digital products." Among the FTAs in which the ROK participates, the e-commerce chapters in those with Australia, the PRC, Colombia, Türkiye, and Viet Nam FTAs, and inside RCEP, do not provide a relevant definition.

Table 7.2: Issues Covered in E-Commerce Provisions of Free Trade Agreements Involving the Republic of Korea

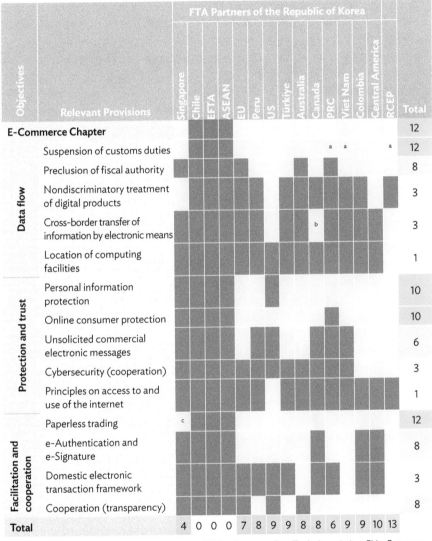

Objectives	Relevant Provisions	Singapore	Chile	EFTA	ASEAN	EU	Peru	US	Türkiye	Australia	Canada	PRC	Viet Nam	Colombia	Central America	RCEP	Total
	E-Commerce Chapter																12
	Suspension of customs duties								a	a					a		12
	Preclusion of fiscal authority																8
Data flow	Nondiscriminatory treatment of digital products																3
	Cross-border transfer of information by electronic means											b					3
	Location of computing facilities																1
	Personal information protection																10
Protection and trust	Online consumer protection																10
	Unsolicited commercial electronic messages																6
	Cybersecurity (cooperation)																3
	Principles on access to and use of the internet																1
	Paperless trading	c															12
Facilitation and cooperation	e-Authentication and e-Signature																8
	Domestic electronic transaction framework																3
	Cooperation (transparency)																8
Total		4	0	0	0	7	8	9	9	8	8	6	9	9	10	13	

ASEAN = Association of Southeast Asian Nations, EFTA = European Free Trade Association, EU = European Union, FTA = free trade agreement, PRC = People's Republic of China, RCEP = Regional Comprehensive Economic Partnership, US = United States.

Notes:
(i) The issues and provisions in the table are not exhaustive.
(ii) Legend: yellow = covered; red = not covered; green = the more categories covered, the darker the cell.

a The relevant provision requires implementation in conformity with the decision of the WTO E-Commerce Work Program.
b The relevant obligation is contained in the cooperation provisions.
c The relevant provision is contained in the trade facilitation chapter.

Source: Author's analysis based on official FTA text.

rules and obligations contained in the other chapters that regulate investment, cross-border trade in services, and financial services.[19]

Other FTAs recognize clearly that the problem of regulatory overlaps between the e-commerce issues and services trade issues exists and explicitly assures that e-commerce provisions would not apply if other provisions state not to. For example, the Korea–Canada FTA openly recognizes that "trade conducted by electronic means" is also covered by other relevant provisions such as those relating to national treatment and market access for goods, cross-border trade in services, financial services, telecommunications, and government procurement.[20] Then, this FTA makes it clear that the e-commerce provisions do not obligate "electronic delivery of digital products" unless other relevant chapters require so.[21]

Similarly, the Korea–China FTA and the Korea–Colombia FTA incorporate a relatively straightforward statement that, if any discrepancy between the e-commerce chapter and the other chapters becomes controversial, then the other chapters would prevail.[22] Those provisions probably shield against an excessively bold application of e-commerce rules and unintended changes to the commitments made under the other FTA chapters.

In the case of the Korea–EU FTA, e-commerce provisions belong to the chapter for "Trade in Services, Establishment and Electronic Commerce." This may be largely reflecting the EU position that regulatory issues on e-commerce are closely related to services trade issues, and that it is not inappropriate to address e-commerce as part of a combined services trade chapter.[23] The EU generally takes the view that electronic supply of digital content and information is a new form of services supply.[24] This position is consistently maintained in the FTA.

In sum, the ROK's FTAs generally show that the ROK has recognized that what is supplied or delivered is accounted for more importantly than how it is supplied or delivered. In principle, the e-commerce chapters are applied only to the extent they are not limited by the provisions of other FTA chapters.

---

[19] Korea–Singapore FTA 14.3, Korea–US FTA 15.2, Korea–Peru FTA 14.3, Korea–Türkiye FTA 2.3, Korea–Australia FTA 15.2, Korea–Central America FTA 14.2.

[20] Korea–Canada FTA 13.1.

[21] In the agreement, "digital product" means computer programs, text, video, images, sound recordings, or other products that are digitally encoded and produced for commercial sale or distribution.

[22] Korea–China FTA 13.2, Korea–Colombia FTA 12.7.

[23] Korea–EU FTA 7.48.

[24] For example, in the EU–Singapore FTA, Article 8.59 for electronic supply of services stipulates, "[f]or greater certainty, the Parties affirm that measure related to the supply of a service using electronic means falls within the scope of the obligations contained in services trade chapters."

7.3.2 Customs Duties and Data Flow

Customs Duties

All FTAs in which the ROK participates contain a bilateral commitment to eliminate customs duties on e-commerce. This implies the multilateral principle of duty-free electronic transmission that WTO members approved to apply temporarily in 1999 is permanent or otherwise extended, at least between the respective FTA partners.

However, there are a few exceptions and variations. First, in some FTAs, the duty-free obligation is systemically linked to the duration of the WTO E-commerce Work Program's decision on the moratorium.[25] For example, the Korea–China FTA affirms that the bilateral duty-free commitment will be effective as long as it is consistent with "the current WTO practice," which is then expounded in a footnote explaining that the parties reserve the right to adjust in accordance with any changes made to the ministerial decision.[26] In any cases where the multilateral moratorium is abandoned, it is an FTA party's right to decide whether to continue the duty-free or not.

Second, most FTAs of the ROK do not include the term "between the parties" in the customs duty provisions of the e-commerce chapter, which likely indicates nonexclusive application of duty-free on electronic transmission. In other words, non-application of customs duties is possibly assured on a most-favored-nation basis. However, some FTAs have removed the customs duties "between the parties." An example is the Korea–Australia FTA, which prohibits imposition of customs duties on electronic transmission "between the parties."[27] As the phrase "between the parties" denotes a bilateral application, the non-imposition of customs duties is a preferential treatment. In this case, the issue of determining the origin is also substantially important and should be elaborated.

Suppose data transmission occurs in a transaction or business between the FTA parties, if the data is actually sent from a third economy where its center or cloud is located, the data's origin subject to preferential treatment under the FTA may not be clear. In the case where the present WTO Moratorium is suspended, and an FTA party intends to impose customs duties on electronic transmission free of multilateral obligations, the data's origin determination will be crucial for guaranteeing the exclusive FTA benefit between the parties. As digitization and digital value chains grow, the issue of origin will become even more complicated.

---

[25] Korea-China FTA 13.3, Vietnam-Korea FTA 10.2, RCEP 12.11.

[26] Korea-China FTA 13.3 and its footnotes 2 and 3.

[27] Korea-Australia FTA 15.3, Korea–Singapore FTA 14.4, Korea–Türkiye FTA 2.4, RCEP 12.11.

Third, what is subject to the removal of customs duty is another important regulatory issue. In general, the ROK's FTAs with other economies in Asia and the Pacific apply zero customs duty to "electronic transmission."[28] However, its FTAs with economies in the Americas generally apply them to "digital products."[29] For example, the FTA with Peru has freed importation and exportation of digital products, and the one with the US has liberalized digital products that are electronically transmitted. Besides their uncertain legal effects, textually different obligations between duty-free "electronic transmissions" and duty-free "digital products" would entail administrative costs for FTA operation in practice.

Internal Taxation

Although e-commerce provisions in most FTAs of the ROK eliminate customs duties, they do not preclude a party's imposition of internal taxes or internal charges on cross-border electronic transmission in general.[30] A few do not have explicit textual basis for recognizing the parties' right to domestic taxes on e-commerce.[31] Even then, fiscal authority is not precluded.

Nevertheless, the relevant provisions require that internal taxes or charges be consistent with FTA rules. The problem is which FTA rules should domestic taxes or charges be consistent with are not specified. In particular, it is not clear if this requirement includes nondiscriminatory tax administration and if there are other FTA rules than nondiscrimination.

Nondiscriminatory Treatment of Digital Products

E-commerce provisions of the ROK's FTAs with Singapore, the US, and Central American economies include obligations for nondiscrimination. They prevent a party from treating digital products less favorably than their like domestic digital products.[32] The gist of the rule is that the obligation is applied with respect to various stages of commercialization—i.e., creation, production, publishment, store, transmission, contracts, and commission—and based on the nationality of persons involved—i.e., the author, performer, producer, developer, or distributor. Above all,

---

[28] Korea–Türkiye FTA 2.4, Korea–Australia FTA 15.3, Korea-China FTA, Vietnam-Korea FTA, RCEP.

[29] Korea–Peru FTA, Korea–US FTA, Korea–Canada FTA, Korea–Central America. In contrast, the Korea–Colombia FTA refers to "importation and exportation of products by electronic means."

[30] Korea–Singapore FTA 14.4, Korea–Peru FTA 14.4, Korea–US FTA 15.3, Korea–Türkiye FTA 2.4, Korea–Canada FTA 13.3, Vietnam-Korea FTA 10.2, Korea–Colombia FTA 12.2, Korea–Central America FTA 14.3, RCEP 12.11.

[31] Korea–EU FTA, ROK–Australia FTA, Korea–China FTA.

[32] Korea–Singapore FTA 14.4, Korea–US FTA 15.3, Korea–Central America 14.3.

it is substantially difficult to legally determine the likeness between digital products from different origins and whether they should be treated less favorably.

Moreover, the Korea–US FTA requires that any favor given to nonparties' digital products be extended to each other. Thus, nondiscrimination is applied based on a most-favored-nation basis between the parties.[33] The added elements regarding a nonparty would further complicate actual application of the nondiscrimination requirements.

Cross-Border Data Flow

Before the RCEP, the ROK's e-commerce provision concerning cross-border flow of information appears only in its FTA with the US.[34] As a rule, the provision prevents parties from restricting the cross-border flow of information.[35] However, the pursuit of seamless data flow to facilitate trade is legally weighed against recognition of personal information protection. Desirable as it might be and given the rising importance of privacy in the digital economy, this article is often cited as an early form of data-related provision in FTAs.

The RCEP contains more detailed rules to regulate cross-border data flow and data protection.[36] Its provisions recognize the parties' discretion to judge on *necessary* restrictions to data flow and *legitimate* public policy objectives,[37] thereby essentially reserving the parties' right to regulate digital trade to a greater extent than the data-related provisions in other digital economy agreements.

An overall assessment of the above-mentioned provisions shows that the ROK has generally supported the principle of data free flow but largely remained passive to accept elaborated data and privacy rules. With the start of the Korea–Singapore Digital Partnership negotiations, however, it became visibly more active to promote policies relating to data economy and accept data-related trade rules.

7.3.3   Protection of Personal Information and Consumers

Personal Information Protection

Most FTAs involving the ROK include e-commerce articles protecting personal information and the online consumer. The data protection provisions generally require parties to adopt or maintain domestic measures to protect personal data

---

[33] Korea–US FTA 15.3.

[34] The Korea–Canada FTA also mentions cross-border flows of information as an essential element to foster vibrant e-commerce (Korea–Canada FTA 13.7).

[35] Korea–US FTA 15.8.

[36] RCEP 12.15.

[37] RCEP 12.15 and Annex 14-A to the Korea–Central America FTA.

of the users in e-commerce.[38] In addition to the general obligation, the FTA with Viet Nam recognizes the need of adequate safeguards for such protection.

By promoting international standards, guidelines, or recommendations, some FTAs aim to restrain domestic enactment of unnecessarily divergent privacy rules and encourage regulatory convergence or harmonization. However, the relevant provisions are different in terms of specific obligations. For example, the ROK's FTA with Türkiye requires full compatibility with international standards for data protection, whereas the FTA with Australia mentions just consideration of international standards and guidelines, and the recommendations of international organizations. In contrast, the Korea–China FTA and the RCEP are among others that do not mention international standards as reference.[39]

Therefore, even if the ROK's domestic system for data protection complies with an international standard, it is hypothetically possible that the other party's assessment on its appropriateness or adequacy may have different results because some FTAs do not recognize international standards as basic criteria.

Online Consumer Protection

Online consumer protection is another key area that FTAs involving the ROK tend to promote. Most of them require parties to maintain transparent and effective measures to protect consumers from fraudulent and deceptive commercial practices.[40] Many call for cooperation between the national agencies to exchange information and share experiences. While the Korea–China FTA does not have relevant provisions, the RCEP now serves to fill the gap. Despite their soft law nature and insufficient legal details, the provisions for online consumer protection are essential to assure that the digital trade environment is trusted and safe, and they have evolved to be default rules in digital trade agreements.

---

[38] Korea–Peru FTA 14.7, Korea–Australia FTA 15.8, Korea–Canada FTA 13.4, Korea–China FTA 13.5, Vietnam-Korea FTA 10.6, Korea–Colombia FTA 12.3, Korea–Central America FTA 14.5.

[39] The Korea–Singapore FTA does not have provisions for personal information protection. This is partly because the agreement was concluded in the early 2000s when e-commerce chapters, including data protection, were not commonly discussed in FTA negotiations. In addition, the Korea–Peru FTA and the Korea–Central America FTA do not have provisions requiring consideration of international standards although they include provisions for personal information protection.

[40] Korea–US FTA 15.5, Korea–Peru FTA 14.5, Korea–Türkiye FTA 2.6, Korea–Australia FTA 15.6, Korea–Canada FTA 13.6, Vietnam-Korea FTA 10.5, Korea–Colombia FTA 12.5, Korea–Central America FTA 14.4.

Other fundamental rules essential to creating a resilient and secure digital ecosystem are concerned with spam messages and cybersecurity. Only a handful of FTAs involving the ROK includes relevant provisions. In those FTAs, parties that are mandated to minimize unsolicited spams and telemarketing, have regulatory dialogues with other parties, and cooperate with each other by exchanging information on technical, educational, and policy approaches.[41]

Principles on Access to and Use of the Internet

The ROK's FTA with the US applies principles on access to and use of the internet for e-commerce.[42] It basically protects consumers' right to use and choose the internet services and digital products, online applications, and services they run and the devices they connect to the Internet. It also aims to protect benefits of competition among networks, applications and services, and content providers. Until the Korea–Singapore DPA enters into force, this FTA remains the only agreement that includes such competition-related provisions.

7.3.4   Facilitation of E-Commerce and Digitalization

Paperless Trading

In general, paperless trading is a goal long and commonly pursued in the regional trading system.[43] The ROK's FTA e-commerce provisions or trade facilitation provisions require the parties to make best efforts to provide the public with electronic trade administration documents and recognize legally the equivalence of other parties' electronic documents.[44]

---

[41] Korea–EU FTA 7.49, Korea–Türkiye FTA 2.9, Korea–Australia FTA 15.9, Korea–Colombia FTA 12.6, Korea–Central America FTA 14.7.

[42] Korea–US FTA 15.7.

[43] Pasadilla (2020) notes that FTAs in general began to include provisions for paperless trading before they dealt with e-commerce issues. Monteiro and Teh (2017) explain that an article mentioning the concept was first adopted in New Zealand and Singapore in 2001, and many economies in Asia and the Pacific adopted the Framework Agreement on Facilitation of Cross-Border Paperless Trade in 2017.

[44] Korea–Singapore FTA 5.13, Korea–EU FTA 7.49 (mentioned as one of the cooperation areas), Korea–US FTA 15.6, Korea–Peru FTA 14.5, Korea–Türkiye FTA 2.8, Korea–Australia FTA 15.7, Korea–Canada FTA 13.5, Korea–China FTA 13.6, Vietnam-Korea FTA 10.7, Korea–Colombia FTA 12.4, Korea–Central America FTA 14.6, RCEP 12.5.

e-Authentication and e-Signature

The e-commerce chapters of most FTAs cover e-authentication and e-signature. They require parties to adopt or maintain a domestic system in which firms can choose for themselves appropriate ways for e-authentication in business and should be given chances to show and verify legal validity of electronic transactions they used before the judicial or administrative authorities.[45] In addition, never should a party deny legal validity of an e-signature just because it is in electronic form.

The use of digital certificates and e-signature is encouraged. FTA rules for e-commerce between the ROK and the PRC, between the ROK and Viet Nam, and between RCEP economies mention mutual recognition as a mechanism to spread use of those electronic tools. The Vietnam-Korea FTA, for example, recommends mutual recognition if the digital certificates and e-signature are based on internationally accepted standards. It emphasizes roles of international standards in developing relevant technology and systems.

Domestic Electronic Transaction Framework

To facilitate e-commerce, economies need to have domestic legal framework for electronic transactions. From a trade perspective, different laws, regulations, and systems between economies can create unnecessary barriers. Some FTAs mention specific international laws and model laws to be used as basis or reference for a party's domestic legal framework. The ROK's agreements with Australia, Viet Nam, and the RCEP all mention that the UNCITRAL Model Law on Electronic Commerce (1996) or the UN Convention on the Use of Electronic Communications in International Contracts (2005) or other applicable international conventions and model laws are to be considered when the parties try to minimize regulatory burdens on e-commerce and establish a business environment that is conducive to industry.[46] The ROK is a signatory of the 1996 UNCITRAL Model Law.[47]

---

[45] Korea–EU FTA 7.49 (mentioned as one of the cooperation areas), Korea–US FTA 15.4, Korea–Peru FTA 14.8, Korea–Türkiye FTA 2.5, Korea–Australia FTA 15.5, Korea–China FTA 13.4, Vietnam-Korea FTA 10.3, RCEP 12.6.

[46] Korea–Australia FTA 15.4, Vietnam-Korea FTA 10.4, RCEP 12.6.

[47] UNCITRAL. Overview of the Status of UNCITRAL Conventions and Model Laws. https://uncitral.un.org/sites/uncitral.un.org/files/media-documents/uncitral/en/overview-status-table.pdf (accessed July 2022).

Cooperation and Transparency

Most of the ROK's FTAs indicate broad areas and various forms to cooperate.[48] Frequently mentioned areas include privacy, spam messages, cybersecurity, consumer protection, and small and medium-sized enterprises (SMEs).[49] Technical assistance, information exchange, and knowledge sharing for enactment and administration of e-commerce legal framework are among the main instruments. FTA parties also need to cooperate in regional and multilateral forums to promote e-commerce development and to help the e-commerce system become more inclusive to SMEs.[50]

7.3.5   Negotiations Ahead: Digital Economy Agreements

Digital trade provisions in the ROK's FTAs are generally geared toward increasing e-commerce and avoiding unnecessary barriers. The scope and content of e-commerce chapters or provisions vary across the FTAs. However, as discussed in this chapter, key obligations of most FTAs involving the ROK include the bilateral lifting of customs duties, along with personal information protection, online consumer protection, and paperless trading. In addition, the promotion of e-authentication and e-signature, the prevention of spam messages, cooperation for cybersecurity and SMEs, and transparency are increasingly prominent.

However, compared with recent digital economy agreements like the DEPA and Singapore–Australia DEA, the ROK's FTA and RCEP provisions concerning e-commerce are limited. They can be augmented across numerous issues. For example, typical digital trade barriers to data free flow are created by domestic regulations and standards on data location, cryptography, and source code, and they form emerging central issues in recent digital trade negotiations. However, FTAs involving the ROK do not address them and, even if RCEP provisions deal somewhat with data localization, the relevant rules are not as rigorous as those in the DEPA and DEAs. In addition, several new provisions in the DEPA center on state-of-the-art digital technologies such as artificial intelligence, digital identities, and cybersecurity, but the ROK's FTAs lack any corresponding e-commerce provisions.

Therefore, gaps can be analyzed between the ROK's current position based on its FTA rules and commitments and a comprehensive and up-to-date set of digital trade rules that generally are incorporated in the DEPA, DEAs, or the Korea–Singapore DPA. The analysis can be conducted in two dimensions: one to find the differences and identify new issues appearing in the DEPA and others, and the other to explore rules and obligations that are legally strengthened in the ROK's FTAs.

---

[48] Korea–US FTA and Korea–Australia FTA do not include a provision dealing exclusively with cooperation.

[49] Korea-Colombia FTA 12.6, Korea-Central America FTA 14.7.

[50] Vietnam-Korea FTA 10.8.

Digital Economy Partnership Agreement Provisions Dealing with New Issues

Through FTAs, the ROK has consistently applied zero customs duties on electronic transmissions and supported protection of personal information and online consumers. However, the DEPA and other DEAs incorporate various provisions new to the ROK. The shaded items in Table 7.3 are not included in the ROK's FTA e-commerce chapters.

To be specific, in the data flow category in Table 7.3, items related to computing facilities, especially for financial services, cryptography of ICT products, and source code of software, for example, have not yet been included in the ROK's agreements and will likely be part of the future agenda. In the ROK's FTAs, data free flow provisions are limitedly stipulated, and nondiscrimination rules are adopted only in respect of the US and Canada, not even of the RCEP economies. Nevertheless, the CPTPP, USMCA, DEPA, and other DEAs commonly include these rules. If the ROK is to join the DEPA, it should ensure that its domestic system conforms. In the Korea–Singapore DEA negotiations, the ROK accepted those provisions for the first time and has to be ready to implement them.

Likewise, the ROK may consider many other items as part of the future digital trade agenda. Items related to online safety and security, and interactive computer services fall under the category of protection and trust, while items related to, for example, e-invoicing, e-payments, and digital identities in the category of e-business facilitation, must be addressed by the ROK in negotiations with the DEPA or other DEA members.

DEPA Provisions Imposing Stronger Obligations

Comparing the ROK's FTAs with the DEPA, many provisions can be improved. From a regulatory perspective, provisions can serve better if they are made clearer, more specific, or legally stronger.

The article on personal information protection is one example. While the RCEP rules are longer and more comprehensive, the DEPA rules are even more detailed. The DEPA basically requires the parties to adopt or maintain a legal framework for privacy protection and then indicates specific criteria to use such as "principles and guidelines of relevant international bodies." The Singapore–Australia DEA even mentions the APEC privacy rules or OECD guidelines for reference.[51] The DEPA and the DEA also specify key principles that a legal framework must include and require nondiscriminatory practices in administering

---

[51] Specifically, these are the APEC Cross-Border Privacy Rules System and the OECD Guidelines Governing the Protection of Privacy and Transborder Flows of Personal Data.

the protection.[52] Those detailed provisions are not found in the ROK's FTAs, which implies that the ROK will have to prepare its domestic system to conform to them in case of its accession to the DEPA.

Another example is the article on paperless trade. The ROK's FTAs commonly encourage electronic submission of administration documents, but generally in the form of soft law. The relevant DEPA rules, however, provide for specific ways to promote a single window customs system and data exchange system. They are more of a guideline or a to-do list to achieve paperless trading. Though in best-endeavor provisions, use of machine-readable administration documents, legal validation of electronic documents, establishment of a single window in accordance with the WTO Trade Facilitation Agreement, and compatible and interoperable single windows that enable data exchange are all among the concrete obligations.

Last, the RCEP is so far the only agreement for the ROK that contains a provision regulating computing facilities. As shown in Table 7.3, while the DEPA and other agreements contain similar provisions, the Singapore–Australia DEA even adopts an article prohibiting financial services-related data localization, and the DEPA goes further to allow businesses the flexibility to choose a data location and data facility.

Therefore, the ROK should be able to embrace a number of such rules elaborated in the DEPA and other DEAs, and is also expected to cope with trading partners' growing demand for effective digital trade governance in future negotiations.

---

[52] The eight principles include limitation on collection, data quality, purpose specification, use limitation, security safeguards, transparency, individual participation, and accountability.

Table 7.3: Issues Covered in Digital Economy Agreements and the Republic of Korea's Free Trade Agreements

DEPA Classification (Module)	Provisions	Number of the ROK's FTAs	RCEP	CPTPP	USMCA	USJDTA	DEPA	ASDEA
Digital product, information, data flow	Customs duties	12	✓	✓	✓	✓	✓	✓
	Nondiscriminatory treatment of digital products	3	–	✓	✓	✓	✓	✓
	Cross-border transfer of information by electronic means	3	✓	✓	✓	✓	✓	✓
	Location of computing facilities	1	✓	–	✓	✓	✓	✓
	Location of computing facilities for financial services	–	–	–	–	–	–	–
	ICT products that use cryptography	–	–	[a]	[a]	–	✓	✓
	Source code	–	–	✓	✓	✓	✓	✓
Protection and trust	Personal information protection	10	✓	✓	✓	✓	✓	✓
	Online consumer protection	10	✓	✓	✓	✓	✓	✓
	Unsolicited commercial electronic messages	6	✓	✓	✓	✓	✓	✓
	Cybersecurity cooperation	3	✓	✓	✓	✓	✓	✓
	Principles on access to and use of the internet	1	–	✓	✓	✓	✓	–
	Online safety and security	[b]	–	–	–	–	✓	✓
	Interactive computer services	–	–	✓	✓	✓	–	✓
E-business facilitation	Paperless trading	12	✓	✓	✓	✓	✓	✓
	e-authentication and e-signature	8	✓	✓	✓	✓	✓	✓
	Domestic electronic transaction framework	3	✓	✓	✓	✓	✓	✓
	Logistics	–	–	–	–	–	–	–
	e-invoicing	–	–	–	–	–	✓	–
	Express shipments	–	–	–	–	–	✓	✓
	e-payments	–	–	–	–	–	✓	✓
	Digital identities	–	–	–	–	–	✓	✓
Infrastructure and interoperability	Internet connection charge sharing	–	–	✓	–	–	–	–
	Submarine telecommunications cable systems	[c]	–	–	–	–	–	–
	Standards and conformity assessment for digital trade	–	–	–	–	–	–	✓

continued on next page

Table 7.3 continued

DEPA Classification (Module)	Provisions	Number of the ROK's FTAs	RCEP	CPTPP	USMCA	USJDTA	DEPA	ASDEA
New emerging technology and cooperation	Fintech and regtech	–	–	–	–	–	✓	✓
	Artificial intelligence	–	–	–	–	–	✓	✓
	Government procurement	–	–	–	–	–	✓	–
	Competition policy	–	–	–	–	–	✓	✓
	Public domain	–	–	–	–	–	✓	–
	Data innovation	–	–	–	–	✓	✓	✓
	Open government data	–	–	–	–	–	✓	✓
	SMEs in digital economy	–	–	–	–	–	✓	✓
	Stakeholder engagement	–	–	–	–	–	✓	✓
	Digital inclusion	–	–	–	–	–	–	–
	Capacity building	–	✓	–	–	–	✓	✓
	Transparency	–	–	–	–	–	–	✓

– = no provision, ASDEA = Australia–Singapore Digital Economy Agreement, CPTTP = Comprehensive and Progressive Trans-Pacific Partnership, DEPA = Digital Economy Partnership Agreement, FTA = free trade agreement, ICT = information and communication technology, RCEP = Regional Comprehensive Economic Partnership, ROK = Republic of Korea, SMEs = small and medium-sized enterprises, USJDTA = United States–Japan Digital Trade Agreement, USMCA = United States–Mexico–Canada Agreement.

[a] Relevant provisions are contained in the Technical Barriers to Trade chapter of the respective agreements.

[b] Liability of intermediary service provider is included as a cooperation area in e-commerce provisions of the Korea–Türkiye FTA.

[c] Relevant provisions are included in the telecommunication chapter of the Korea–United States FTA.

Note: The issues and provisions in the table are not comprehensive.

Source: Author's analysis.

7.4   Conclusion

Aside from the WTO e-commerce negotiations, a framework for digital trade governance emerged through regional trade negotiations. FTA provisions have solidified the basic rules and procedures to deal with e-commerce problems and, gradually, data flow and data protection form central issues in digital trade negotiations. Many other areas are not as fully tackled as the data issues and, therefore, more works on those remaining areas are expected to continue in the future.

The Republic of Korea (ROK), having formed an extensive FTA network with major trading partners around the world, is at a crossroads, uncertain of whether to join with enthusiasm the global discussions about a new digital trade order or respond passively to the demands for playing a certain role in rulemaking. Its recent decisions to join the CPTPP and the DEPA, as well as the conclusion of the DPA with Singapore, represent only part of these important policy considerations.

As examined in this chapter, there are many issues in the RTAs that digital trade negotiators must continue to work on. Among the main points, first is the potential problem from the systemic link between zero customs duty on electronic transmission and the WTO decision. Second, data governance rules encompassing data free flow and privacy protection need further elaboration. Third, for flourishing e-businesses, interoperability of technologies and systems is the key obligation, but needs to be accompanied by real and effective actions and cooperation. Also, while some DEPA and DEA provisions point to bold new areas such as artificial intelligence, digital identities, cybersecurity, and fintech, along with diverse ways to encourage digital transformation, they fall short of providing concrete rules.

Another challenge concerns enlargement of those digital trade agreements. As the case of the ROK shows, FTA e-commerce rules differ from one agreement to another. Formation of RTAs inevitably leads to a fragmented global system and incurs unnecessary costs. However, the breadth and intensity of obligations in an agreement is basically an outcome of various factors, including the parties' capacity and willingness to accept them. Therefore, any attempt to enlarge the DEA participation should be accompanied by far-reaching efforts in international communities to help increase economies' relevant capacity and cooperate to share information and regulatory experience.

The final point to make is that, even though sector-specific trade openness is largely regulated by existing commitments in the GATS and nonconforming FTA provisions, digital trade law will have increasing influence on the delivery of cross-border digital services. Digitalized areas like computer services, telecommunication services, or business services will increasingly benefit from freer cross-border data flows. Even financial services, which typically are explicitly excluded from e-commerce negotiations, will need to ensure an environment with a freer but more secure and safer cross-border information flows.

As WTO and RTA negotiations on digital trade and trade-related aspects of the digital economy proceed, discussions need to focus more on changing markets and digital services. Digital trade rules need to be more responsive to real problems and practices in emerging areas and, at the same time, be coherent with development of other international rules and standards.

Bibliography

Aaronson, S. A., and P. Leblond. 2018. Another Digital Divide: The Rise of Data Realms and Its Implications for the WTO. *Journal of International Economic Law.* 21. pp. 245–272.

Andrenelli, A., and J. L. González. 2019. Electronic Transmissions and International Trade—Shedding New Light on the Moratorium Debate. *OECD Trade Policy Papers.* No. 233. Paris: Organisation for Economic Co-operation and Development (OECD).

Burri, M. 2020a. Adapting Trade Rules for the Age of Big Data. In A. Taubman and J. Watal, eds. *Trade in Knowledge: Economic, Legal and Policy Aspects.* Cambridge: Cambridge University Press.

———. 2020b. Data Flows and Global Trade Law: Tracing Developments in Preferential Trade Agreements. In M. Burri, ed. *Big Data and Global Trade Law.* Cambridge: Cambridge University Press.

Burri, M. and R. Polanco. 2020. Digital Trade Provisions in Preferential Trade Agreements: Introducing a New Dataset. *Journal of international Economic Law. 23* (1). pp. 187–220.

Casalini, F. and J. L. González. 2019. Trade and Cross-Border Data Flow. *OECD Trade Policy Papers.* No. 220. Paris: OECD.

Choi, C. 2010. The Effect of the Internet on Services Trade. *Economic Letters.* 109. pp. 102–104.

Duval, Y. and A. Kravchenko, eds. 2017. *Studies in Trade, Investment and Innovation No. 87: Digital Trade Facilitation in Asia and the Pacific.* Bangkok: United Nations Economic and Social Commission for Asia and the Pacific (UNESCAP).

Gao, H. 2011. Google's China Problem: A Case Study on Trade, Technology and Human Rights under the GATS. *Asian Journal of WTO and International Health Law and Policy.* 6. pp. 349–385.

González, J. L. and M. A. Jouanjean. 2017. Digital Trade: Developing a Framework for Analysis. *OECD Trade Policy Papers.* No. 205. Paris: OECD.

González, J. L., and J. Ferencz. 2018. Digital Trade and Market Openness. *OECD Trade Policy Papers*. No. 217. Paris: OECD.

Jaller, L., S. Gaillard, and M. Molinuevo. 2020. *The Regulation of Digital Trade: Key Policies and   International Trends*. Washington, DC: World Bank.

Miroudot, S. and C. Cadestin. 2017. Services in Global Value Chains: From Inputs to Value-Creating Activities. *OECD Trade Policy Papers*. No. 197. Paris: OECD.

Mitchell, A. D., and N. Mishra. 2020. Digital Trade Integration in Preferential Trade Agreements. *ARTNeT Working Paper Series*. No. 191. May. Bangkok: UNESCAP.

Monteiro, J. A. and R. Teh. 2017. Provisions on Electronic Commerce in Regional Trade Agreements. *WTO Working Paper*. No. ERSD-2017-11. Geneva: World Trade Organization.

Pasadilla, G. 2020. E-commerce Provisions in RTAs: Implications for Negotiations and Capacity Building. *ARTNeT Working Paper Series*. No. 192. June. Bangkok: UNESCAP.

Pasadilla, G., Y. Duval, and W. Anukoonwattaka. 2020. Next Generation Nontariff Measures: Emerging Data Policies and Barriers to Digital Trade. *ARTNeT Working Paper Series*. No. 187. June. Bangkok: UNESCAP.

Peng, S. Y. 2007. Trade in Telecommunications Services: Doha and Beyond. *Journal of World Trade*. 41 (3). pp. 289–310.

———. 2016. GATS and the Over-the-Top Services: A Legal Outlook. *Journal of World Trade*. 50 (1). pp. 21–46.

———. 2020. A New Trade Regime for the Servitization of Manufacturing: Rethinking the Goods-Services Dichotomy. *Journal of World Trade*. 54 (5). pp. 699–726.

Sen, N. 2018. Understanding the Role of the WTO in International Data Flows: Taking the Liberalization or the Regulatory Autonomy Path? *Journal of International Economic Law*. 21 (2). pp. 323–348.

Weber, R. and R. Baisch. 2013. Tensions between Developing and Traditional GATS Classifications in IT Markets. *Hong Kong Law Journal*. 43. pp. 77–110.

Wolfe, R. 2019. Learning about Digital Trade: Privacy and E-commerce in CETA and TPP. *World Trade Review*. 18 (S1). pp. S63–S84.

World Trade Organization (WTO). 1998. *The Work Programme on Electronic Commerce*. WT/L/274. Geneva.

———. 2001. *Dedicated Discussion on Electronic Commerce Under the Auspices of the General Council on 15 June 2001: Summary by the Secretariat of the Issues Raised*. WT/GC/W/436. Geneva.

———. 2018. *Work Programme on Electronic Commerce: The E-commerce Moratorium on Customs Duties and Electronic Transmissions: Need for a Re-think (Communication from India and South Africa)*. WT/GC/W/747. Geneva.

————. 2019. *Joint Statement on Electronic Commerce.* WT/L/1056. Geneva.

————. 2019. *Work Programme on Electronic Commerce: The E-commerce Moratorium and Implications for Developing Countries (Communication from India and South Africa).* WT/GC/W/774. Geneva.

Wu, T. 2006. The World Trade Law of Censorship and Internet Filtering. *Chicago Journal of International Law.* 7 (1). pp. 263–287.

8 | ENSURING CYBERSECURITY FOR DIGITAL SERVICES TRADE

Lennon Yao-Chung Chang and Han-Wei Liu

8.1 Introduction

Digital technologies are not only transforming conditions for international trade but also how criminals behave. Cybercriminals are not only chasing money but also collecting data online for diverse purposes, including monetary gain, revenge, and political purposes. Cybercrime is a worldwide concern. The old criminology adage "where there's money, there's crime" is now joined by "where there is data, there is crime."

Insecurity in the global cyberspace is often in the news. In July 2022, 23 terabytes of personal data from the People's Republic of China (PRC) police agency were for sale online. The dataset includes a billion records, mostly on PRC citizens, and is the largest ever sale of data on record (Tidy 2022; Xiao 2022). In June 2021, Colonial Pipeline, the largest pipeline operator in the United States (US), providing about 45% of the nation's east coast's fuel supply, was forced to close its business due to cyberattacks (BBC News 2021). That same month, JBS, the world's largest meat processor, paid an $11 million ransom to resolve a cyberattack (Bunge and Newman 2021). Economies in Asia and the Pacific are also suffering from serious cyberattacks. For example, AXA, one of the world's biggest cyber insurance companies, suffered a serious ransomware attack at its Asian offices in May 2021 (Ikeda 2021). Kaspersky, an information security service provider, counted more than 2.7 million ransomware activities in the Association of Southeast Asian Nations (ASEAN) in the first three quarters of 2020 (Interpol 2021). In recent years, ransomware attacks have crippled critical infrastructure in the US and Asian economies and disrupted global supply chains. It shows that no firm is safe from insidious cyberattacks, especially so in least developed countries (LDCs), which do not have adequate cyber-capacity and awareness.

With the broader adoption of information and communication technology (ICT), including various emerging technologies such as artificial intelligence, big data, cloud computing, and the Internet of Things, cyberattacks are credible challenges policy makers are facing. The risks of cyberattack trigger different regulatory responses, or lack of response due to limited capacity. Insofar as regulatory interventions affect imports, exports, and foreign investment, they can raise concerns from the perspective of international trade law. Cybersecurity has emerged as a source of commercial, legal, and geopolitical conflict. It is therefore on the agenda of policy makers across areas, including trade.

A common approach can help enhance cybersecurity and facilitate digital trade. Divergent, or even protectionist approaches, can create obstacles to digital trade. Without a clear understanding of cybersecurity laws and policies, industry stakeholders can struggle to adapt to evolving restrictions. Similarly, trade policy makers need to map the issues and reconfigure the global trading system. The aim of this chapter is not to offer an account of cybersecurity governance in the digital trade context. Rather, by illustrating the overall trend in regulatory responses to cybersecurity, it seeks to identify common ground and differences and how well Asia and Pacific economies have adopted them. This inquiry could not only help reveal the implications of domestic regulations of cybersecurity for the global trading system, but more crucially, help map the differences in capacity and readiness to react to emerging threats in cyberspace. Such maps are the key for policy makers to work toward building a resilient digital economy.

The terms "cybersecurity" and "cybercrime" go beyond technical definitions and reflect how policy makers perceive concerns and react to them as a matter for regulation. This chapter provides a deeper understanding of regulatory concerns by identifying common cybersecurity threats in Asia, while offering an overview of international and national responses, in particular approaches that can disrupt the open internet and digital trade the most, such as data localization measures.

The Council of Europe's Convention on Cybercrime (Budapest Convention) is perhaps the most important international initiative to help like-minded nations manage some of these cybersecurity concerns. The Budapest Convention could serve as a good point to reflect upon the economy's readiness in developed and developing economies in the field. Key features of preferential trade agreements (PTAs) explored in this chapter can help moderate trade concerns related to cybersecurity issues, directly or indirectly, and—as also discussed in this chapter—can be supported by more informal arrangements.

8.2   Cybersecurity as a Regulatory Concern

The development of technology and the internet is a double-edged sword. On the one hand, it has transformed our everyday life, from ways we communicate with people to how we do business. The work, study, and business operated from home during the coronavirus disease (COVID-19) pandemic would not be possible without the support of new technology and the internet. However, the development of technology and the internet also provides criminals with a new tool to commit the crime. As the internet was built initially for research purposes rather than commercial use, security mechanisms were not considered in the design. The borderless characteristics of the internet also create barriers to investigating crime. Routine Activity Theory teaches that a crime happens when a potential offender meets a suitable target when capable guardians are not present. Cyberspace has created ample space where guardians are not capable most of the time due to a range of reasons illustrated below.

8.2.1   Defining Cybersecurity and Cybercrime

Defining the term "cybersecurity" can be as complex as managing trade concerns around cybersecurity. While no universally agreed definition of this term exists, from a technical and data-driven perspective, cybersecurity is often linked to the CIA Triad—*confidentiality, integrity,* and *availability*—of information.[1] A well-known definition along this line comes from the International Telecommunication Union, which refers to cybersecurity as a

> collection of tools, policies, security concepts, security safeguards, guidelines, risk management approaches, actions, training, best practices, assurance and technologies that can be used to protect the cyber environment and organization and user's assets... Cybersecurity strives to ensure the attainment and maintenance of the security properties of the organization and user's assets against relevant security risks in the cyber environment.[2]

The National Institute of Standards and Technology of the US, as related in Kissel (2013) and its updates, elaborates on each of these dimensions:

- *Confidentiality*—"Preserving authorized restrictions on information access and disclosure, including means for protecting personal privacy and proprietary information."
- *Integrity*—"Guarding against improper information modification or destruction, and includes ensuring information nonrepudiation and authenticity. Data integrity covers data in storage, during processing, and while in transit. Typical measures include file permissions and user access controls."

---

[1] International Organization for Standardization. ISO/IEC 27032:2012 (Information Technology—Security Techniques—Guidelines for Cybersecurity). https://www.iso.org/obp/ui/#iso:std:iso-iec:27032:ed-1:v1:en (accessed July 2022).

[2] International Telecommunication Union (ITU). Definition of Cyberspace. https://www.itu.int/en/ITU-T/studygroups/com17/Pages/cybersecurity.aspx (accessed July 2022).

- *Availability*—"Ensuring timely and reliable access to and use of information. It is ensured by hardware maintenance, regular and timely system upgrades, but also disaster recovery plans."

Defining cybersecurity, however, is more than a technical issue. This term is often colored by politics, which elevates it as a geopolitical concern (Koh 2020; Meltzer and Kerry 2019). In some economies, cybersecurity is widely perceived to include any digital information that can threaten social or political stability—which could be framed as a matter of internet sovereignty and national security. The PRC and Viet Nam are prime examples.[3] Under its Cybersecurity Law, for instance, the PRC conceptualizes cybersecurity as a matter of "safeguarding the cyberspace sovereignty, national security and public interests, protecting the lawful rights and interests of citizens, legal persons, and other organizations, and promoting the sound development of economic and social information technology" (Article 1 of the PRC Cybersecurity Law). Broadly framed, cybersecurity could be seen as concerning both the traditional CIA Triad and information distributed online—including, notably, disinformation, fake news, or misinformation.[4]

While it is important to understand the linkage between cybersecurity and digital trade, one should not ignore the impact of cybercrime on digital trade. Cybercrime refers to criminal offenses that are committed using and/or targeting computers and telecommunications (Smith, Grabosky, and Urbas 2001). It is argued that "cybercrime" tends to be used "metaphorically and emotively rather than scientifically or legally" (Wall 2007). Just like the term "white collar crime" has been used for about 50 years, academia uses these terms to "delimit the scope of computer-related misconduct" (Smith, Grabosky, and Urbas 2001). On one hand, cybercrime can be conventional crime facilitated by the internet, such as online fraud and telecommunication scams. On the other hand, it can include new crimes developed out of the advancement of computing technologies, such as hacking, Denial of Service (DoS) or Distributed Denial of Service (DDoS) attacks, phishing, and botnets.

---

[3] Cybersecurity Law of the PRC, effective 1 June 2017 (English translation available at Westlaw China); Law on Cybersecurity of Viet Nam, effective 12 June 2018 (English translation prepared by Allens Linklaters, https://www.allens.com.au/insights-news/insights/2018/06/vietnam-issues-a-stringent-new-cybersecurity-law/).

[4] Even in the Western world, it is not uncommon to see governments address the threats of fake news in the context of cybersecurity. See, for example, Buckmaster and Wils (2019).

Similar to cybersecurity, there is no universally agreed definition of cybercrime. That said, academics have classified cybercrime into three general forms (Grabosky 2016) while noting that the three types somewhat overlap:

(i)   Crimes where the computer is used as the instrument of crime, such as phishing, producing, and disseminating child pornography;

(ii) Crimes where the computer is the target of crime, such as denial of service attack; and

(iii) Crimes where the computer is incidental to the offense, such as maintaining records of criminal transactions such as money laundering and drug dealing.

Indeed, remarkable overlap can be seen between the computer as instrumental and the computer as incidental. These two types of cybercrime are mainly conventional crimes facilitated by new technology, which can be called "cyber-enabled crime." On the other hand, for crimes where the computer is the target of crime, these are crimes that did not exist before the digital age and are highly dependent on new technology. Thus, they can be called "cyber-dependent crime" (McGuire and Dowling 2013).

Statistics from government and industry demonstrate the drastic increase in the number, and increasing seriousness, of cybercrime. According to the 2020 Internet Crime Report, the Federal Bureau of Investigation's Internet Crime Complaint Centre (IC3) received about 800,000 cybercrime complaints, which is 2.5 times higher than in 2016 (298,728). The financial loss from these crimes reaches $4.2 billion in 2020, about three times more than it was in 2016 ($1.5 billion). The top cybercrime types are phishing (including vishing, smishing, and pharming), nonpayment and nondelivery, extortion, personal data breach, and identity theft.

8.2.2   Identifying Emerging Threats in Cyberspace

From the definition and classification of cybercrime and cybersecurity, we can see that digital trade and services are not only impacted by weaknesses in technology and systems, but can also be impacted by users who control or use the technology. Some prevalent and emerging threats that might impact digital trade, especially for developing economies and LDCs in Asia, include the following:

• Botnets—These are still very popular and are used to commit cybercrime and breach cybersecurity. A botnet is a network of bot-infected computers. A bot-infected computer is a computer that contains a malicious computer program, malware, which allows the computer to be controlled remotely. Usually, the program is installed secretly without the owner's understanding. The use of botnets as springboards to launch a cyberattack or cybercrime creates barriers to crime investigation. Large botnets can contain millions of bot-infected computers and can be used to launch a DDoS, a massive attack to disrupt traffic of a targeted server or network by flooding the bandwidth. This can cause severe damage to critical infrastructure, such as online banking, and interrupt digital transactions. It has been deemed the new architecture of cyber-organized crime (Chang 2012). They are also used to disseminate *ransomware*, a type of malicious computer software used by criminals to encrypt victims' files and data and ask for a ransom payment to get codes to decrypt the file. For example, the Colonial Pipeline and the JBS USA holdings were ransomware attacks. Reports have shown that ASEAN economies are suffering from ransomware attacks (Thomas 2019).

- *ATM heists*—Using sophisticated malicious computer software, international organized crime syndicates have stolen money from automatic teller machines (ATMs). This has occurred not only in developed economies like the US. It has also happened in developing and middle-income economies in Asia (Chang 2017).

- *Phishing*—This has been reported as a way criminals gain access to ATMs. When phishing, criminals obtain confidential user information, such as the login ID and password for online banking, personal data, a business login, and credit card details. Using social engineering skills, criminals masquerade as a trusted entity, luring the victim to open an e-mail, click on a link or text message and/or to fill out a fake form. It can be done by sending an e-mail, by voice message (*vishing*), by SMS text (*smishing*), and by redirecting the link to a fake website, rather than a legitimate one (*pharming*). As mentioned, phishing is on the top of IC3's list of cybercrimes. Phishing is usually not personalized or targeted, and expecting anyone to take the bait.

- *Advanced persistent threat (APT)*—This is similar to phishing but more targeted and is becoming popular. The malicious software and/or social engineering skills designed for advanced persistent threat (APT) are usually customized, targeting a specific entity or region. Also, they are designed usually for sensitive data such as government classified information, trade secrets, and intellectual property, rather than for direct financial gain. For example, PLATINUM, a malicious computer software, was designed to access sensitive government data in South and Southeast Asian economies (Microsoft 2016).

- *Business email compromise*—Such a scam can easily be launched using information about an entity/company acquired through APT. According to Trend Micro, business email compromise (BEC) is "a type of scam targeting companies who conduct wire transfers and have suppliers abroad." While this has been highlighted in the IC3 report as a serious issue, it is actually critical in Asia, especially for companies in economies that are under sanctions, as they usually need to use another company outside the country to accept a money transfer, which allows criminals to take the role as agents.

In response to these cybersecurity and cybercrime issues, more and more economies have introduced cybersecurity laws and personal data protection laws. While these regulatory initiatives have their merits, the free flow of information can be impeded by how each country designs and implements them, leading to a fragmented internet. The introduction of cybersecurity and data protection laws are pushing in the direction of a localized internet and are a constraint on a free and open internet. The control of data and data flow might significantly hamper the development of digital trade and services and would create barriers to trade negotiation. The power to allow a government to shut down the internet to manage damaging and uncontrollable events to the government (e.g., spreading of misinformation or information operations) also needs to be considered while developing digital trade and services. Last, digital literacy, and especially cybersecurity awareness, is key to promoting successful digital trade and services.

8.2.3   International and National Responses

Cybercrime and cybersecurity concerns are being tackled through international and national measures. The Council of Europe drafted the Convention on Cybercrime (the Budapest Convention) in 1989 to account for the "borderless" nature of cybercrime. It was opened for signature by both member and nonmember states and entered into force on 1 July 2004 after ratification by five member economies.[5] The Budapest Convention is viewed as the first international treaty focusing on combating cybercrime and has been noted by the United Nations (UN) General Assembly (resolution 56/121), which invited its member states to become signatories (Chang 2012).

The Budapest Convention aims to facilitate adoption of adequate international legal instruments against cybercrime. Computer-related offenses relating to the confidentiality, integrity, and availability of computer data are among them. They include (i) illegal access to a computer system; (ii) interception of nonpublic transmissions of computer data to, from, or within a computer system; (iii) interference with computer data; (iv) interference with

---

[5] According to the Council of Europe, only after ratification by five states (including at least three members) would the Convention enter into force. Albania, Croatia, Estonia, Hungary, and Lithuania were the first five states to ratify.

computer systems, such as computer sabotage; and (v) the misuse of computer-related devices (e.g., "hacker tools"), including the production, sale, procurement for use, import, or distribution of such devices. It also covers cyber-enabled crimes such as the traditional offenses of fraud and forgery when carried out through a computer system, child sexual exploitation using the internet, and offenses relating to copyright infringement. On the procedural part, it regulated real-time data sharing and asked its signatories to create 24/7 contact points for an international computer crime assistance network. While 66 economies, including Australia, Japan, the Philippines, and the US, have ratified or acceded to the Budapest Convention, the Russian Federation, supported by the PRC, is proposing a separate treaty at the UN level (Chang 2012), sharing similarities with the Budapest Convention while presenting significant differences in enforcement, with more autonomy given to states in their own investigation (ADB 2021).

Australia has promoted the Budapest Convention. In its International Cyber and Critical Technology Engagement Strategy, the Australian government supports economies in the Indo-Pacific region to build cyber resilience and promote the convention. It has also become an essential part of Australia's development cooperation program, which helps developing and least developed economies in Asia and the Pacific to improve their regulations and capacity on cybersecurity (Government of Australia, DFAT 2021).

In the past few years, while economies in Asia and the Pacific have developed cybersecurity and cybercrime laws, not all are aligned with the Budapest Convention. While most economies in the region are strongly aligned with the convention, some developing economies are weakly aligned and would benefit from developing their legal systems to improve cybersecurity and combat cybercrime (Chang 2020).

Cyberattacks can cause a chain reaction (Chang 2012). While it is hard to stop an attack from happening, it is crucial to reduce the harm that an attack could cause to society. Therefore, besides the harmonization of laws on cybercrime and cybersecurity, a risk-based approach has also been adopted by many economies to reduce the harm caused by cyberattacks, especially cyberattacks targeting critical infrastructure. For example, the US introduced the Federal Information Security Management Act, regulating computer incident information sharing among the critical infrastructure industry. Similar approaches have been adopted by Asian economies to encourage the critical infrastructure industry to share their computer incidents so that other companies can take measures in advance. In order to protect national security and prevent cyber espionage, economies like the PRC also require software companies and service providers to make source codes available for review (Dou 2015).

Research has shown the need to help economies strengthen their laws and regulations to combat cybercrime and maintain cybersecurity. We see that cyber capacity building and raising cybersecurity awareness have become essential for aid programs and trade negotiations. For example, the Australian government recently launched the International Cyber and Critical Technology Engagement Strategy. The key for this is to support economies in the Indo-Pacific region, especially LDCs, to draft laws that meet the international standard, such as the Budapest Convention, and equip them with better cyber environments by building a risk-based approach to ensure cybersecurity.

8.3   Regulatory Cooperation: The State of Play

The lack of cybersecurity is costly and can undermine the trust of consumers and businesses in engaging in the digital context. Protecting confidence in an online world involves cross-border collaboration between the public and private sectors, as individuals, businesses, and governments that operate through the global networks can face the same threats (Meltzer and Kerry 2019). Many of the regulatory models—such as Australia, the PRC, and the US—feature the "risk-based" approach by identifying "critical infrastructure" and imposing strict obligations on the relevant operators. The PRC and others have gone even further by mandating local storage of data and obtaining source codes. Others, such as developing economies and LDCs in the ASEAN, however, are yet to maintain adequate measures.

World Trade Organization and Preferential Trade Agreements

The internet and the way we trade in terms of goods and services around it was entirely different from today when the World Trade Organization (WTO) was established in the 1990s. The WTO is therefore not well-equipped with tools to address cybersecurity explicitly—or measures in its name, except certain disciplines such as nondiscrimination (e.g., General Agreement on Trade in Services [GATS] Article II), security exception (e.g., GATS Article XIV *bis*), and general exception (e.g., GATS Article XIV) that may be applicable.[6] These exceptions, however, are far from satisfactory to manage trade conflicts that arise from cybersecurity. For one, these rules are subject to the judicial interpretation after the fact and on a case-by-case basis. There is room for WTO members to maneuver. Another, and more crucial reason, is that where a member defends itself under the security exception, WTO adjudicators may find it politically sensitive to review the disputed

---

[6] Marrakesh Agreement Establishing the World Trade Organization, opened for signature 15 April 1994, 1867 UNTS 3 (entered into force 1 January 1995) Annex 1A (General Agreement on Tariffs and Trade 1994 or GATT), Annex 1B (General Agreement on Trade in Services or GATS). Mitchell and Hepburn (2017) argued for instance that the former European Union (EU)–US Safe Harbor arrangement may violate the most-favored-nation (MFN) obligation under GATS Article II:1.

measures. There is significant uncertainty, as Tania Voon remarks, around the security exception (Voon 2019). Some economies, hence, attempt to reconfigure the rules to provide greater certainty and clarity for businesses and policy makers both within and outside the WTO context. Within the WTO, for instance, the consolidated negotiating text on e-commerce recently released seems to signal the willingness of some members to tackle these recurring issues in the digital age (WTO 2020). While it remains to be seen how WTO members come up with new solutions, the new development of preferential trade agreements (PTAs) is a good reference point to identify the key instruments for trade policy makers to harness trade concerns around cybersecurity. We now consider them in turn.

Cybersecurity Cooperation Clause

Recent PTAs often feature a provision dedicated to cybersecurity—under the title of "Cybersecurity,"[7] "Cooperation on Cybersecurity Matters,"[8] or "Cybersecurity Cooperation."[9]

However, given the complex nature of cybersecurity and the capacity gap among economies, the cybersecurity clauses typically take the form of "soft law" rather than "hard law"—they are not binding, enforceable commitments. Using the expressions "recognize," "shall endeavor to," or something along this line, these PTAs seek to shape the confidence in digital trade and focus on capacity building and information sharing. To illustrate, let us consider some of the US-led PTAs. Article 19.15 of the United States–Mexico–Canada Agreement (USMCA) states that:

> (a) 1. The Parties recognize that threats to cybersecurity undermine confidence in digital trade. Accordingly, the Parties shall endeavor to:
>
> 7.2.1.1 build the capabilities of their respective national entities responsible for cybersecurity incident response; and
>
> 7.2.1.2 strengthen existing collaboration mechanisms for cooperating to identify and mitigate malicious intrusions or dissemination of malicious code that affect electronic networks, and use those mechanisms to swiftly address cybersecurity incidents, as well as for the sharing of information for awareness and best practices.

---

[7] Agreement between the United States of America, the United Mexican States, and Canada (USMCA), Chapter 28, 30 November 2018, Article 19.15; Agreement between the United States and Japan Concerning Digital Trade (US–Japan DTA), signed 7 October 2019, Article 19; Regional Comprehensive Economic Partnership Agreement (RCEP), Article 12.13.

[8] Comprehensive and Progressive Agreement for Trans-Pacific Partnership (CPTPP), Chapter 25, 8 March to 30 December 2018, [2018] A.T.S. 23 (incorporating, by reference, the provisions from the Trans-Pacific Partnership), Article 14.16.

[9] Digital Economy Partnership Agreement (DEPA), Chile–New Zealand–Singapore, NZTS. B2020-02, signed 12 June 2020, Article 5.1.

The US–Japan Digital Trade Agreement (US–Japan DTA) also features a cybersecurity provision (Article 19), copied nearly word for word from Article 19.15 of the USMCA. Likewise, Article 14.16 of the Comprehensive and Progressive Agreement for Trans-Pacific Partnership (CPTPP) provides that the signatories recognize the importance of "building the capabilities of their national entities responsible for computer security incident response," and collaboration to "identify and mitigate malicious intrusions or dissemination of malicious code" that affect their electronic networks.

Arrangements of this sort can also be found in PTAs that involve Asian economies, such as the Regional Comprehensive Economic Partnership (RCEP),[10] the world's largest trading bloc with a diverse group of nations—including ASEAN states; the Digital Economy Partnership Agreement (DEPA), between New Zealand, Singapore, and Chile;[11] and the Australia–Singapore Digital Economy Agreement (DEA),[12] among others.

Notably, DEPA and the Australia–Singapore DEA have two unique features compared with others. First, while they both recognize the role of capacity building, they underscore in particular the importance of "workforce development in the area of cybersecurity, including through possible initiatives relating to mutual recognition of qualifications, diversity and equality."[13] Second, both DEPA and the Australia–Singapore DEA add a provision called "Online Safety and Security" or "Creating a Safe Online Environment" on top of a general clause on cybersecurity.[14] Article 5.2 of DEPA, for instance, reads:

(1) The Parties recognise that a safe and secure online environment supports the digital economy.

(2) The Parties recognise the importance of taking a multi-stakeholder approach to addressing online safety and security issues.

(3) The Parties shall endeavour to cooperate to advance collaborative solutions to global issues affecting online safety and security.

It is also noteworthy that, while new PTAs do not require signatories to adopt specific legislation, some do highlight the "risk-based" approach as a guiding principle for parties to regulate cybersecurity. USMCA Article 19.15 states:

---

[10] RCEP, Article 12.13.

[11] DEPA, Article 5.1

[12] Australia–Singapore DEA, effective 8 December 2020, Article 34.

[13] DEPA, Article 5.1. Note, however, that Article 34 (2)(c) of the Australia–Singapore DEA contains similar language: "The Parties recognise the importance of (c) workforce development in the area of cybersecurity, including possible initiatives relating to mutual recognition of qualifications, diversity and equality."

[14] DEPA, Article 5.2; Australia–Singapore DEA, Article 18.

2. Given the evolving nature of cybersecurity threats, the Parties recognize that risk-based approaches may be more effective than prescriptive regulation in addressing those threats. Accordingly, each Party shall endeavor to employ, and encourage enterprises within its jurisdiction to use, risk-based approaches that rely on consensus-based standards and risk management best practices to identify and protect against cybersecurity risks and to detect, respond to, and recover from cybersecurity events.

This risk-based approach is consistent with the recommendation of the Organisation for Economic Co-operation and Development (OECD), which states that the "treatment of the risk should aim to reduce the risk to an acceptable level relative to the economic and social benefits expected from those activities while taking into account the potential impact on the legitimate interests of others" (OECD 2015). [15]

Cross-Border Data Flow and Data Localization

As noted, it is not uncommon to see economies restrict cross-border data flow or mandate local data storage in the name of cybersecurity or data protection. Consider, for instance, data localization measures. Although some cast doubt on its role in combating cybercrime (Chander and Uyên 2015), others consider data localization an effective tool for law enforcement authorities to gather evidence to identify and arrest cybercriminals (Selby 2017). For some nations, it is argued that, data localization can help resolve the practical difficulty of accessing evidence through the Mutual Law Enforcement Assistance Treaty and lessen the comparative disadvantage in intelligence agencies (Selby 2017). In recent years, trade policy makers have reacted to the growing concerns by committing to cross-border data flow—subject to certain conditions—and restricting data localization measures.

The CPTPP is, again, a prime example. Article 14.11, while recognizing there may be different regulatory approaches toward data transfer, requires that the "Party shall allow the cross-border transfer of information by electronic means, including personal information, when this activity is for the conduct of the business of a covered person." Article 14.13 further provides that data localization measures are prohibited unless they meet certain qualifications:

---

[15] In this regard, regulatory frameworks of, notably, the US, the EU, and Australia also underscore the risk-based approach. See, for example, Australian Cyber Security Centre. Using the Information Security Manual. Canberra. https://www.cyber.gov.au/acsc/view-all-content/advice/using-information-security-manual (accessed 21 July 2022).

2. No Party shall require a covered person to use or locate computing facilities in that Party's territory as a condition for conducting business in that territory.

3. Nothing in this Article shall prevent a Party from adopting or maintaining measures inconsistent with paragraph 2 to achieve a legitimate public policy objective, if the measure: (a) is not applied in a manner which would constitute a means of arbitrary or unjustifiable discrimination or a disguised restriction on trade; and (b) does not impose restrictions on the use or location of computing facilities greater than are required to achieve the objective.

In other words, the CPTPP attempts to facilitate digital trade by balancing cross-border information flow and the public interests of the signatories. USMCA Articles 19.11 and 19.12, US–Japan DTA Articles 11 and 12, DEPA Articles 4.3 and 4.4, Australia–Singapore DEA Articles 17 and 24, and RCEP Articles 12.14 and 12.15 generally follow a similar logic, though with some variants.

Some observations are warranted. First, some of these new PTAs contain references to the principles or guidelines developed by relevant international bodies in crafting their regulatory frameworks on personal information protection or facilitating cross-border data flow. For instance, Article 17 of the Australia–Singapore DEA refers to the APEC Cross-Border Privacy Rules as a "valid mechanism to facilitate cross-border information transfer while protecting information."

Second, the US–Japan DTA extends the data localization provision to cover "Financial Services Computing Facilities for Covered Financial Services Suppliers" (Article 13). Third, while the RCEP and the CPTPP ban data localization, certain flexibility is made available to developing economies in terms of enforcement timelines.

Nondisclosure of Source Code

Requiring source codes can sometimes be framed as a matter of cybersecurity regulation (Meltzer and Kerry 2019). Some of the recent PTAs have addressed this concern. For instance, CPTPP Article 14.17 reads:

1. No Party shall require the transfer of, or access to, source code of software owned by a person of another Party, as a condition for the import, distribution, sale, or use of such software, or of products containing such software, in its territory.

2. For the purposes of this Article, software subject to paragraph 1 is limited to mass-market software or products containing such software and does not include software used for critical infrastructure.

3. Nothing in this Article shall preclude: (a) the inclusion or implementation of terms and conditions related to the provision

of source code in commercially negotiated contracts; or (b) a Party from requiring the modification of source code of software necessary for that software to comply with laws or regulations which are not inconsistent with this Agreement.

4. This Article shall not be construed to affect requirements that relate to patent applications or granted patents, including any orders made by a judicial authority in relation to patent disputes, subject to safeguards against unauthorized disclosure under the law or practice of a Party.

Source code provisions also exist in other US-led PTAs, such as USMCA Article 19.16 and US–Japan DTA Article 17. It can also be found in Article 28 of the Australia–Singapore DEA. However, neither the DEPA nor the RCEP has such a clause, except a reference in Article 12.16 of RCEP that mentions "current and emerging issues, such as ... source code" shall be considered when signatories have a dialogue on e-commerce.

Nondisclosure of Encryption Technologies

As in the case of source codes, forced transfer of encryption technologies can also be framed—though not necessarily justifiably—as part of cybersecurity matters. The CPTPP is the first PTA that responds to it. In Annex 8-B, Section A, entitled "Information and Communication Technology (ICT) Products that Use Cryptography," the CPTPP defines *cryptography* as "the principles, means or methods for the transformation of data to hide its information content, prevent its undetected modification or prevent its unauthorized use; and is limited to the transformation of information using one or more secret parameters, for example, crypto variables, or associated key management," and refers to *encryption* as the conversion of data (plaintext) into a form that cannot be easily understood without subsequent reconversion (ciphertext) through the use of a cryptographic algorithm."[16] It then prohibits governments from requiring transfer or access to specific technologies as a condition for market access. In the relevant part, it states:

3. With respect to a product that uses cryptography and is designed for commercial applications, no Party shall impose or maintain a technical regulation or conformity assessment procedure that requires a manufacturer or supplier of the product, as a condition of the manufacture, sale, distribution, import or use of the product, to:

---

[16] CPTPP, Annex 8-B.2. Liu (2017) provides a legal and geopolitical analysis.

(a) transfer or provide access to a particular technology, production process or other information, for example, a private key or other secret parameter, algorithm specification or other design detail, that is proprietary to the manufacturer or supplier and relates to the cryptography in the product, to the Party or a person in the Party's territory;

(b) partner with a person in its territory; or

(c) use or integrate a particular cryptographic algorithm or cipher, other than where the manufacture, sale, distribution, import or use of the product is by or for the government of the Party.[17]

However, the CPTPP also considers the needs of public law enforcement by clarifying that this section "shall not be construed to prevent a Party's law enforcement authorities from requiring service suppliers using encryption they control to provide, pursuant to that Party's legal procedures, unencrypted communications."[18] USMCA Article 12.C.2, US–Japan DTA Article 21, DEPA Article 3.4, and Australia–Singapore DEA Article 7 feature similar arrangements, though there is no analogous clause in the RCEP.

Memorandums of Understanding

Beyond trade negotiations, some economies have or are currently engaging one another through an informal, nonbinding memorandum of understanding (MOU) to facilitate regulatory cooperation on cybersecurity. Australia is a notable example. It has signed MOUs with Singapore, Indonesia, Papua New Guinea, Thailand, and others in relation to cybersecurity matters.[19] These MOUs feature similar language as seen in the cybersecurity clause in recent PTAs mentioned above—though they often provide more detail.

---

[17] CPTPP, Annex 8-B.3.

[18] CPTPP, Annex 8-B.5

[19] Australia–Singapore MOU on Cybersecurity Cooperation. https://www.csa.gov.sg/news/press-releases/singapore-signs-mou-with-australia-to-enhance-cybersecurity-collaboration; MOU between the Government of the Republic of Indonesia and the Government of Australia on Cyber Cooperation (AU–Indonesia MOU on Cyber Cooperation). https://www.dfat.gov.au/international-relations/themes/cyber-affairs/Pages/mou-indonesia-australia-cyber-cooperation; MOU between the Government of Australia and the Government of Papua New Guinea Relating to Cybersecurity Cooperation (AU–PNG MOU on Cyber Security Cooperation). https://www.dfat.gov.au/international-relations/themes/cyber-affairs/Pages/mou-between-papua-new-guinea-and-australia-relating-to-cyber-security-cooperation; Australia–UK–Thailand MOU on Cyber and Digital Cooperation. https://www.dfat.gov.au/international-relations/themes/cyber-affairs/Pages/mou-on-cyber-and-digital-cooperation-australia-thailand.

The Australia–Indonesia MOU, for instance, emphasizes the significance of sharing information and best practice and capacity building. For capacity building, in particular, the MOU (paragraph 2) sets out more specific plans by stating that:

(i)   Participants will support skills and knowledge development in cyber security and cyber policy through short-term training programs and long-term awards (including scholarships for master's and PhD programs);

(ii) Participants will facilitate links between institutions working in the field of cyber security including government, business, or private sector and academia;

(iii) Participants will explore linking research institutions and universities to strengthen teaching and research outcomes in cyber affairs; and

(iv) Participants will explore opportunities to promote international law, norms, and responsible behaviors in cyberspace.

Nevertheless, these MOUs go beyond the typical cybersecurity clause in the PTAs by addressing cybercrime issues or institutionalizing regulatory cooperation. On the former, for instance, the Australia–Indonesia MOU has a provision that both parties "will promote stronger cyber forensic and investigation capacities" (paragraph 2). On the latter, the MOU between Australia and Papua New Guinea states that both will work toward its objectives through a series of "Joint Cybersecurity Initiatives"—funded by Australia—including "establishment of a Cyber Security Operations Centre" to monitor threats and controls, and "enhancement of Papua New Guinea's newly established Computer Emergency Response Team," among others (paragraph 5).

These MOUs on engagement in cybersecurity should be considered with recent regional efforts. The ASEAN's Political-Security Community Blueprint 2025 has addressed the need to combat cybercrimes through regional collaboration (ASEAN Secretariat 2016). In 2019, the ASEAN also issued a "Statement on Cybersecurity Cooperation" with the European Union,[20] and "Joint Chairs' Statement" following its Cyber Policy Dialogue with Australia.[21] More broadly, in the context of APEC, various initiatives are working toward the same goal. For instance, the APEC Cybersecurity Strategy, developed by the APEC Information Working Group in 2002, identified six issue areas—legal developments, information sharing and cooperation initiative, security and technical

---

[20] ASEAN Secretariat. ASEAN–EU Statement on Cybersecurity Cooperation. https://asean.org/asean-eu-statement-on-cybersecurity-cooperation (accessed July 2022)

[21] Government of Australia, Department of Foreign Affairs and Trade. Joint Chairs' Statement: ASEAN-Australia Cyber Policy Dialogue. https://www.dfat.gov.au/international-relations/themes/cyber-affairs/Pages/joint-chairs-statement-asean-australia-cyber-policy-dialogue (accessed July 2022).

guidelines, public awareness, training and education, and wireless security to "serve as the basis of APEC's efforts on cybercrime and critical infrastructure protection"(NATO CCDCOE 2018). This was followed by the APEC Strategy to Ensure Trusted, Secure and Sustainable Online Environment and the APEC Framework for Securing the Digital Economy (APEC 2005, 2019).

There are, of course, other instruments to help build trust in cyberspace and facilitate digital trade. Certification schemes created by the EU Cybersecurity Act[22] and the development of relevant international standards by international standard-setting bodies such as the International Organization for Standardization (ISO) (Dupendant 2016) are prime examples.

8.4   Conclusion

Ensuring cybersecurity and preventing cybercrime is essential for promoting digital trade in services. Digital trade in services will not be successful if the users and clients cannot trust each other. This is especially important for LDCs where digital services are flourishing as the internet expands. It is challenging for these economies to put more resources into issues relating to cybersecurity and cybercrime, given the many priorities competing for government expenditure.

Inquiries so far lead us to make several general recommendations. First, a consensus has formed that cybersecurity presents significant issues across the global supply chain. However, different laws and policies introduced in the name of cybersecurity—which sometimes is framed and elevated as a national security issue—have raised trade barrier concerns in recent years. Such policies not only shape cyberspace within economies, they also increase transaction and communication costs for all economies by fragmenting the internet.

Second, and relatedly, while some regulatory responses may be overreactions and unnecessary to achieve their legitimate policy purposes, one should not overlook the issues around underreaction. Developing economies and LDCs have a daunting task to grapple with the mixed opportunities of ICT. While digital technologies help accelerate social and economic development, they come with costs. Cybercrimes are borderless, as this chapter has noted. Developing economies—particularly LDCs with inadequate regulatory frameworks and limited human capacity and financial resources—find it challenging to react to these threats effectively (ITU 2022). It is problematic for economies to tap into the booming internet and maximize socioeconomic benefits unless there

---

[22] European Union Agency for Cybersecurity (ENISA). EU Cybersecurity Certification Framework. https://www.enisa.europa.eu/topics/standards/certification (accessed July 2021).

is a secure infrastructure to protect the organizations' assets and resources at different levels—organizational, human, financial, and technical. It is also vital to prevent the clients of digital services and digital trade from becoming victims.

Third, to tackle the ramifications of these regulatory reactions (or lack thereof) for digital trade, there is a need for a new set of rules, which will require cooperation among like-minded economies. It could occur within the existing multilateral trading system—as in the WTO e-commerce negotiations or new PTAs. These new generation trade agreements have begun to reinvent the rules—ranging from cybersecurity cooperation, cross-border information flow, data localization, source code, to encryption. Some of these new rules are "harder" than others—particularly, at cooperation on cybersecurity. Moreover, some offer a grace period for developing economies and LDCs to gradually fit into the new setting. Such arrangements are welcome because they properly acknowledge the gap between economies with different endowments in handling cybersecurity matters. However, more actions are needed. Such a gap, as well as the trade concerns in connection with cybersecurity, can be moderated through other informal arrangements such as MOUs. Of course, the gap could also be narrowed if international organizations like the Asian Development Bank or others can play a more active role in assisting developing economies and LDCs in capacity building. Proper cooperation within and outside the WTO can therefore rebuild the trust in the online environment and facilitate the sustainable growth of global digital trade in the long term.

Bibliography

Asia-Pacific Economic Cooperation (APEC). 2005. *APEC Strategy to Ensure Trusted, Secure and Sustainable Online Environment* (Inter-Sessionally Endorsed of the Senior Officials in November 2005). https://www.apec.org/-/media/Files/Groups/TEL/05_TEL_APECStrategy.pdf.

———. 2019. *APEC Framework for Securing the Digital Economy.* https://www.apec.org/Publications/2019/11/APEC-Framework-for-Securing-the-Digital-Economy.

Asian Development Bank (ADB). 2021. *E-Commerce in CAREC Countries: Laws and Policies.* Manila.

ASEAN Secretariat. 2016. *ASEAN Political-Security Community Blueprint 2025.* Jakarta.

BBC News. 2021. Colonial Pipeline Boss 'Deeply Sorry' for Cyber Attack. 8 June. https://www.bbc.com/news/business-57403214.

Buckmaster, L., and T. Wils. 2019. *Parliamentary Library Briefing Book: Responding to Fake News.* Canberra: Parliament of Australia. https://www.aph.gov.au/

About_Parliament/Parliamentary_Departments/Parliamentary_Library/ pubs/BriefingBook46p/FakeNews.

Bunge, J., and J. Newman. 2021. Ransomware Attack Roiled Meat Giant JBS, Then Spilled Over to Farmers and Restaurants. *Wall Street Journal*. 11 June. https://www.wsj.com/articles/ransomware-attack-roiled-meat-giant-jbs-.

Chander, A. and P. L. Uyên. 2015. Data Nationalism. *Emory Law Journal*. 64 (3). pp. 732–733.

Chang, L. Y. C. 2012. *Cybercrime in the Greater China Region*. Cheltenham, UK: Edward Elgar.

———. 2017. Cybercrime and Cyber Security in ASEAN. In J. H. Liu, M. Travers. and L. Yao-Chung Chang , eds. *Comparative Criminology in Asia*. New York: Springer.

———. 2020. Legislative Frameworks Against Cybercrime: The Budapest Convention and Asia. In T. Holt and A. Bossler, eds. *The Palgrave Handbook of International Cybercrime and Cyberdeviance*. London: Palgrave Macmillan.

Dou, E. 2015. IBM Allows Chinese Government to Review Source Code. *Wall Street Journal*. 16 October. https://www.wsj.com/articles/ibm-allows-chinese-government-to-review-source-code-1444989039.

Dupendant, J. 2016. *International Regulatory Co-operation and International Organisations: The Case of the International Organization for Standardization (ISO)*. Paris: Organisation for Economic Co-operation and Development / Geneva: International Organization for Standardization.

Government of Australia, Department of Foreign Affairs and Trade (DFAT). 2021. *International Cyber and Critical Technology Engagement Strategy*. Canberra.

Grabosky, P. 2016. *Cybercrime*. Oxford: Oxford University Press.

Ikeda, S. 2021. Ransomware Attack Reported at Insurance Giant AXA One Week After It Changes Cyber Insurance Policies in France. *CPO Magazine*. 25 May. https://www.cpomagazine.com/cyber-security/ransomware-attack-reported-at-insurance-giant-axa-one-week-after-it-changes-cyber-insurance-policies-in-france/.

International Telecommunication Union (ITU). 2022. *Enhancing Cybersecurity in Least Developed Countries*. Geneva.

Interpol. 2021. Interpol Report Charts Top Cyberthreats in Southeast Asia. 22 January. https://www.interpol.int/en/News-and-Events/News/2021/ INTERPOL-report-charts-top-cyberthreats-in-Southeast-Asia.

Kissel, R., ed. 2013. Glossary of Key Information: Security Terms. *NIST Interagency or Internal Report*. 7298 Rev. 2. Gaithersburg, MD: National Institute of Standards and Technology, US Department of Commerce.

Koh, D. 2020. The Geopolitics of Cybersecurity: Cooperation Among States Must Underpin Efforts to Create a Safer, More Secure, and Interoperable Cyberspace. *The Diplomat.* 9 December. https://thediplomat.com/2020/12/the-geopolitics-of-cybersecurity/.

Liu, H. W. 2017. Inside the Black Box: Political Economy of the Trans-Pacific Partnership's Encryption Clause. *Journal of World Trade.* 51 (2). pp. 309–334.

———. 2019. Data Localization and Digital Trade Barriers: ASEAN in Megaregionalism. In P. L. Hsieh and B. Mercurio, eds. *ASEAN Law in the New Regional Economic Order: Global Trends and Shifting Paradigms.* Cambridge, UK: Cambridge University Press.

McGuire, M., and S. Dowling. 2013. Cybercrime: A Review of the Evidence. *Research Report.* 75. October. London: United Kingdom Home Office.

Meltzer, J. P. and C. F. Kerry. 2019. *Cybersecurity and Digital Trade: Getting it Right.* Washington, DC: The Brookings Institution.

Microsoft. 2016. Platinum: Targeted Attacks in South and Southeast Asia. *Microsoft Security Intelligence Report.* 20. Redmond, WA.

Mitchell, A. D., and J. Hepburn. 2017. Don't Fence Me In: Reforming Trade and Investment Law to Better Facilitate Cross-Border Data Transfer. *Yale Journal of Law and Technology.* 19. pp. 182–237.

NATO Cooperative Cyber Defence Centre of Excellence (CCDCOE). 2018. *APEC Cyber Security Strategy.* https://ccdcoe.org/uploads/2018/10/APEC-020823-CyberSecurityStrategy.pdf.

Organisation for Economic Co-operation and Development (OECD). 2015. *Digital Security Risk Management for Economic and Social Prosperity: OECD Recommendation and Companion Document.* Paris: OECD Publishing.

Selby, J. 2017. Data Localization Laws: Trade Barriers or Legitimate Responses to Cybersecurity Risks, or Both? *International Journal of Law and Information Technology.* 25 (3). pp. 213–232.

Smith, R., P. Grabosky, and G. Urbas. 2001. *Cyber Criminals on Trial.* Cambridge, UK: Cambridge University Press.

Thomas, J. 2019. Ransomware Could Cripple ASEAN. *The ASEAN Post.* 10 September. https://theaseanpost.com/article/ransomware-could-cripple-asean.

Tidy, J. 2022. Security Warning After Sale of Stolen Chinese Data. *BBC.* 9 July. https://www.bbc.com/news/technology-62097594.

Voon, T. 2019. The Security Exception in WTO Law: Entering a New Era. *AJIL Unbound.* 113. pp. 45–50.

Wall, D. S. 2007. *Cybercrime: The Transformation of Crime in the information Age.* Cambridge, UK: Polity Press.

World Trade Organization (WTO). 2020. *Negotiations on e-Commerce Continue, Eyeing a Consolidated Text by the End of the Year.* 23 October. https://www.wto.org/english/news_e/news20_e/ecom_26oct20_e.htm.

Xiao, B. 2022. Private Information of More Than 100 Australians Exposed Amid Huge China Police Data Leak. *ABC.* 8 July. https://www.abc.net.au/news/2022-07-08/australian-citizens-exposed-in-shanghai-police-data-leak/101214904.

TRADE IN DIGITAL SERVICES AND INTERNATIONAL TAXATION: IMPLICATIONS FOR DEVELOPING ASIA

Bruno da Silva and Rolando Avendano

The rise of the digital economy has offered opportunities to expand trade in digital services in Asia and the Pacific. Technology firms and digital intermediation platforms from the region are leading the expansion by delivering traditional services through digital tools and providing a range of new digitally intensive services. As digital service providers do not need physical retail presence to operate, their expansion has created scope for firms to lower taxable income artificially, with potential losses of revenue in the jurisdiction where profits are generated. The rapid emergence of technology firms in Asia means that these taxation losses could be more significant than in other developing regions.

Reforms of international tax rules endorsed by 137 jurisdictions will be important for Asia's prospects on digital services trade. Proposals for new nexus and profit allocation rules for taxing rights beyond physical presence directly target automated digital service providers. As the region hosts some of the largest providers of digital services, a global minimum tax may impact the sector. In parallel, Asian economies have gradually introduced measures to levy indirect taxes on imported digitally delivered services. Some economies have also adopted unilateral tax measures on digital services. Understanding their impact and ensuring consistency with trade rules and regional agreements are essential.

9.1 Digital Services Tax Models in Asia and the Pacific

Concerns over multinationals tax avoidance practices have been raised in the context of the Organisation for Economic Co-operation and Development (OECD)/G20 Base Erosion and Profit Shifting initiative since 2013, with the increasing role of digitalization underscoring the need to adapt the international tax framework. Digital services are part of the discussion because they rely on features bringing challenges to national tax systems: reduced need for physical presence, reliance on data and other intangible assets, and growing mobility of business processes and users. In response to these challenges, several economies have adopted unilateral measures targeting digital services to enhance tax revenues (Noonan and Plekhanova 2020). Most unilateral measures taken by Asian economies in the area of digital services can be classified into four main categories:

Digital permanent establishment. Measures to introduce amendments to domestic nexus rules to accommodate the concept of permanent establishment (PE) have been adopted in the region. These measures aim to expand the definition of nexus by accounting for significant economic presence and allowing for the taxation of profits of a nonresident corporation regardless of its physical presence in the taxing jurisdiction. Changes to the PE model include, for example, steps that base economic presence on local revenue or the number of users.

Indirect taxes on imported digital services. Economies can impose a value-added tax (VAT) or goods and services tax (GST) on goods and services that are supplied in their territory, impacting the services sectors such as internet advertising and digital intermediation services. Several Asian economies have made progress in adopting nondiscriminatory VAT or GST rules in relation to cross-border transactions.[1]

Withholding taxes. Some economies have expanded the scope of withholding taxes and the use of sector turnover taxes. A state can use a withholding tax by classifying business profits as royalties, or by introducing a fee for online digital services. The Philippines and Malaysia, for example, have included payments for the right to use software, visual images, or sound transmissions under the scope of royalties. Nonresidents providing digital services in the local market can be required to establish a local office and be subject to income tax. This often falls outside trade agreements and double taxation agreements.

Digital services taxes. These are taxes levied on the supply of a category of e-services, charged at a fixed rate, and generally applied at the place where the services are supplied. They have gained traction among economies as they are not covered by double taxation agreements. Digital services taxes (DSTs) can vary in scope of activities, revenue thresholds, and tax rates.

Table 9.1 provides a summary of recent unilateral measures covering digital services taken by Asian economies. Measures diverge in scope, mechanism, and sector, with some targeting e-commerce as well as a variety of digital services.

[1] International guidelines have been developed for making digital platforms liable for assessing, collecting, and remitting the VAT or GST due on the online sales they facilitate (OECD 2020).

Table 9.1: Recent Digital Services Tax Measures in Selected Asian Economies

Economy	Status	Effectivity Date	Type	Description
India	Enacted	1 April 2022	Digital PE	Revenue related to the digital PE
	Enacted	1 October 2020	WHT	Gross amount of sale of goods or provision of service facilitated through digital or electronic facility or platform
	Enacted	1 June 2016	Equalization levy	Gross amount of online advertising payments
	Enacted	1 April 2020	Equalization levy	Online sale of goods, provision of services or services facilitation (when operatory provides platform for others to supply service)
Indonesia	Enacted	31 March 2020	Digital PE	Revenue related to the digital PE
	Enacted	31 March 2020	Electronic transaction tax	Imposed on e-commerce sales when the digital PE cannot be applied due to the provision of a tax treaty
Japan	Announced	8 March 2021		Currently in discussion. Tax measures the allocation of tax rights to market economies (Pillar 1) for digital companies and the like, and evaluation of a DST based on case studies in other economies
Malaysia	Enacted	13 May 2019	WHT	
Pakistan	Enacted	1 July 2018	WHT	Payments for offshore digital services (online advertising, designing, creating, hosting or maintenance of websites, uploading, storing or distributing digital content, etc.) performed by nonresident persons
Singapore	Waiting for global solution	7 Dec 2020		To be based on international consensus on issues relating to the taxation of the digital economy
Taipei,China	Enacted	24 July 2019		Payments for online advertisement for e-services (online games, videos, audio broadcast, movies, music platform services, etc.) supplied to Taipei,China customers by foreign service providers without fixed place of business or business agent in Taipei,China (ESS providers)

continued on next page

Table 9.1 *continued*

Economy	Status	Effectivity Date	Type	Description
Thailand	Proposed	To be determined	WHT	Income from e-commerce supplies of goods and services, including online advertising, gaming, shopping, and others
Türkiye	Enacted	1 March 2020	DST	Gross revenue derived from in-scope services (i.e., digital advertising services; sales of any audible, visual, or digital content services for the provision and operation of a digital platform)
Viet Nam	Enacted	1 January 2021	WHT	Income derived by nonresidents from digital and e-commerce operations in Viet Nam

DST = digital services trade, PE = permanent establishment, WHT = withholding tax.

Sources: International Monetary Fund (2021); KPMG (2021); and national tax administrations.

9.2. International Tax Reforms: Implications for Digital Services Trade

9.2.1. A New Right to Tax without Physical Presence

An important component of the agreement reached by members of the OECD/G20 Inclusive Framework in October 2021 is the creation a new taxing right to market economies which is independent from physical presence. The new taxing right allows to overcome the limitations of the PE concept (either the fixed base or dependent agent as provided in Article 5 of Double Tax Treaties) and to prevent double taxation.

Pillar One in the multilateral solution brings together three previously competing proposals into one solution.

Amount A: Setting a New Taxing Right Based on the Residual Profit of Multinationals

Amount A provides for a new taxing right on the residual profit of multinational enterprises (MNEs) when they meet a threshold in size and profitability. It refers to a certain percentage of the deemed "residual profit" of an MNE. Amount A is based on global financial accounts of profit before taxes where part of the income is allocated to jurisdictions based on a pro rata revenue allocation. The new taxing right allows for market jurisdictions (those where goods and services are consumed) to tax part of the MNE's profits even in the absence of physical taxable presence. Amount A is applicable to all MNEs that meet two quantitative thresholds: a global turnover exceeding €20 billion (which may be reduced to €10 billion after 7 years of its implementation), and a profitability threshold above 10%. These MNEs will be subject to Amount A liability irrespective of the type of activity developed.

In addition, a significant part of that global revenue needs to be derived from foreign sources (the "*de minimis* foreign source in-scope revenue test"). Therefore, in-scope MNEs will be the ones deriving at least €1 million in revenue from a particular jurisdiction. For smaller jurisdictions with GDP lower than €40 billion, the nexus will be set at €250,000. This nexus rule will apply solely to determine whether a jurisdiction qualifies for the Amount A allocation. However, extractives and regulated financial services will be excluded.

Amount B: A Fixed Return for Marketing and Distribution Activities

Amount B proposes a fixed return for standard ("baseline") marketing and distribution activities taking place physically in a market jurisdiction. It is based on the arm's length principle. It tries to create a simplified approach to deal with market distributors. Contrarily to Amount A, it could be applicable to all MNE groups. The genesis behind Amount B is the perception that a significant number of disputes under the Mutual Agreement Procedure have dealt with determining the appropriate remuneration for marketing and distribution functions and that developing economies experienced particular difficulties in dealing with these transfer pricing disputes. Therefore, Amount B seeks to simplify the administrative burden put on tax administrations, lower the compliance costs for taxpayers, enhance tax certainty, and reduce tax disputes. For that purpose, it sets a fixed return—that is deemed to be in accordance with the existing arm's length principle—for marketing and distribution functions.

Tax Certainty

The third fundamental component of Pillar One is an overall enforcement of tax certainty through innovative and effective dispute prevention and resolution mechanisms. While aspects of the agreement need to be completed, multinationals headquartered in Asia and the Pacific will likely generate a significant share of the residual profit to be reallocated among jurisdictions, with a disproportional contribution from information and communication technology and technology firms (IMF 2021).

Pillar One also aims to improve tax certainty through innovative and effective dispute prevention and resolution mechanisms (Box 9.1).

Box 9.1. A Dispute Prevention and Resolution Mechanism for Taxing Rights

The Organisation for Economic Co-operation and Development Pillar One Blueprint proposes a mandatory binding dispute prevention procedure to provide early certainty on the application of the new taxing right. For the assessment of the filed Amount A self-assessment return and dispute resolution, a similar procedure would apply. The multinational enterprise (MNE) group would submit a request to apply the early certainty procedure to the "lead" tax administration (which should correspond to the country where the ultimate parent entity is located). The lead tax administration would conduct an initial review of the request to assess whether a review panel is needed.

For the assessment of a filed Amount A self-assessment return or a dispute resolution request, this would also first be reviewed by the lead tax administration to make such an assessment. If the lead tax administration concludes that a panel review is needed, a panel comprising representatives of six to eight affected tax administrations would be set up. Besides the lead tax authority, this panel would consist of jurisdictions from which relief is sought and recipient market jurisdictions under Amount A. The conclusion reached by the panel could be accepted or rejected by the MNE group. If the review panel is unable to reach a conclusion, a "determination panel" would be constituted with the obligation to reach a decision.

The outcome of this process would be binding for the MNE group and the tax administrations involved. If the MNE group does not accept the review or determination panel's decision, it may withdraw its request and use domestic administrative and judicial review procedures in the respective jurisdictions. For issues beyond Amount A, the Pillar One Blueprint proposes to improve existing dispute prevention mechanisms and develop new ones.

Source: OECD (2021).

Implementation

To ensure proper implementation of Pillar One, model rules have been developed within the OECD Inclusive Framework, with three main spheres for implementation:

- **Domestic legislation to create taxing rights consistent with the design of Amount A.** Each jurisdiction part of the agreement on Pillar One should adopt rules like identifying taxpayers, tax base, taxable period, tax rates, all consistent with Amount A design.
- **Public international law to overcome obstacles in tax treaties as regards Amount A.** This should be achieved with the development of a new multilateral convention. This new self-standing multilateral treaty would rule the implementation of Amount A. It is required as to overcome

existing treaty barriers such as Article 7 (Business Profits) of Double Tax Treaties. The Multilateral Convention will supersede bilateral tax treaties in force. It will also ensure a coordinated and consistent approach, for dealing with identifying paying entities and who bears the double tax relief. The same applies as regards the new tax certainty process.

- **Guidance to supplement the domestic and international legislation.** Its role will be to support and supplement domestic legislation and provisions of public international law. The Multilateral Convention and domestic law will be the primary means of applying Pillar One and will contain detailed rules.

9.2.2 A Global Minimum Corporate Tax for Multinational Enterprises

A second key component of the multilateral agreement endorsed by 137 jurisdictions is that multinationals, regardless of their sector and country of operation, will pay a minimum 15% of corporate income tax. This Pillar Two gives economies the right to "tax back" profit that is currently taxed below the minimum agreed rate. It essentially operates as a "top-up" tax, up to the minimum rate.

Together with achieving a minimum taxation on income, Pillar Two aims to considerably reduce incentives of MNEs to shift profits to low-tax jurisdictions and strengthen the transparency and predictability for tax administrations and firms.

These goals are achieved with two sets of interrelated rules that protect source economies against base-eroding payments and ensure that all international businesses pay a minimum level of tax on the income in each jurisdiction in which they operate. The two sets of rules are discussed in the succeeding paragraphs.

The Subject to Tax Rule

The subject to tax rule (STTR) is a treaty-based provision that applies for certain payments (at least interest and royalties and also a list of other covered payments) between connected persons. The rule is applicable where payments are subject to a nominal rate below 9% at the level of the recipient. The nominal rate adjusted for reductions in the tax base directly related to the income or entity receiving it. It allows the source jurisdiction to impose a tax on the gross amount of the payment only up to the difference between the agreed minimum rate and the adjusted nominal tax rate on the payment. The amount is creditable under the effective tax rate (ETR) of the second set of rules, the GloBe rules. In other words, the amount charged through the application of the STTR will be accounted for when calculating the ETR in the context of the application of the GloBE rules described below.

GloBE Rules

GloBE rules involve the income inclusion rule (IIR) and the undertaxed payments rule (UTPR) that operate through domestic legislation.[2]
    The IIR is the primary rule, while the UTPR works as a backstop. Both apply under the same €750 million threshold as the country-by-country reporting and exclude the same entities as under Pillar One. The mechanism for applying these rules is by reference to the effective tax rate by jurisdiction. Whenever the ETR in a jurisdiction is below the minimum agreed rate there will be a top-up tax percentage to bring the ETR in that jurisdiction up to the minimum rate of 15%. The calculation of the effective tax rate corresponds to the ratio of adjusted covered taxes paid over the net GloBE income obtained in the jurisdiction. A substance-based income exclusion allows to reduce the amount of GloBE income (Box 9.2). The substance-based income exclusion is based on a fixed return of payroll expenses in a jurisdiction and a fixed percentage of the carrying value of tangible assets in a jurisdiction. The IIR operates like a controlled foreign company rule. The UTPR is applicable when the IIR cannot be applied—i.e., when the top-up tax has not been caught under the IIR.
    There is, however, a *de minimis* exclusion for jurisdictions where the MNE has aggregated revenues of less than €10 million and profits of less than €1 million. These conditions are cumulative and when met, the MNE does not have to compute the ETR—and consequently potentially apply to GloBE rules—in the respective jurisdiction. This *de minimis* exclusion is justified by the fact that the top-up tax that could be collected under GloBE rules would not be as significant as the compliance and administrative burden related to the calculation of the ETR and application of the GloBE rules.
    An important element for jurisdictions is the option to adopt a qualified domestic minimum top-up tax (QDMTT). In applying the GloBE rules in a jurisdiction, it is relevant to analyze whether a constituent entity that is otherwise low taxed is subject to a QDMTT. The QMDTT reduces the jurisdictional top-up tax (eventually to 0). The QMDTT may be of relevance to prevent the tax base of otherwise low-taxed income from moving to another jurisdiction due to being caught by the application of the GloBE rules. In other words, the QMDTT offers the possibility for jurisdictions with the ETR below the minimum rate to collect the additional tax up to the minimum rate, preventing such tax difference from

---

[2] The IIR may be complemented by the switch over rule (SoR), which is also a treaty-based rule and aims to facilitate the application of the IIR whenever a country applies the exemption method in tax treaties to relief double taxation of business profits.

moving to another jurisdiction via the application of the IIR or the UTPR. In order to meet the condition of being "qualified," a QMDTT must have the following characteristics: (i) it determines the excess profits of the constituent entity in a manner equivalent to the GloBE rules; (ii) it increases domestic tax liability with respect to domestic excess profits to the minimum rate; and (iii) it is implemented and administered in a way that is consistent with the outcomes provided by the GloBE rules and commentary, and provided that the jurisdiction provides no benefits in relation to such rules.

Box 9.2: Substance-Based Income Exclusion

The substance-based income exclusion is relevant to determine the excess profit, which corresponds to the amount of profits to which the top-up tax percentage is applied (i.e., the excess points between the agreed minimum tax rate of 15% and the effective tax rate in a jurisdiction). The substance-based income exclusion is calculated using payroll expenses and the carrying value (original cost minus depreciation) of tangible assets, and allows for exclusion of a fixed return, which is subtracted from the Net GloBE income as regards payroll expenses and tangible assets developed in a jurisdiction. These two activities are chosen because they are less mobile factors and therefore less likely to lead to tax induced behavior. The fixed return is 5%, but there is a transition period of 10 years in which the fixed return starts at 10% for payroll expenses and 8% for tangible assets. The initial percentage will be declining annually by 0.2 percentage points for the first 5 years, and by 0.4 percentage points for tangible assets and by 0.8 percentage points for payroll for the last 5 years.

Source: Regional consultation on international tax matters for Asia and the Pacific (June 2022).

Implementation

As regards to implementation, Pillar Two will require amendments to domestic and international laws. The GloBE implementation entails domestic law amendments, while the STTR requires changes as to existing bilateral tax treaties. Importantly, Pillar Two will be based on a common approach: economies will not be required to implement the rules but if they opt to do so, they should follow the agreed framework and rules order.

To ensure proper implementation and effective coordination of these rules, model legislation and guidance are being developed and combined with a multilateral review process for the implemented rules. It is expected that a process will identify what are considered low-tax jurisdictions for the purposes of STTR application, i.e., jurisdictions that apply a nominal tax of less than 9%. Furthermore, the development of a multilateral convention is also being considered. While a multilateral convention is not a prerequisite for the GloBE, it may be relevant for the coordinated implementation of the STTR. For the purposes of effective administration, an important design tool for Pillar Two would be a shared filing mechanism to ensure smooth exchange of MNEs' information and an appropriate mechanism for dispute prevention and resolution.

9.2.3   A New Provision for Double Taxation Treaties

In parallel to the multilateral solution, a new article in double tax treaties was approved in April 2021 under the United Nations (UN) Model Tax Convention as a solution to tax income from digital services. The approach takes into account concerns of feasibility, administrability, and distribution of taxing rights expressed by developing economies.[3] The new Article 12B entitles the source country to levy tax on gross income—typically through a withholding tax mechanism—on payments from automated digital services.[4] The right to tax income from digital services is granted to a contracting state where payment originates even if the service is provided in another jurisdiction.

The obligation to levy a tax is placed on the payer of the service, which should apply the provided double tax treaty rate whenever the recipient is the beneficial owner of that income. In contrast to the OECD/G20 Inclusive Framework Agreement, it does not require a new nexus rule or an alternative to the permanent establishment definition.[5]

Economies may introduce the new provision in the renegotiation of or signature of future double taxation treaties, which will need to be complemented by domestic legislation. They may also consider including some thresholds to limit the administrative burden for small-sized or new taxpayers. However, the renegotiation or conclusion of new double tax treaties is a burdensome process, also dependent on the relative bargaining power of developing economies and contracting partners as for the inclusion of this provision. The potential of this instrument will depend on the widespread inclusion of the provision in existing double taxation treaties.

---

[3] The UN Committee of Experts on International Cooperation in Tax Matters (UN Tax Committee) started this process in 2017, with the formation of the Subcommittee on Tax Challenges related to the Taxation of Digitalized Economy. The subcommittee considered several approaches to tax digitalized transactions from the perspective of developing countries.

[4] Examples of automated digital services include online advertising, supply of user data, social media platforms, cloud computing, online search engines, and online gaming.

[5] The new provision does not introduce any quantitative thresholds and applies to business-to-consumer services. While the applicable tax rate on digital services is to be negotiated bilaterally by the contracting parties in their respective double taxation treaties, a modest rate of 3%–4% is recommended.

In April 2022, Article 12B was included in the UN Model Tax Convention, and some developing economies may be considering its adoption given that double taxation treaties are intended to be simpler and easier to administer when compared with the complexities surrounding Amount A under Pillar One.

9.2.4 Extending Value-Added Tax to Digital Services

While developing a multilateral solution, economies have made efforts toward implementation of a framework to introduce VAT on imports of digitally delivered services and goods. An advantage of this approach is the consensus that rules establishing the allocation of VAT taxing rights are determined by the destination principle. Under this principle, the taxing right is located at the place of consumption. Tax administrations in Asia and the Pacific have made progress in this direction, allowing for compliance and revenue collection. Governments have also recognized that the VAT challenges of the digital economy require a globally coordinated response to ensure minimal cost and effective cooperation. International guidelines have been developed for making digital platforms liable for assessing, collecting, and remitting the VAT or GST due on the online sales they facilitate. Firm survey data also suggest VAT or GST rules for digital goods and services as their preferred alternative (WEF 2021).

As of 2021, more than 60 economies have adopted domestic legislation and undertaken reforms to capture VAT tax in digital services and low-value imported goods (Box 9.3). Most of these have implemented the vendor collection model, in which liability for tax payment rests with the nonresident services provider.

9.3 Policy Considerations for International Tax Reforms

Gains from increasing tax revenues may be modest. With implementation of the multilateral agreement starting in 2023, estimations suggest that the proposed reforms could increase global corporate income tax revenues by 6% or about $150 billion a year (OECD 2021).[6] Estimated gains from profit reallocation would be relatively modest (0.5% of global corporate income tax revenues) and larger among low- and middle-income economies. Revenues from a global minimum tax are estimated around 2%–4% of global corporate income tax, with larger gains for high-income economies. Recent estimates by the International Monetary Fund (2021) for Asia and the Pacific suggest a modest gain for economies in the region,

---

[6] These results assume that the US global intangible low-taxed income (GILTI) regime is replaced with a per-country minimum tax at a higher rate, leading to a considerably higher increase in revenues.

Box 9.3: VAT Digital Toolkit for Asia-Pacific

Introduced in March 2022, the VAT Digital Toolkit for Asia-Pacific aims to assist tax authorities in the region with the design and implementation of reforms to ensure the effective collection of value-added taxes (VAT) on e-commerce activities. VAT is a crucial source of tax revenue for several Asian economies, and challenges exist for tax collection on online services and digital products, and on online sales of low-value imported goods. Where no reforms have been implemented in response to digitalization, VAT revenue losses have increased, together with increasing competition for domestic firms with foreign suppliers.

The toolkit is based on core standards and principles reflected in a policy framework around four pillars: (i) creating the appropriate legal basis for jurisdictions to assert the right to impose VAT, (ii) ensuring VAT collection from nonresident suppliers through simplified registration and collection mechanisms, (iii) improving efficiency by requiring digital platforms to collect and remit VAT on sales carried through their platforms, and (iv) enhancing VAT compliance by nonresident suppliers and digital platforms.

The standards and recommendations have been implemented in over 70 jurisdictions with encouraging results, including improved VAT revenue collected and higher compliance. Efforts for improving VAT standards and recommendations aim to support economies' wider strategies to address the tax challenges from digitalization.

Source: OECD, World Bank Group, and ADB (2022).

with investment hubs and some economies potentially losing some tax revenue. Considering the heterogenous type of jurisdictions in Asia and the Pacific, the revenue impact of the multilateral solution may be wide-ranging.

Unilateral tax measures find favor but prompt retaliation and impact trade rules. While a multilateral solution is adopted, unilateral tax measures involving digital services are on the rise. These measures, however legitimate for raising tax revenue, have shown to be costly and potentially trigger retaliatory trade measures. From the perspective of businesses, they can also increase prices for consumers or result in suppliers not serving markets where measures are implemented. Estimations on the effects of trade retaliation measures to digital services taxes (DSTs) suggest a possible fall of global trade by 1% (OECD 2021). The most notable example of trade retaliation to unilateral tax measures probably comes from the United States (US). Following the adoption of DSTs by some economies, the US started a Section 301 of Trade Act investigations, considering that such measures could be discriminatory and inconsistent. As a result, the US imposed tariffs on goods imports from these economies. The measure was suspended while multilateral negotiations on international taxation at the OECD/G20 level were being finalized.[7]

The surge in unilateral measures stresses the importance of consistency between World Trade Organization (WTO) trade rules and the new international tax framework. While key provisions in the General Agreement on Trade in Services (GATS) relate to nondiscrimination, international trade rules do not comprehensively encompass taxation issues (Low 2020). From the WTO perspective, most concerns about DSTs are associated with ensuring nondiscrimination, which is based on most favored nation (MFN) and national treatment principles (Mavroidis 2020). As for goods, MFN rules under the GATS require that all WTO members receive the same treatment. The national treatment principle requires that service suppliers of other members be treated no less favorably than domestic suppliers. However, in contrast to goods, national treatment in services is negotiated sector by sector, and not all obligations apply for all services (Low 2020). The GATS also includes provisions allowing exceptions to the MFN and national treatment principles.[8] While DSTs differ in their mechanism, they will need to be analyzed under the GATS framework to establish whether they can lead to legal or actual discriminatory treatment.

As regional trade agreements gradually include more elaborate provisions for digital services trade, they will require further alignment with current proposals for international tax policy.[9]

A global minimum tax brings investment and competition challenges. While the adoption of a global minimum tax may improve tax revenue, it could also bring challenges for existing investment policy frameworks in the region. The global minimum tax may impact policies in developing Asia for attracting foreign direct investment through special investment regimes as the tax advantage provided to MNEs for investing may be neutralized—at least up to the minimum agreed tax rate—in the country where the ultimate parent of the multinational is based. Policy makers will need to consider in the coming years to what extent tax incentives for attracting investment can be implementable or effective under the new international tax framework.

Reforms in the international tax framework may also have implications for competition in digital services sectors. As cross-border digital services expand, the compliance of foreign digital service providers to register and remit VATs or

---

[7] US authorities found the introduction of a DST to be discriminatory in intent and effect. As a result, the US could levy duties of up to 25% on imports from France. This measure could probably lead to more retaliatory measures.

[8] These are related to the existence of a double taxation agreement, in the case of MFN, or to ensure "the equitable or effective" imposition of direct taxes.

[9] As of 2017, nearly 9% of the 275 existing regional trade agreements notified to the WTO specified a right to impose an internal tax or charge on digital products.

GSTs on their operations is increasingly important. A tax framework including foreign suppliers of digital services may be a mechanism to ensure they have the same opportunities as domestic suppliers.

Compliance and implementation measures will need to be developed. From the perspective of both governments and firms, implementation of the OECD/G20 Inclusive Framework multilateral solution will increase compliance costs while at the same time provide tax certainty. To ensure proper implementation, efforts to upgrade the current tax framework and tax practices will be needed. Jurisdictions will need to develop domestic legislation implemented in association with a multilateral review of the implemented rules. International law will need to be developed to overcome obstacles in tax treaties, in particular the development of a new multilateral convention that addresses existing treaty barriers such as Article 7 (Business Profits) of double taxation treaties. For tax administrations, an important design tool for the appropriate application of the agreement relies on the existence of a shared filing mechanism as to ensure an effective exchange of information on MNEs and appropriate mechanism for dispute prevention and resolution.

9.4   Conclusion

The benefits and risks of digital services taxes and other unilateral measures should be weighed carefully. While these measures can moderately increase tax revenue, economies need to consider the possible effects of their implementation. Evidence suggests that DSTs could lead to trade disputes with partner economies, trigger compensatory measures, and prompt MNEs to reconsider their investment in some sectors. Under the OECD/G20 Inclusive Framework, participating members have also agreed to refrain from imposing DSTs in the future. Looking forward, consistency between existing WTO rules and the international tax framework will be important. While WTO rules are not fully adaptable to the tax challenges of digital services, future negotiations on market access and national treatment commitments under the GATS could contribute to a more structured approach to the taxation of digital services.

Consensus has emerged on the adequacy and feasibility of alternative measures, in particular the implementation of rules to ensure effective VAT or GST collection on imported digital services. Developing Asia should continue to use VAT as a mechanism to capture cross-border digital transaction as a source of revenue. As a tax imposed on a destination principle, the taxing right under VAT is allocated to the jurisdiction in which consumption occurs, which encourages its applicability for digital services. Economies in the region can build on these examples to reduce administrative costs and improve compliance. While awaiting the implementation of the OECD/G20 Inclusive Framework Agreement, double tax treaties may provide another mechanism for granting taxing rights to digital services through the recently introduced Article 12B of the Model Tax Convention.

Although a multilateral agreement has been reached, regional and international cooperation will be essential to ensure its implementation. Notwithstanding the agreement, in developing Asia, consistent efforts will be needed to adapt and design new domestic legislation, upgrade double tax treaties, and account for other international law amendments. Regional cooperation can also contribute to ensuring effective exchange of information for tax purposes, developing appropriate mechanisms for dispute prevention and resolution on taxation, and technical assistance for modernization of tax administrations.

Jurisdictions in the region should consider assessing and eventually revising their preferential tax regimes so as to determine whether additional substance requirements are needed (to meet the substance-based income exclusion) and whether to introduce a qualified minimum domestic top-up tax.

Bibliography

Asian Development Bank (ADB). 2021. *Asian Economic Integration Report 2021: Making Digital Platforms Work for Asia and the Pacific.* Manila.

———. 2022. *Asian Development Outlook 2022: Strengthening Taxes for Sustainable Development.* Manila.

Bradbury, D., T. Hanappi, and A. Moore. 2018. Estimating the Fiscal Effects of Base Erosion and Profit Shifting: Data Availability and Analytical Issues. *Transnational Corporations.* 25 (2). pp. 91–106.

Eden, L. 2020. Winners and Losers: The OECD's Economic Impact Assessment of Pillar One. *Tax Management International Journal.* 49 (12). pp. 597–609.

Grimes, A., C. Ren, and P. Stevens. 2012. The Need for Speed: Impacts of Internet Connectivity on Firm Productivity. *Journal of Productivity Analysis.* 37. pp. 187–201.

Ikeda, S. 2021. Ransomware Attack Reported at Insurance Giant AXA One Week After It Changes Cyber Insurance Policies in France. *CPO Magazine.* 25 May. https://www.cpomagazine.com/cyber-security/ransomware-attack-reported-at-insurance-giant-axa-one-week-after-it-changes-cyber-insurance-policies-in-france/.

International Monetary Fund (IMF). 2021. Digitalization and Taxation in Asia. *Departmental Paper.* No. 2021/017. Washington, DC.

KPMG. 2021. *Taxation of the Digitalized Economy: Developments Summary.* May. Amstelveen.

Low, P. 2020. Digital Services Taxes, Trade and Development. *Working Paper.* No. 2020-07. Adelaide: University of Adelaide.

Mavroidis, P. C. 2020. And You Put the Load Right on Me: Digital Taxes, Tax Discrimination and Trade in Services. *Trade, Law and Development.* 12 (1). pp. 75–108.

Noonan, C., and V. Plekhanova. 2020. Taxation of Digital Services under Trade Agreements. *Journal of International Economic Law.* 23. pp. 1015–1039.

Organisation for Economic Co-operation and Development (OECD). 2018. *Tax Challenges Arising from Digitalisation—Interim Report 2018: Inclusive Framework on BEPS, OECD/G20 Base Erosion and Profit Shifting Project.* Paris: OECD Publishing.

——. 2019. *The Role of Digital Platforms in the Collection of VAT/GST on Online Sales.* Paris: OECD Publishing.

——. 2020. *Tax Challenges Arising from Digitalisation–Economic Impact Assessment: Inclusive Framework on BEPS, OECD/G20 Base Erosion and Profit Shifting Project.* Paris: OECD Publishing.

——. 2021. *Two-Pillar Solution to Address the Tax Challenges Arising from the Digitalisation of the Economy.* October. Paris: OECD Publishing.

OECD, World Bank Group, and ADB. 2022. *VAT Digital Toolkit for Asia-Pacific.* https://www.oecd.org/tax/consumption/vat-digital-toolkit-for-asia-pacific.pdf.

United Nations (UN). 2020. *Committee of Experts on International Cooperation in Tax Matters, 20th Session.* E/C.18.2020/CRP.25. 30 May. New York.

——. 2021. *Committee of Experts on International Cooperation in Tax Matters, 22nd Session.* E/C.18/2021/CRP.16. April. New York.

World Economic Forum (WEF). 2021. Digital Trade in Services and Taxation. *White Paper.* October. https://www.weforum.org/whitepapers/digital-trade-in-services-andtaxation.

10 CONCLUSIONS AND POLICY RECOMMENDATIONS

Jong Woo Kang, Pramila Crivelli, and Mara Claire Tayag

Discussions and analyses on international trade and investment have been centered on manufacturing. Services trade remains poorly understood and its drivers and effects are rather elusive compared with "traditional" trade in merchandise goods. The traditional dichotomy in terms of tradability has largely treated services as nontradable, with less potential to globalize than trade in goods; although, trade in services has flourished since the General Agreement on Trade in Services came into force in 1995, at the end of the Uruguay Round of multilateral trade negotiations. Yet, businesses and consumers are finding greater and practical ways of transforming services tradable across borders. More recently, the uptake of digital technologies is propelling all regions of the world into the Fourth Industrial Revolution, and digital enablement has ushered in a powerful new phase of services unbundling.

Services trade is growing fast, not only because consumer preferences are changing as incomes rise, but also due to the "servicification" of manufacturing. And a wide variety of services, such as financial services, professional services, and logistics are becoming an integral part of global and intra-industry trade as stand-alone industries or as part of the back-office or in-house arms of large manufacturing businesses. While economies are endeavoring to develop domestic service industries, cross-border service transactions are growing exponentially. Digitalization is reinforcing this rapid transformation toward a services economy by fostering the easier, faster, and cheaper transaction of services for the convenience of suppliers and consumers alike, and lowering costs by cutting out intermediary agents. This "third unbundling" is likely a worldwide phenomenon, enabling the fragmentation of "jobs" into more specialized "tasks"—for example, separating software engineering, data analytics, remote high-tech service providers, knowledge product providers, or web designers, among others, which allows separate tasks to be performed remotely but to interact in real time. Those who embrace this evolutionary transformation will thrive, whereas those who are clumsy will fall behind.

This book, in shedding some light on the latest episode in the services globalization story, clearly describes the transition from traditional trade in services, through digital enablement, to trade in "digitally delivered" and "digitally deliverable" services, or more simply trade in digital services. The "digital" aspect of the issues dealt with in this book highlights the key role of data, the internet, and other technology-related infrastructure as the bedrock of flourishing digital services and digital services trade. Its cross-border transaction nature also implicates regulatory and governance environment across economies.

One big challenge in discussing digital services trade is its conceptual vagueness and the blurry boundary of its current scope. This book attempts to provide clearer delineation of digitally deliverable services trade based on the frameworks of the Organisation for Economic Co-operation and Development (OECD), the World Trade Organization (WTO), and the United Nations Conference on Trade and Development (UNCTAD), and to describe regional and sector performances based on this framework.

The analysis shows that Asia and the Pacific is at the forefront of digital services trade, having demonstrated the fastest rate of growth in this sector over recent decades. The region is also showing rapid growth in the relative share of digital services trade in total services trade, although has yet to catch up with the global average. Cross-country analysis has shown that the region is still far behind economies in the European Union and North America in the share of digital services exports in total goods and services exports. This leads to a lower revealed comparative advantage for the region.

Within Asia and the Pacific, economies are also at different stages of development in trade of digital services—from nascent through emerging to strong players. The range of digital services traded in the region reflects this diversity. It spans traditional call center services based on cost, location, and time zone advantages; advanced artificial intelligence and cloud-based services based on skills and domain competence; services linked to goods trade and manufacturing competitiveness; embedded services; and services supporting e-commerce such as fintech.

To plug the gap with other regions and economies more advanced in digital services trade performance, this book emphasizes four key dimensions where economies in Asia and the Pacific need to put focus: (i) human capital development, (ii) digital connectivity, (iii) information and communication technology (ICT) investment, and (iv) an enabling policy and regulatory environment, including for freedom to access the internet.

The length and quality of education is associated with greater trade in digital services, with the total expected years of schooling seen to be positively associated with an economy's performance in trade in digital services. In addition, the importance of upskilling and reskilling the workforce cannot be overstated, especially considering existing skill-based barriers to the uptake of digital technology. Digital technologies are also the foundation for fostering innovation that allows small and medium-sized enterprises to become competitive providers of digital services. The development of digital services exports in the region therefore hinges on the availability, accessibility, affordability, and quality of broadband services. Rapid growth of mobile penetration bodes well. ICT investments, which constitute the physical underpinnings of digital services trade, should therefore comprise internet infrastructure, computing facilities, software programs, and data processing equipment. Freer internet regulations could enable even economies with low digitalization to better reap the benefits of digital services trade. The policy environment should enable business opportunities in digital services to thrive while ensuring consumer protection.

As part of their development strategy, governments can pave the way for digital services exports—positively associated with economic growth—by adopting policies and programs that improve the country's performance in one or more of the four key dimensions as drivers of digital services competitiveness. Other efforts could include investing in digital infrastructure and skills, not only expanding the digital competency base but reducing the digital divide, supporting startups by providing funding, tax incentives, and piloting opportunities, while enacting supporting legislation on cross-border data transfers and data protection, among other measures.

Simulation scenarios of trade liberalization and deregulation of digital services sectors through computable general equilibrium modeling using ADB's Multi-Regional Input-Output Table data demonstrate positive impacts on digital services trade from both types of policy measure, while the impacts on other sectors are smaller. Both scenarios also lead to clear gains in backward and forward global value chain participation regionally and globally across manufacturing and services sectors. Indeed, the gains are not confined to the digital services sectors where a positive policy shock is simulated but are spread over other sectors. Interestingly, both trade liberalization and the deregulation of digital services sectors could garner real income impact for regional economies, with deregulation generating larger gains by far. From a welfare perspective, this reinforces the importance of implementing nondiscriminatory regulatory cost reduction measures besides trade policy reforms at the border. Trade liberalization efforts should therefore embrace reform in domestic markets.

Digital services trade and other sectors of the economy can generate mutual synergies. Growth in e-commerce for merchandise goods, itself enabled by digital services platforms, creates opportunities for digital services exports such as financial services, logistics, and software development. Growth of manufacturing provides opportunities for embedding digital services and applications in manufacturing design, production, and shipment, enabling indirect exports of digital services.

On the other hand, restrictive data-related policies, in particular on cross-border data flows, could significantly limit digital services trade. Using a unique dataset, this book assesses which of the restrictions on (i) data localization policies, (ii) local storage requirements, and (iii) conditional flow regimes on cross-border data exchange most impinge trade in digital services for Asia and the rest of the world. The results show that globally, data localization and local storage requirements, in particular, hold back digital services trade, but that the role of conditional flow regimes is more complex. While many of the data flow restrictions are adopted and implemented from various legitimate policy perspectives such as protection of privacy and personal data, and protection against the threat of cybersecurity, economies need to weigh their positive effects against their negative impact on digital trade flows.

In enhancing the competitiveness of digital services and narrowing the digital divide, governments should consider the possible trade-offs and differential impacts—for example, for skilled versus unskilled workers and urban versus rural areas. While expansion in digital services trade could help reduce poverty and improve welfare through its overall positive impact on wages and cost reductions, the worsening income inequality among those with different skill sets as well as potentially yawning divergence between urban and rural households remain concerns. This requires policy makers' continued attention to the sector, geographic, and gender distribution effects of the benefits from digital services trade.

International trade rules need to catch up with the fast-changing regulatory environment for digital services trade. WTO trade rules as well as bilateral and regional trade agreements provide an emerging international regulatory framework, governing conditions for digital services production, marketing, dissemination, and sales. The transition into the digital economy and growing awareness of the need to fill the void in regulatory space will likely prompt more discussion and negotiation about regulation in the areas of data flows, privacy, data protection, and cybersecurity, among other realms. Although more and more digital trade-specific trade agreements are expected to emerge, heightened effort is needed to create clearer guidelines for digital services trade and digital trade at large. The WTO Joint Initiative on Trade-Related Aspects of E-Commerce would constitute a significant step forward in filling some gaps in international digital services trade governance. WTO members in Asia and the Pacific could also consider joining the WTO's Joint Initiative on Services Domestic Regulation, given that a commitment to principles for good regulatory practice will help to cut trade costs, including for digital services.

Widespread adoption of international standards in ICT has already demonstrably increased interoperability and security across technology platforms, decreased barriers to trade, ensured quality, and built trust in digital services. Beyond trade negotiation, it is clearly in the interests of digital services competitiveness for regional governments to participate in opportunities for digital regulatory cooperation. The adoption of common standards could help economies avoid redundant efforts and technical duplication, achieve better interoperability, and reduce trade costs. Recognition of regulatory outcomes, whether autonomous or by mutual arrangement, and preferably reducing the risk of discrimination to a minimum by designing mutual recognition agreements in an open and transparent manner, provides guarantees to any party wishing to join.

International trade and regulatory cooperation require specific skills and expertise on trade and international economic laws that developing economies may not always possess, to engage in discussions, evaluate proposals, draft legislation and agreements, and develop constructive negotiating positions. In ensuring an inclusive process, the importance of capacity-building assistance cannot be overstated. Developing economies need assistance to enhance awareness and understanding on how to align digital regulatory regimes with international standards, principles, and guidelines, as well as support in designing and drafting the necessary domestic reforms. Technical assistance is, therefore, urgently needed for developing economies that want to improve and upgrade data protection laws and regulation in the context of greater digitalization. The WTO negotiations offer an opportunity for more developed WTO members to commit to this effect.

While digitalization brings more convenience and efficiency, it can entail greater vulnerabilities in security and pursuant social and economic costs. The importance of putting in place appropriate risk management tools against cybersecurity crimes cannot be emphasized enough. As cybersecurity increasingly becomes a precondition for cross-border data flows, economies aspiring to competitiveness in digital services exports will need to strive for greater international regulatory cooperation on cybersecurity. Asia and the Pacific should encourage the use of transparent, globally competitive and market-driven cybersecurity standards and practices, and avoid adoption of domestic measures that constrain competition and innovation. The objective should be to ensure interoperability of cybersecurity frameworks while reducing the costs of regulatory friction.

Digital services are important in current discussions on international tax policy. Digitization means that mode 1 is trending in the direction of taking over as the dominant mode for services trade. Absent common frameworks for taxation of cross-border digital services, unilateral measures to capture tax revenue associated with cross-border delivery of digital services have proliferated in the region. Meanwhile, an international push is under way to resolve the underlying issues through international agreement on new taxation frameworks for digital services trade. Ongoing international tax cooperation could ensure fair taxation across borders.

The prospects for developing economies in Asia and the Pacific to take part in digital services trade are promising. Opportunities are likely to intensify in the post-pandemic period as consumers and producers continue to embrace online purchasing, digital transactions, and remote delivery of services. These long-term shifts in behavior, production structure, and labor market needs offer all economies new possibilities to develop competitive advantages in digital services. Whether policy makers are ready to seize this opportunity, which supportive measures they take to nurture an enabling environment, and how effectively they open the windows for necessary investments and innovation will characterize the future landscape of digital services and digital services trade for the region.

CPSIA information can be obtained
at www.ICGtesting.com
Printed in the USA
JSHW071113160523
41776JS00007B/212

9 789292 698621